D0899064

May 2017

EXPERIENCING FILM MUSIC

The Listener's Companion
Gregg Akkerman, Series Editor

Titles in **The Listener's Companion** provide readers with a deeper understanding of key musical genres and the work of major artists and composers. Aimed at nonspecialists, each volume explains in clear and accessible language how to *listen* to works from particular artists, composers, and genres. Looking at both the context in which the music first appeared and has since been heard, authors explore with readers the environments in which key musical works were written and performed.

EXPERIENCING FILM MUSIC

A Listener's Companion

Kenneth LaFave

ROWMAN & LITTLEFIELD
Lanham • Boulder • New York • London

Published by Rowman & Littlefield
A wholly owned subsidiary of The Rowman & Littlefield Publishing Group,
Inc.
4501 Forbes Boulevard, Suite 200, Lanham, Maryland 20706
www.rowman.com

Unit A, Whitacre Mews, 26-34 Stannary Street, London SE11 4AB

British Library Cataloguing in Publication Information Available

Library of Congress Cataloging-in-Publication Data

Names: LaFave, Kenneth.
Title: Experiencing film music : a listener's companion / Kenneth LaFave.
Description: Lanham : Rowman & Littlefield, [2017] | Series: The listener's companion | Includes
bibliographical references and index.
Identifiers: LCCN 2016043501 (print) | LCCN 2016044142 (ebook) | ISBN 9781442258419
(cloth : alk. paper) | ISBN 9781442258426 (electronic)
Subjects: LCSH: Motion picture music—Analysis, appreciation.
Classification: LCC ML2075 .L32 2017 (print) | LCC ML2075 (ebook) | DDC 781.5/42—dc23 LC
record available at https://lccn.loc.gov/2016043501

♾ ™ The paper used in this publication meets the minimum requirements of
American National Standard for Information Sciences Permanence of Paper
for Printed Library Materials, ANSI/NISO Z39.48-1992.

Printed in the United States of America

For my sons, Max and Emmett LaFave. May music always be with you.

CONTENTS

SERIES EDITOR'S FOREWORD

The goal of the Listener's Companion series is to give readers a deeper understanding of pivotal musical genres and the creative work of its iconic composers and performers. This is accomplished in an inclusive manner that does not necessitate extensive music training or elitist shoulder rubbing. Authors of the series place the reader in specific listening experiences in which the music is examined in its historical context with regard to both compositional and societal parameters. By positioning the reader in the real or supposed environment of the music's creation, the author provides for a deeper enjoyment and appreciation of the art form. Series authors, often drawing on their own expertise as both performers and scholars, deliver to readers a broad understanding of major musical genres and the achievements of artists within those genres as lived listening experiences.

As a student of music composition in graduate school, I was told by my professors on various occasions that while film music might be considered suitable for earning an income, it should not be equated with "legitimate" genres of music. It was somehow more temporary and rather pedestrian. While I can't argue with certainty that they were wrong, I can enthusiastically report that their opinions have proven irrelevant. Film music has fully embedded itself into the popular culture at all levels. For generations now, we can easily conjure up visions of shark attack by simply humming two notes back and forth. The playful theme from the Harry Potter movies is immediately recognizable by millions of muggles throughout the world. The "hero" themes in the

Star Wars, Indiana Jones, or *The Lord of the Rings* movies are equally familiar and prone to eliciting emotions of excitement. And community orchestras are able to program more esoteric concerts because of the revenue collected by their "Music of Hollywood" offerings.

Despite the worldwide recognition and acceptance of film music as a loved, relevant, and "serious" form, there is still a lack of academic writing on how to appreciate and listen to the genre. Fortunately, the *Listener's Companion* series is well positioned to address this issue and author Kenneth LaFave has completed this excellent book. I am most impressed by his ability to take music that is originally intended to support a visual medium and break it down in language without jargon in a manner that is educational without becoming ponderous. Film music has risen to new heights, and LaFave is the skilled communicator worthy of guiding us up to the vista.

Gregg Akkerman

ACKNOWLEDGMENTS

I wish to thank Diane Daou for reading every word and for her unflagging encouragement along the way. For their various contributions of patience, critical observation, and general assistance, thanks go also to Gregg Akkerman, Natalie Mandziuk, Susan Simpson, and Emmett and Max LaFave.

TIMELINE

1895   A guitarist accompanies the first public screening of a film in Paris.

1896–1927   Musicians across the United States accompany silent movies. From solo pianists, organists, and guitarists to eighty-piece orchestras, musicians rely largely on the classical catalog to supply appropriate emotional backdrop for screen images.

1908   Classical composer Camille Saint-Saëns writes the first known original music for a film, *L'Assassinat du Duc de Guise.*

1915   Joseph Carl Breil composes one of the first designated scores for a Hollywood feature, *Birth of a Nation.* It combines original cues with classical and folk-song sources.

1927   *The Jazz Singer* opens. The first talkie causes a panic in the film industry, which retools for sound, putting thousands of musicians out of work and focusing all future movie-music creation in Hollywood studios.

1929   Max Steiner arrives in Hollywood from Austria via England and New York. Throughout the 1930s, along with fellow European immigrants such as Franz Waxman and Erich Wolfgang Korngold—many of them escapees from Nazism—Steiner will establish the Hollywood soundtrack sound: orchestral scores derived in character from the late romantic period of Western symphonic music, such as Mahler and Richard Strauss.

1933   Steiner composes *King Kong*, the earliest full-length score to exhibit the new sound of original symphonic music, over producer David Selznick's preference for classical music cues.

1938   Korngold wins the first Oscar ever given to a composer for an original score, *The Adventures of Robin Hood*. Previous music awards had gone to music departments, rather than to individuals.

1939   *Gone with the Wind*'s epic visuals are matched by Steiner's epic score, topped by the sweeping "Tara's Theme."

1941   Composer Bernard Herrmann makes his debut with no less a film than Orson Welles's *Citizen Kane*.

1944   David Raksin's theme for *Laura* sets the standard for memorable movie melodies. Written as an instrumental, its popularity demands words that are added a year later.

1949   Aaron Copland scores *The Heiress*, which will win him an Oscar, the first awarded to a composer of classical concert music.

1954   Leonard Bernstein writes some of the most expressive music ever composed for a film in *On the Waterfront*. Inconsistently effective in the context of the film, it thrives in the concert hall.

1955   *The Man with the Golden Arm* becomes the first major mainstream film to use jazz and jazz-inflected music as its background score, as composed by Elmer Bernstein with input from jazz trumpeter Shorty Rogers.

1959   Sword-and-sandal music reaches a peak of mastery in Miklos Rozsa's score to *Ben-Hur*.

1960   The brass chords and jagged rhythms of the Western reach a peak in Elmer Bernstein's score to *The Magnificent Seven*.

1960   Bernard Herrmann's screeching violins help send Janet Leigh to her end in *Psycho*, the peak of the composer's six-film association with director Alfred Hitchcock.

1961   Henry Mancini and Johnny Mercer initiate a golden age of movie theme songs with "Moon River," written for *Breakfast at Tiffany's*.

1962   Young Maurice Jarre composes the iconic score to *Lawrence of Arabia*.

1964–1966   Ennio Morricone throws out clichés and reinvents movie music for cowboys in Sergio Leone's "spaghetti Westerns," culminating in *The Good, The Bad, and the Ugly* (1966).

1968   Stanley Kubrick's *2001: A Space Odyssey* rejects the standard model, replacing Alex North's original music with the classical selections he had used as temp tracks, including the famous employment of Richard Strauss's *Also Sprach Zarathustra*.

1972   Nino Rota bridges the worlds of diegetic and background music in Francis Ford Coppola's *The Godfather*.

1974   Jerry Goldsmith saves the day for Roman Polanski's *Chinatown*, replacing a misfired score in only ten days and turning sneak-peek audiences' reactions from negative to enthusiastic.

1975   Two perfect notes turn a shark from menacing to outright scary via John Williams for *Jaws*.

1977   John Williams strikingly returns the epic movie soundtrack sound to post-romantic symphonic gestures, following a decade-plus of drift toward pop songs and more contemporary sounds, and in doing so produces the number-one music score on many people's lists, the original *Star Wars*.

1982 While enjoying unprecedented near-hegemony in penning scores for major releases and beginning his concert music career, Williams manages to compose what is probably his masterpiece, the score to *E.T. The Extra-Terrestrial*.

1989–1994 The incredible popularity of Disney's animated musicals leads to confusion for the voters at the Academy of Motion Picture Arts and Sciences, culminating in a brief (1995–1998) split of the award into two parts: dramatic on the one hand, and musical or comedy on the other.

1996 Rachel Portman composes the first score to win an Oscar for a woman composer (musical or comedy), *Emma*.

1997 The soundtrack recording of James Horner's *Titanic* score becomes the first (and as of 2016, only) original film score soundtrack to go platinum.

2001–2003 Peter Jackson's *The Lord of the Rings* trilogy gains emotional traction via Howard Shore's almost constant background score.

2001–present The popularity of film music takes on new forms, including original scores written to older silent films and screenings of sound-films that feature live musical accompaniment instead of recorded soundtracks. New composers, many of them comprising a fresh generation of European, Mexican, and South American musicians, make their appearance, including Gustavo Santaolalla and Alexandre Desplat.

INTRODUCTION

Music and film are parallel experiences: they are linear, they are narrative. —Todd Haynes, director (*Far from Heaven, Carol*)

The purpose of this book is to explore incidental music's role in American films. By *incidental music*, I mean background music or underscoring. The very word "incidental" is, in a way, an insult to an artistic ingredient that is far from incidental (in the sense of referring to an accompanying element of relatively minor importance) to the greater art it serves, and yet the terms "background music" and "underscoring" also place its role behind the scenes. With the understanding that we are not referring to musicals (song-based films), we will from now on simply use phrases such as "movie music" and "film scores" to refer to our subject.

Visual action and music have gone together since humans first learned to dance. And music has shored up words since Homer sang the *Iliad*—or, to restrict ourselves to instrumental music only, since the staging of plays by the great tragedians of ancient Athens. Music of the *kithara* (a sort of harp) and *aulos* (a flute) went right along with the words of Sophocles and Euripides, "underscoring" them, as we would now say. Incidental music for plays was common in modern stagecraft as well. Two of the best-known concert works of the nineteenth century had their origins as incidental music for plays: Bizet's *L'Arlésienne* Suites, and Grieg's *Peer Gynt* Suites. So when cinema was birthed, there was already a long, if informal, tradition of music accompanying dramatic action. Early cinema was silent as to words, but it is telling that live music was a component from the start, first in improvised music by a single pianist or other solo player, often borrowing from the classical canon, and later in original scores especially designated for the film at hand and played by forces ranging from small chamber ensembles to full-sized orchestras. With the advent of sound, music became an integral part of the finished cinematic product.

Music is typically the last thing to be added to a film. Given the power of music to create and alter mood and emotions, this is remarkable. Unless the director has some idea of what the music will be like at the start, that means a vital part of the film's content is reserved for one person, in the final weeks of the process, to control. Perhaps this is why so many successful film scores are the result of an intimate artistic relationship between director and composer—Hitchcock and Herrmann, the Coen brothers and Carter Burwell, and of course, Spielberg and Williams come to mind. When a director knows a composer's skill set and is musically savvy enough to ask for specifics, the result can be a more integrated final product than if the composer is simply brought in at the last minute. On the other hand, the right composer at the last minute can make an enormous positive difference, if the composer knows how to look at film. The famous story of Jerry Goldsmith's last-minute save of *Chinatown* is case in point.

Here are the twenty-five best film scores and their composers, according to the American Film Institute (AFI):

1. *Star Wars* (John Williams, 1977)
2. *Gone with the Wind* (Max Steiner, 1939)
3. *Lawrence of Arabia* (Maurice Jarre, 1962)
4. *Psycho* (Bernard Herrmann, 1960)
5. *The Godfather* (Nino Rota, 1972)
6. *Jaws* (John Williams, 1975)
7. *Laura* (David Raksin, 1944)
8. *The Magnificent Seven* (Elmer Bernstein, 1960)
9. *Chinatown* (Jerry Goldsmith, 1974)
10. *High Noon* (Dimitri Tiomkin, 1952)
11. *The Adventures of Robin Hood* (Erich Wolfgang Korngold, 1938)
12. *Vertigo* (Bernard Herrmann, 1958)
13. *King Kong* (Max Steiner, 1933)

14. *E.T. The Extra-Terrestrial* (John Williams, 1982)
15. *Out of Africa* (John Barry, 1985)
16. *Sunset Boulevard* (Franz Waxman, 1950)
17. *To Kill a Mockingbird* (Elmer Bernstein, 1962)
18. *Planet of the Apes* (Jerry Goldsmith, 1968)
19. *A Streetcar Named Desire* (Alex North, 1951)
20. *The Pink Panther* (Henry Mancini, 1964)
21. *Ben-Hur* (Miklos Rozsa, 1959)
22. *On the Waterfront* (Leonard Bernstein, 1954)
23. *The Mission* (Ennio Morricone, 1986)
24. *On Golden Pond* (Dave Grusin, 1981)
25. *How the West Was Won* (Alfred Newman, 1962)

A number of things jump out. One is that great film scoring (taking these scores as the models) is apparently a thing of the past. The most recent film on the list is *The Mission*, from thirty years ago as of this writing (2016). The list was compiled in 2005, so it can be forgiven a certain datedness. But surely a score or two from the 1990s or the first years of the twenty-first century might have been found.

Another is that comedies apparently don't make for "great" film scores. Of the twenty-five, only *The Pink Panther* is pure comedy, the others falling under the headings of epic, thriller, drama, adventure, Western, or romantic comedy.

Still another is that great movie music generally comes from great movies. There are exceptions here. *Planet of the Apes* is a silly exercise in making thin sci-fi seem profound, and *How the West Was Won* is a pseudo-historic potboiler. *The Mission* is ambitious but flawed, and both *Out of Africa* and *On Golden Pond* are overly sentimental. But the remaining twenty make up a list of landmarks, masterpieces, and box office explosions. One can also sense a prejudice on the part of the list's compilers for making sure that all the major screen composers were listed, even if that meant choosing to name the best-known movies they scored rather than their best musical efforts. This is clearly true of number fifteen. The music for *Out of Africa* is well made, but it is hardly Barry's best. That would be *The Lion in Winter* (1968). Similarly, while it is great to have *The Pink Panther* on board as the token comedy, Mancini's music for *Breakfast at Tiffany's* (1961) is that much richer.

No female composers made the list, but that is hardly surprising, as film scoring seems to be one of the last of the "old boys" clubs in show business. Women writers and directors work regularly, though not as much or as often as their male counterparts. Women film composers, on the other hand, are today nearly nonexistent; in the decades represented by the AFI list, they were completely missing. (Strange that this remains the case today, when both the worlds of classical composition and jazz have opened to female artists as never before.)

Nor do the nineteen composers named above include any musicians of color. African American composers such as Duke Ellington and Quincy Jones have scored movies, but, as with female composers, it remains rare indeed to see the name of a composer of color following the words "Music by" in screen credits.

It's illuminating to compare this list, voted on by film and film-music experts, with the Oscar winners for the years represented. Only nine of AFI's Top 25 also won Oscars for the best original score. To be frank, that award has been suspect since its beginning, when it was given not to the composer, but to the sound engineer. When composers at last were recognized as the actual creators of the music, the awards frequently made no sense. For example, the best-score Oscar for 1939 did not go, as one would almost be willing to bet a fortune it did, to *Gone with the Wind*, but to Herbert Stothart's incidental music for *The Wizard of Oz*—not the Harold Arlen-Yip Harburg songs (which won no Oscar), but the orchestral cues *between* the songs.

Another thing stands out when you stop to think over these scores in your head; it's a certain distinction that I will employ throughout. To grasp this distinction, consider two of the scores, both by John Williams: *Star Wars* and *Jaws*. Play parts of them over from memory. You will almost certainly hear the main theme from *Star Wars* with ease, the first sixteen notes being ingrained in the public ear. But thinking of *Jaws* will produce only two notes a half-step apart. These two will seesaw back and forth, slowly at first, then faster, in a deep bass register. Can any two pieces of music be more different in structure? One is a full-blooded melody, heroic in shape—rising, falling briefly, then rising again and yet again, both times on the backs of fanfare-like triplets. In short, it is a *theme*. The other is just a gesture, the simplest imaginable, which depends for effect on the sinister implications of the bass register and increasingly menacing repetitions. It is a *motive*. While there are exceptions, most of the film scores above and, indeed, most of the film scores ever written fall into one of these two categories: theme-based scoring, and motive-based scoring. The most obvious instances of the former are scores headed by a theme song or a short vocal work. "Do Not Forsake Me, O My Darling" is a Western-flavored song that dominates Dimitri Tiomkin's score for *High Noon*, to such an extent that even the final, famous, eight-minute gun battle consists of the theme broken up and reassembled in ever-intensifying orchestral salvos. By contrast, Bernard Herrmann's music for *Psycho* is a series of dissonant motives in the strings that culminate in the famous "screeching" strings of the shower scene. You come away from *High Noon* with a tune in your head. You come away from *Psycho* with a musical impression of terror, but no remembered melody. Of course, composers frequently employ both motives and themes, but the choice to put one or the other in the forefront affects the nature of both the score and the film it serves. (Williams's cues for *Jaws* do, in fact, include some beautiful thematic writing. But you don't recall it, do you?)

And before we leave the matter just touched on, let's underline this all-important point: the final and only real reason for movie music *is* to serve the movie. The task of a film score is to enhance its film's overall identity, character, and even meaning. This subservience is frequently simplified as "a film score's job is to be unnoticed" (so as to blend in with the other cinematic elements). In actuality, it's more complicated than that: the film score's task is to be both unnoticed and indispensable at the same time. A film composer is primarily a cinema artist who must contribute to the whole without distracting from it.

I have organized the book more or less according to genre, but don't be disappointed if you look for, say, *2001: A Space Odyssey* in chapter 8, "Science Fiction and Fantasy"—a reasonable enough expectation—but find it instead in chapter 9, which is devoted to films that use ready-made music. And while "epic" certainly fits the Star Wars series, you will not find those films in chapter 4, but in the aforementioned chapter on sci-fi and fantasy. As I said, the book is organized along the lines of genre—more or less.

Finally, it should be noted that this list of 25 was selected from 250 nominees, and that the 250 in turn represent a small sampling of the many thousands of film scores composed over the past ninety years. I have, of course, watched these twenty-five winners and done a certain amount of study of their various musical elements, and I have also watched and studied a fairly large sampling of the other 225 nominees. But I cannot claim to have watched, let alone studied in any sense, all of the major releases pertinent to a discussion of film music. I doubt that would even be possible. The number of additional films required for viewing would easily approach 1,000 (many more if I were to expand my purview to include Europe, Japan, and Bollywood), and while I love movies, I do not have at my disposal the 2,000-plus hours—roughly the equivalent of working a full-time position for a year—necessary for such an enterprise.

In other words, this book is not offered as a scholarly last word on the art of writing music for the cinema. (For that, the reader should turn to the books of Christopher Palmer and James Wierzbicki.) It is, rather, a set of observations on the history of that art and some of its major practitioners, a look at how they worked and why the music they wrote sounded the way it did, along with some hints about how to appreciate their music in the context of film. (Because my focus is the experience of music in film, I will usually refer to cues by titles I invent, rather than those listed on original soundtrack recordings. Obviously, no moviegoer encountering a moment of music will know the cue by the title given it by the composer. They will know it by the effect it has. In cases where soundtrack recordings are mentioned, however, I will use the composer's cue titles.) Because a film's music relates to its story, this book contains spoilers; be warned. Also be warned that it may not necessarily reference your favorite film composer in sufficient quantity—or at all. The text reflects my own tastes and particular interests. Beyond that, readers are advised to explore film music on their own, using this book as a guide.

I

THE NOT-SO-SILENT ERA

Silent films were the least silent cinematic experience in history. Except for movies screened in those rare locales where a piano was unavailable or a guitarist couldn't be found, the showing of a "silent" film always provided a live musical experience that paralleled the visuals on the screen. With small- to medium-budget releases, accompanying music was chosen by local musicians. Most cinema musicians kept a book of classical music pieces arranged according to the mood required. My grandmother, Alma Gensbechler, played piano for silent movies as a teenager in the 1920s. She told me once that Schubert was her favorite composer to call upon. Typical moments were Schubert's "Ave Maria" for scenes of holy rectitude, and the opening of "Erlkonig" to suggest the approach of a sinister person or event.

A guitarist played the music on December 28, 1895, in Paris, when the Lumiere brothers presented the first public cinema screening, a set of ten brief films—each under a minute in length—with such thrilling titles as "The Baby's Meal," "Workers Leaving the Factory," and "Bathing in the Sea." There's no record of what pieces the guitarist played, but instantly the idea was born that music and moving pictures were an ideal pairing. Something else was likely born that historic evening, for while the projected pictures gave the audience information, the music almost certainly provided the only clues as to what the audience might *feel* while watching. After all, it's one thing to watch a baby eat her meal to the slow strum of some placid chords, and quite another to watch her eat as an up-tempo piece is played.

There was precedent for the combination of silent, moving images and music in the stage form called *melodrama*. Today, melodrama usually refers to a drama absurdly broad in its depictions of good and evil, as when a villain ties an ingénue to a train track. But its original meaning comes from the eighteenth century, when no less a personage than philosopher-author Jean-Jacques Rousseau wrote *Pygmalion*, based on the Greek myth, as a sort of hybrid dramatic-musical work. Rousseau's idea was to alternate recited words with pantomimed action, all to the unifying accompaniment of original instrumental music. He wrote *Pygmalion* in 1770, the same year he also wrote his epoch-defining work of political philosophy, *The Social Contract*. Both, in their separate ways, were successful: *The Social Contract* in sparking the liberal ideas that would form the basis of the French Revolution, and *Pygmalion* in founding a form that was soon to sweep the theaters of Europe. The music for *Pygmalion* was mostly by Henry Coignet, though the overture was apparently composed by Rousseau himself, an amateur composer of some skill when he was not writing philosophy or penning popular novels such as *Julie; or, the New Eloise*. Having innovated the form, Rousseau never touched it again, but melodrama (from the Greek *melos*, for "music," and the French *drame*, as in "drama") took off in a big way, particularly in Germany. A reciter would tell a story, sometimes animating it himself, but more often accompanied by silent actors who pantomimed the action recited. Music filled the emotional gap between narration and action. Essentially, that is what film music continues to do today.

The popularity of melodrama led to the widespread use of incidental scores in staged plays. Beethoven and Schubert composed incidental scores for dramas, and two standard works in the current orchestral repertoire—Bizet's *L'Arlésienne* Suites and Grieg's *Peer Gynt* Suites— began as incidental music. So by the time cinema emerged at the end of the nineteenth century, audiences had come to expect instrumental music to be part of a dramatic experience. Even though the first films, which were little more than mini-documentaries about daily life, were hardly "dramatic," and despite the fact they lacked the element of the spoken word, they called out for music to help shape that space between the image of the action on the screen and the audience's reception of the image.

For American musicians, "silent" film was a godsend. Pianists, organists, and guitarists had new employment opportunities, and in the bigger cities, whole orchestras were organized to accompany major releases. Duke Ellington, while honing his art in Harlem in the 1920s, used to escape from time to time to catch a film, but really to hear the amazing orchestras that New York City could deploy for "mere" movie music. What is today the Rochester Philharmonic Orchestra in Rochester, New York, began as a silent-film orchestra.

No less a figure than twentieth-century French philosopher Jean-Paul Sartre extolled the importance of music in conveying the emotional content of music for silent film:

> I liked the incurable muteness of my heroes. But no, they weren't mute, since they knew how to make themselves understood. We communicated by means of music; *it was the sound of their inner life*. Persecuted innocence did better than merely show or speak of suffering; it permeated me with its pain by means of the melody that issued from it. I would read the conversations [on the title cards that flashed on screen between the images] but I heard the hope and bitterness. . . . (T)he young widow who wept on screen was not I, and yet she and I had only one soul: Chopin's funeral march; no more was needed for her tears to wet my eyes. . . . (E)ven before the traitor betrayed, his crime entered me; when all seemed peaceful in the castle, sinister chords exposed the murderer's presence. How happy were those cowboys, those musketeers, those detectives; their future was there, in that premonitory music, and governed the present. An unbroken song blended with their lives, led them on to victory or death by moving toward its own end. (*The Words: The Autobiography of Jean-Paul Sartre*; emphasis mine)

Who does not recognize in this description the role of film music even today? In the simplest horror movie, the opening of a door is just the opening of a door—unless the music tells us, as it so often does, that something terrible lurks behind that door. In some ways, cinema without music is largely about the conveyance of information. Unlike the stage, where the energy and the presence of actors charges the air with feeling, cinema is primarily the art of presenting fluid visual images. Within these images, actors speak words that expose their character and, at length, a story, but the actors' energy is "up there," so to speak, caught on the screen. It can only reach us via the parallel experience provided by the music. In addition, as noted by Sartre, we can know things about a scene that the actor does not know. The best directors understand this primacy of composed images, as well as the role of music in filling the emotional gap. Think of Stanley Kubrick's visually stunning films and the carefully chosen music that goes with them.

As the popularity of cinema grew, so did the need for musicians, and the need for guidance in the selection of accompanying pieces. Cue sheets were assembled and sent to theaters along with the films, so that musicians—whether a solitary pianist, a string quartet, or a full orchestra—would know the kind of music needed. Overtures were important. The overture—which has now disappeared from film—was a prefatory piece of music that set the mood or suggested the coming action. Overtures were de rigueur for stage plays and operas, and so it seemed natural to preface films with overtures as well. These were generally taken from the pre-composed classical repertoire. A list of overtures used by the orchestra at New York's Rialto Theatre between 1918 and 1921 includes pieces by Tchaikovsky, Wagner, Liszt, Mendelssohn, Verdi, Sibelius, Saint-Saëns, Rossini, Elgar, and Dvořák. Liszt dominates the list.

Beyond the overture, cue sheets, while exact as to the placement of the music, were less exact about the actual music to be used. Sometimes they consisted of mere descriptions of the emotional states at certain points of the film. The cue sheet for the release of the Warner Bros. feature film, *The Desired Woman*, released in 1927 at the sunset of the silent era, contains more than seventy cues linked precisely to scenes in the film and paired with specific emotional ideas and musical indications such as "Dramatic disappearance," "Tense *mysterioso*," "Sentimental—'I love your eyes,'" "Dramatic love tragedy," and "Threatening—*agitato appassionata*." It was left to the musician(s) to determine which specific classical pieces would fit the demand for the emotions or states depicted.

On the other hand, the cue sheet for *The Desert's Price* (1925) accompanies each of its several dozen cues with four to eight measures of music in the style desired. The musician was expected to play music of the sort indicated by the handful of measures, or perhaps to play those measures and expand on them for the length of the cue. Making music for the silents was a highly creative endeavor.

Still, most musicians don't catalog music in their heads according to such sensibilities as "romantic," "tragic," and so forth, and still fewer are capable of improvising original music to fit those verbal descriptions. It fell then to music directors of the film orchestras to come up with albums of sheet music that compiled a range of classical and light classical pieces indexed as "romantic," "tragic," "humorous," and so on. These differed from the cue sheets, as these were not intended for a single film but as a reference guide to possible music for any film. Because of this, experiencing the same movie in two different theaters with different accompanying musicians could be very different experiences, indeed. One musician might choose to accompany a dramatic passage with some intense Liszt, while another might choose to improvise a series of diminished chords.

The need for pieces of music to suggest this emotion led to a cottage industry for minor composers, who would pump out pieces capturing the sorts of musical gestures usually associated with said emotion, and intended specifically for use in the movies. The important thing to keep in mind is that by "romantic," the film composer meant the sort of arching melody and plaintive harmony generally associated with romanticism in nineteenth-century classical music. By "dramatic," the film composer meant the kind of roiling, minor-key, chromatic measures associated with struggle in nineteenth-century symphonies. Film music unerringly aped the gestures of classical music in its late nineteenth-century mode. This doesn't mean the music was bad or even necessarily derivative, but that it adapted the language of classical concert music to the needs of the new medium. From the start, then, moviegoers heard a certain kind of classical music as "movie music." Within this context, that music could be obvious and stereotyped, or it might be (rarely) original and brilliant. But the core sound—the sound expected by moviegoers—was a certain orchestral texture exhibiting particular harmonic and melodic vocabularies. This has never, essentially, changed. The genius of John Williams is partly because he understands this and consequently makes music that masterfully exploits these expectations.

One of the lesser-known uses of music in silent film had to do with creating a mood for actors on a set. This was not music destined to be heard by audiences, but music played as shooting progressed. A violinist or guitarist in an outdoor shoot, or a pianist during an inside shoot, would play music that fit the scene for whatever circumstances were at hand. This practice disappeared with the advent of sound, only to be resurrected as innovation by director Terrence Malick, who asked Hans Zimmer to compose music for *The Thin Red Line* (1999) before shooting began, and then played back some of it during filming.

Early on, the idea came to directors to ask composers to assemble dedicated scores—music put together specifically for Movie XYZ, and required as part of that film's screening. This is a major aesthetic change. Instead of leaving the selection and performance of music up to local musicians throughout the country, the screening of a film came with specific, written musical cues to be performed by those musicians. The combination of screen image and live music was now more unified. The earliest major example of a composer writing an original score for a film goes to French composer Camille Saint-Saëns for *L'Assassinat du Duc de Guise* in 1908. The most celebrated example in Hollywood was Joseph Carl Breil's score for D. W. Griffith's notorious *Birth of a Nation* in 1915. An ode to the vanquished south and to the Ku Klux Klan, *Birth of a Nation* was documented as having caused at least one murder of a black man by an enraged white man inspired by the movie. In strictly cinematic terms, however, the film was a success, including Breil's score, which was a compilation of original music, classical excerpts, and folk-song arrangements. (Breil—b. 1870, d. 1926—was a fascinating figure, a trained operatic tenor whose long-range ambition was the composing of operas. He died at the age of fifty-five, partly the result of a breakdown following the failure of one of his operas.)

The mix of original with adapted material dominated the dedicated film scores of the silent era, and even held sway into the first years of talkies. Max Steiner's score for *Gone with the Wind* (1939) is riddled with found pieces of music, many of them by Stephen Foster. Little by little, the consensus was reached that an original score should be not merely a compilation of bits with original cues between, but music shaped for the action and characters on screen from original material, exactly as the script was made, not from scraps of this and that but out of whole cloth for the purpose of telling a story.

Hungarian-born composer-conductor Erno Rapee (1891–1945) was one of the major composers of dedicated film scores in the last years of silent film, with credits including *Nero* (1922), *The Waltz Dream* (1925), and *The Prince and the Dancer* (1926). But dedicated scores were for the biggest releases only, and most movies continued to feature local musicians playing cues of their own choosing. To that end, Rapee also published a catalog of suggested cues for various moods portrayed in cinema.

The advent of sound was a disaster for American musicians. Talkies came with their own sound, including music, meaning where once hundreds, if not thousands, of musicians throughout the land were employed to provide live music for a film, now only a fraction of that number were employed by one studio in a single town to do the same. There must have been an extraordinary freedom on the part of musicians in the era of so-called silent film. The creativity of coming up with appropriate music for a romantic scene or a tragic episode must have been exhilarating. Except where dedicated scores came with movies, directors were not in charge of this vital aspect of the cinema—musicians were. Sound on film transferred that power to the director, who now more than ever was the single artistic vision behind the myriad disciplines involved in making a movie.

When silent films left the current scene and entered history, their musical aspect temporarily disappeared. For a long time, silent-film viewers looked at silent film without musical accompaniment, which is to say, they missed fully half of the experience. Toward the end of the twentieth century, silent-film release on video began to reinstate the music, and in some cases great silent films whose dedicated scores had been lost were given new scores by living composers. Major examples included Richard Einhorn's luminescent 1994 score for Carl Dreyer's *The Passion of Joan of Arc* (1928), and two rival scores for Abel Gance's *Napoleon* (1927) by Carmine Coppola and Carl Davis, both released the same year, 1980.

City Lights (1931), a masterful silent film made by Charlie Chaplin after the era of talkies had commenced, boasts one of the most fully realized scores in silent-film history—or in the history of cinema, for that matter. The popularity of both the movie and its music continue today in the form of live-accompaniment screenings, such as the one presented by the New York Philharmonic in May 2016. That Chaplin composed the music himself, with the assistance of composer Arthur Johnston, is evidence of the director's understanding of the importance of music as an equal in the cinematic experience, as well as testimony to the incredible range of Chapin's talents. The score is a model of how to use music in silent film, and in particular comic silent film. We'll see in a later chapter that comedies, for reasons pertaining to the nature of their unchanging characters, can sometimes get away without any music at all. But *City Lights* is as much romance as it is comedy; one could even see it as a romance with comedy attached. The characters undergo change, just as in a drama, and for that, music works wonders.

Properly employed, music can also create or underline the rhythms of the comic visuals. In an early scene in *City Lights*, the Tramp is admiring a nude statue outside a shop on a busy street. The music is faux-elegant, a lilting little waltz. As the Tramp steps back to admire the statue, a space opens in the sidewalk behind him where a workman eventually emerges. The comedy comes from the Tramp's ignorance of this gap in the sidewalk. Innocently, he steps back and forth, barely escaping a fall. The music stops and starts accordingly, creating from the Tramp's movements a little dance that enhances the comedy and underlines our expectations that the Tramp will fall in (which he eventually does).

The scene immediately following that one introduces us to the Tramp's love interest, a blind woman who sells flowers on the street. The music here is borrowed: Chaplin used the song "La Violatera" (The Woman Who Sells Violets) as the theme associated with the blind woman, and at first failed to credit the song's composer, José Padilla. A lawsuit soon changed that, and today the credits cite Padilla as the writer of that song. In hindsight, it's difficult to understand why Chaplin did not simply write a tune of his own, as he was clearly capable of doing. His next and final silent-film masterpiece, *Modern Times* (1936), would also feature his own music, this time topped by the song we now know as "Smile," as rich a melody as might be imagined.

We are next introduced to the alcoholic rich man who intends to hang himself by the riverfront. The music here is typical of what would come to be called *Mickey Mouse*—a musical cue that hits each movement comically on the nose, from the Tramp walking down the stairs to the waterfront with his characteristic gait, to him jumping around while holding his foot after the rich man accidentally drops a rock on it, to the panicky *allegro* that plays as the Tramp flails about in the river when he, and not the rich man, ends up in it! The very next comic scene takes an opposite musical tack, providing genteel parlor music at the rich man's home that proceeds in apparently blissful ignorance of the fact that the rich man, still quite drunk, is pouring whisky down the Tramp's pants.

This more in-the-background approach will continue to alternate with Mickey Mouse stuff, such as the slide whistle that accompanies the Tramp slurping a spaghetti noodle, or the drums and cymbals that signal the rich man's misfiring car.

Several musical ideas follow the characters and the action around. One is the Padilla melody for the girl, and there are also a walking theme for the Tramp and a frantic main theme in a *presto agitato* three-beat pattern that shows up whenever the Tramp is about to get himself in trouble of some sort, as when he approaches the boxing ring. Best of all is the music in the ring itself, a pairing of staccato strings and twittering flute that turn the play between the Tramp, his opponent, and the referee into a surreal dance. The film's tender ending, one of the most famous in film history, is cradled by glowing music that might very well fit a saint's benediction.

In the chapter on comedy, we'll examine whether comedy even needs music in the way that drama needs it. Indeed, most of the out-and-out comic moments in *City Lights* amount almost to musicalized sound effects. The true music of Chaplin's lush score occurs in those scenes associated with character (the rich man's music, the Tramp's walk, etc.) and especially with romance. The film is a comedy-romance, not merely a stumble-and-pratfall comedy, and music for such a story is needed to make characters' emotions spring to life. No emotional cues are needed for slipping on a banana peel.

The *City Lights* score shows clearly that many of the methods and traits associated with soundtrack music of the talking pictures were already in place during the silent era. The term "Mickey Mouse" would come to be used in the 1930s to refer to hitting a visual on the nose with a sound; this happens, for example, in Max Steiner's score to *King Kong* (1933; see chapter 2). Steiner is even thought of as the king of Mickey Mouse. But what he did in *King Kong* was not that different from what silent-movie musicians were doing in live performance in the 1920s. The coordination of sight and sound can, after all, take only so many forms, and the two main forms are perfectly illustrated in *City Lights*: atmospheric music, or music to set a mood, whether present in a scene or in anticipation of something, as when some foreboding measures of music tell us a terrible truth unknown to the actors; or the underlining of an action with a parallel musical event—the Mickey Mouse.

As of 1927, filmmakers and moviegoers had no idea of what was coming. A total change in the art form was at hand with the introduction of sound on film. It cannot be overemphasized that silent films were rarely if ever silent: music—live music—played a prominent role. With the exception of certain large-scale releases featuring dedicated scores overseen by the directors, musicians were in charge of the music for movies. Now that responsibility would go to directors and, inevitably, some of those directors would be musically adept, and others wholly ignorant. The level of that ignorance could be astounding, as exemplified by the famous incident that gave the title to composer André Previn's Hollywood memoir. When producer Irving Thalberg (*Grand Hotel*, 1932, and *Mutiny on the Bounty*, 1935) heard a passage in one score that he found unsettling, he asked a musician what kind of music the passage consisted of. "Minor chords," he was told. Out went a Thalberg memo to his music department: "No minor chords."

In some sense, the history of film music after the silent era is a massive postscript. Music dominated the silent-film experience, not only because it was constant or nearly so, but because it was live. Live music with film is a wholly different experience from music on a film soundtrack, as anyone who attends the various live-music-with-film productions now popular (2016) in the United States can attest. While the screen unrolls a series of pre-recorded, flat images, live musicians generate in-the-moment commentary. Seeing *The Godfather* or *The Fellowship of the Ring* with live music not only underlines the importance of the music in telling the story, it also draws a line between the story and its emotive content. Hearing a live-music accompaniment to a movie makes it clear that the music could be other than what it is, that what is felt when Michael Corleone visits his namesake village or Frodo announces that he will take the Ring on its deadly journey might easily be other feelings, given other music.

The realization that silent film needs music has given rise to a number of contemporary (late twentieth- and early twenty-first-century) composers who make a living (or nearly so) of supplying music for the vast catalog of silent films that lie mostly in repose, awaiting rediscovery. A more vibrant possibility—one not yet widely explored aside from the Godfrey Reggio/Philip Glass collaboration on *Koyaanisqatsi* and companion films—is the creation of new silent films in tandem with original music. One imagines composers submitting scores to directors for realization on the silent screen, as well as composers scoring silent films already shot. Such undertakings would continue the art of silent film that was cut short in 1927.

2

MAX STEINER AND THE
FIRST GENERATION

In 1896, a little Viennese boy named Max was taken to the great Johannes Brahms for piano lessons. The following year, Brahms died, and in Paris, the first studios dedicated solely to the emerging art of the cinema were built. The connection? Max was Max Steiner, the composer ultimately most responsible for the way movie music sounds.

Classical music was the artistic predecessor of film music. Without the tradition of Beethoven, Brahms, Strauss, and Mahler, film music as we know it simply would not exist. From the earliest sound films with dedicated scores down to the present time (2016), the majority of movies have included music played by the instruments of the Western classical orchestra—bowed strings, woodwinds, brass, and percussion—and composed by people trained in the classical mode. Steiner set the standard for this. Not only did little Max study piano with Brahms, he studied conducting with Gustav Mahler, and at age fifteen composed an operetta, *The Beautiful Greek Girl*, that enjoyed a one-year run in his native Vienna. By the time he landed in Hollywood in 1929, Max Steiner was an accomplished, forty-one-year-old composer of symphonies and stage works who brought a wealth of classical-music knowledge to the sound stages of the new "talking motion pictures."

Why does this matter? After all, classical music, as we have seen, was already widely used to accompany many silent films. Wasn't it only natural that it would become the language of the new sound films? While it may seem inevitable in retrospect, the scoring of original music couched in classical language and style was not a foregone conclusion. As of 1929, two years after *The Jazz Singer* introduced the world to sound on film, Hollywood was still struggling with how to handle music in the new medium. Musicals—song-and-dance movies like *The Jazz Singer*—dominated the first talkies, and these seemed at first to embody the perfect and only use of music in the context of the new technology. Background music for dramas and songless comedies was another matter entirely. Most producers and many directors felt that audiences would be startled to hear music underneath a movie's dialogue and action. Live music during a silent film was one thing; audiences knew where the music was coming from. But background music on the actual soundtrack of a film, unless it was performed by on-screen musicians and heard by the actors (called "diegetic music"), would seem to emanate from some unidentified place and confuse audiences, or so producers' thinking went. It took years to convince honchos at the major studios that audiences were not that stupid.

Max Steiner (1888–1971) was one of the men who did the convincing. Steiner's early success as a Viennese *wunderkind* had led him to London in 1910, where he enjoyed celebrity status and success. But with the outbreak of World War I in 1914, Steiner's Austrian birth marked him as a potential "enemy alien," and for a while, incarceration loomed over his head. Thanks to a friend in high places, Steiner escaped that fate and left for the safety of the New World; he landed in New York harbor in December 1914 and never looked back. For a decade and a half, the burgeoning theater life of New York made good use of Steiner's talents as an orchestrator, arranger, and conductor, and he was kept busy working on operettas and musicals that included George and Ira Gershwin's *Lady Be Good*. When another of those musicals, a minor show called *Rio Rita*, was bought by RKO Pictures in Hollywood, Steiner traveled to Los Angeles to adapt his orchestrations for the movie version and conduct the studio orchestra. RKO was impressed by Steiner's abilities and asked him to stay on. Whether it was the thrill of a new art form, the lure of considerable money, the warm California weather, or a combination of all three, Steiner said yes, thereby launching, in 1929 at the age of forty-one, a career that would earn him the title "Father of Film Music."

At first, Steiner's job as music director for RKO consisted of merely doing what he'd done in New York: orchestrating and conducting musicals, the most frequently produced genre in the first few years of talkies. But by 1931, the public had started to grow weary of the endless stream of song and dance, and Steiner was at last asked to do what he would become matchless at: compose an original score. The movie was *Cimarron*, a Western based on Edna Ferber's novel of the same name. Steiner's music comprised a handful of cues that barely made their presence known. Such music as there was, however, was not mere general mood music, but measures shaped for the action in the frames. This is what we now think of movie music as doing, but in 1931, it was new. The progress of Steiner's scores from *Cimarron* to *King Kong* (1933) to *Gone with the Wind* (1939) is, in a way, the story of the development of film music itself. Let's watch and listen to *King Kong*, and then move on to *Gone with the Wind* to get an idea of how Steiner (along with other classically trained composers) in the 1930s set the course of movie music for decades to come.

King Kong opens with three somber chords against a credit: "RADIO PICTURES PRESENTS," and then this disappears and the title rushes toward the screen to fill the frame with letters as big as the ape they signify—*KING KONG*. As this happens, Steiner's music, in strongly profiled four-beat meter, continues in a somber mood to which is added a charge of menace. Thickly orchestrated chords, heavy on the brass, dominate for a minute or so, fading to a quiet, almost sweet string theme as the screen is emblazoned with the words of an Arabian proverb about beauty and the beast. The pairing of a "masculine" or aggressive theme with a "feminine" or lyrical one in the opening titles will become standard Hollywood practice.

The first surprise comes in the form of a negative: There is no music for a very long time. As the actors play out the film-within-a-film exposition—on board a ship in a remote oceanic location, a filmmaker searches for a famous beast said to exist on a certain island, in order to use it in his new movie on the theme of "beauty and the beast"—the music is notable by its absence. At last, around twenty minutes in, Steiner's music enters with a fog that has suddenly surrounded the ship. The fog is made both more atmospheric and more ominous by Steiner's use of harp over strings. A series of solo woodwind instruments play long, sustained notes for the strings until at last, at a crucial moment, a French horn enters on a high note that hangs over the strings like the fog over the sea. This kind of literal tone painting and the general use of

Impressionist gestures will become common currency for scenes of obscure beauty or indistinct dangers.

The eerie fog music dissipates and slips directly into low brass playing darkly orchestrated, pulsing minor chords over pseudo-native drum music. The accompanying visual is the siting of the island, an intimidating piece of desolate real estate dominated by a jutting geographical feature called "Skull Mountain." We see the filmmaker talking casually to the ship's captain. In one of the first truly creative cues in film music history, Steiner's music ignores the filmmaker's idle chatter and plays instead to the captain's nervous concern about the strange fog and the day ahead. This will be one of the signs of a truly gifted film composer: the ability to write to the true emotions of a scene in which the dialogue is only a distraction.

Once the music has started up again, it doesn't seem to want to stop. As the ship's crew and the cast of the film-within-a-film gather to go ashore, the music continues, but changes yet again. The brass instruments have unveiled for us the treacheries of Skull Mountain before we've even arrived. Now it's time for low strings, in a quiet, unaccompanied melody, to sketch the dangers we have yet to encounter. The people going ashore are all chipper and hale, but the music has a sickly pall. Thanks to Steiner, the audience knows something the actors do not—there is serious trouble ahead. This, too, will become a familiar trope in film scores: music that tells the moviegoer what's about to happen, before the characters on the screen have an inkling. The cliché would be the innocent victim blithely entering her home, while unknown to her but seen clearly by the audience a murderer waits in the shadows. The role of the music in such a case is not to reflect the cheery swing of the incipient victim's stride, but the danger set to end it.

When the landing party reaches the shore, they see a native dance, and the apparent preparation of a human sacrifice. (Such blatantly racist depictions of "native" activity were common for a very long time in Hollywood.) The situation is dicey at best, and as the tension mounts, so does the volume and intensity of Steiner's music. The filmmaker decides to start rolling his camera from a discrete distance, but just as he does, the chief spots him. At this moment, the nearly eight-minute cue abruptly halts. We have just been carried from the ship to the shore to the brink of a disaster on the magic carpet of Steiner's score. The visuals have outlined the action, but the emotions of the landing party have been told exclusively through the music, from the strangeness of the thick fog, to the captain's apprehensions, to the adventurous landing, to the frightening view of the observed ritual. The music briefly leaves, but it returns as the chief of the natives explains in his language (a made-up one, presumably) the fate of the girl at the center of this ritual. The last syllable of the chief's utterance is "KONG!" And on that very word, Steiner's music strikes a loud, fully diminished seventh chord, and stops.

A moment of respect for the fully diminished seventh chord. That term is merely the technical label for a certain four-note chord in which all the notes are equidistant from each other. This tightness of spacing and the specific character of the distances between notes—minor thirds—produce an unmistakably dark sound—a "scary" sound, if you will. The fully diminished seventh chord will show up throughout Hollywood history whenever there is something the movie audience ought to find frightening. It will be the best friend of the composer who writes horror-movie music, but all composers will make use of it at one time or another.

So far, Steiner's remarkable little score has given evidence of two things that will become very familiar as we watch the history of film scoring evolve. One of those things is the definition of a general task incumbent on all composers who write for the cinema, and the other is a term for a certain technique. We'll start with the fun one, the term frequently used as a pejorative: Mickey Mouse.

For a film composer to Mickey Mouse a score means to coordinate the music exactly with the visuals/action/dialogue. The loud, fully diminished seventh chord sounding at the same instant the chief said "KONG" was a classic Mickey Mouse move. Researchers who have investigated the origins of the term trace it back to the early 1930s, and some specifically to Steiner, who engaged frequently in this technique. The obvious reference is to the Disney cartoon character, who made his debut in 1928, almost simultaneously with the advent of sound itself. Ironically, the rodent's first released film, *Steamboat Willie*, did not utilize a Mickey Mouse score. Instead, Wilfred Jackson's arrangements of folk songs breeze by like so much filler as the animated characters go through all sorts of antics. The second and third to be released (though they were the first and second made), *Gallopin' Gaucho* and *Plane Crazy*, featured Carl Stalling scores that inclined a little more in that direction, though more along the lines of coordinating the rhythms of a character walking with the beat of the music, for example. It's more likely that the Mickey Mousing here referred to the slapstick of obvious sound effects, like a thud when a character fell or an animal making its characteristic "moo" or "quack." The musical equivalent was read as a chord or beat hitting a visual cue directly, as the fully diminished seventh chord hit "KONG" on the button.

The second thing evidenced by Steiner's score is by far the more important: the creation of a film's rhythm. Cinematic rhythm is complex. In the hands of a master filmmaker, rhythm is created by the pace and composition of the visuals; music, to the extent that it has a role, enhances the rhythm already present. This requires, of course, a composer exceptionally sensitive to how a director creates a flow from one scene to the next, and patterns of tension and release within each scene. But *King Kong* was not Ingmar Bergman. The directors—yes, there were two of them, Merian C. Cooper and Ernest B. Schoedsack— seemed simply to point and shoot, and the acting ranged from mediocre to flatulent. Look at the eight minutes just described twice—once with the sound on and then with the sound muted—and you will know which element, visuals or music, is creating any sense whatsoever of tension and forward motion. The original *King Kong* is a magnificent cartoon of a movie, and its designation of "Greatest Horror Film of All Time" (*Rotten Tomatoes*) has to do with sentimentality, the relative level of innovation for the time (it features an early use of stop-motion animation), and Steiner's music, which tells the audience what to feel when the screen is filled with empty images and limp dialogue.

The score continues in this function off and on throughout the movie's one hundred minutes. In 1933, so much music in such a prominent role was unprecedented, and the credit for encouraging Steiner goes to producer David O. Selznick, the son of a silent-movie producer and new to RKO Pictures at the time. Music was an important part of a film to Selznick, who often oversaw its production directly—sometimes to his composers' frustration. Selznick's preference was for mood music over Mickey Mouse, which sometimes led to angry memos between him and Steiner. In the end, though, *King Kong* balances the two aesthetics. When we first see the monstrous Kong, the music tells us to pull back in awe. When the beautiful Ann (Fay Wray) is kidnapped to be given as a sacrifice to the beast, the music tells us to be frightened. It is precisely for this that Steiner's score has been called breakthrough: for the first time, music played a major role in how an audience experiences a film. It is still background, but indispensable background. For the next several decades, music would play this essential part in the cinematic art, at least in Hollywood. Sometime after the 1980s, and especially with the advent of the twenty-first century, this function began to fade. The reason was the screen's greatly increased ability, with computer-generated imagery (CGI) and other technical advances, to engage audiences visually. A look at Peter Jackson's 2005 *King Kong* remake will show that music, by this time, has taken a back seat to those things. Instead of a score like Steiner's, engaging with the action of the film, James Newton Howard's music stays discretely at the rear, providing only the most general frameworks of feeling.

There's a fine line between Mickey Mousing a score in the pejorative sense, and writing truly descriptive music that matches the visuals. Steiner crosses back and forth over that line in the last minutes of *King Kong*. When the great ape ascends the Empire State Building, Fay Wray in hand, the music climbs with him as a four-note motive is sounded, then transposed higher, and again still higher. The origin of Mickey Mouse as a term referring to this kind of writing is obscure, but its earliest appearance in print comes from *A Smattering of Ignorance*, pianist/raconteur Oscar Levant's 1939 memoir. Levant, a Hollywood favorite and insider, defined the term and then wrote of Steiner's groundbreaking score for *King Kong*:

> It offered him a chance to write the kind of music no one had heard before—or since. Full of weird chords, strident background noises, rumblings and heavings, it was one of the most enthusiastically written scores ever to be composed in Hollywood. Indeed, it was always my feeling that is should have been advertised as a concert of Steiner's music with accompanying pictures on the screen.

I fault Levant on only one point: while the sort of music Steiner wrote for *King Kong* had indeed not been heard before, it had been heard again—in later Steiner scores and in scores by his colleagues—because it set the standard for how Hollywood music should work. And its like would be heard again and again in the years after 1939, as Hollywood movie music came to play an important role in conveying the emotions of screen action and dialogue. Levant also identified the opposite of Mickey Mouse music as the setting of a general mood or atmosphere, and credited Alfred Newman with that school of cinematic composition. Newman, whose breakthrough film was the stark drama *Street Scene* (1931), will be discussed later.

The early 1930s saw the de facto establishment of both Mickey Mouse and background mood music. To do Mickey Mouse right meant the composer had to use a click track and coordinate the precise moment of, say, an arrow hitting a cowboy in the chest, with the stinging chord that signaled impact and pain. Steiner pioneered the technique, which is today, in a technologically advanced form, a commonplace trade skill for film composers.

The year 1934 welcomed the arrival in Hollywood of two other European immigrants who would soon join Steiner among the greats of film composition. Like Steiner, they brought with them ideas of the classical mainstream. Unlike Steiner, they fled a menace far more dangerous than English internment. In 1934, twenty-eight-year-old composer Franz Waxman (1906–1967) strolled the streets of Berlin, where lately he had scored his first film and begun for himself, or so he thought, a career as a composer for German cinema. But when Nazi thugs beat him to the cries of *"Juden!"* Waxman decided his talents might better be used elsewhere. He and his wife left for Paris, and proceeded to Hollywood in late 1934. Erich Wolfgang Korngold (1897–1957) made an entrance just as dramatic, though in a different way. A celebrated prodigy in his native Austria, Korngold did not need the movies. His opera, *Die Tote Stade*, composed when he was only twenty, had put him in demand and, wherever he went, musicians asked him for scores. (Korngold was among the composers, including the likes of Ravel and Prokofiev, commissioned to write a Left-Hand Concerto for the pianist Paul Wittgenstein—the brother of philosopher Ludwig Wittgenstein—whose right arm had been blown off during World War I.) In 1934 he paid a somewhat casual visit to Hollywood to score one film, *A Midsummer Night's Dream*, then afterward alternated between composing concert music in Austria and film music in Hollywood. Korngold's scores for *Captain Blood* (1935) and *Anthony Adverse* (1936) defined the rhythmic profile of "adventure" music. In 1938, after much coaxing, Korngold left Austria once more for California, this time to write music for *The Adventures of Robin Hood*. His intent was to return home as usual, but when Hitler annexed Austria,

Korngold, who was Jewish, thought better of it and remained. "*The Adventures of Robin Hood* saved my life," he would later say.

Waxman's first Hollywood triumph was *The Bride of Frankenstein* (1935). His cues contained gestures that would become standard for as long as horror films were made, among them the tremolo-ing strings and dissonant brass in the scene where the Frankenstein monster is reintroduced to his maker; the *pianissimo* parallel chromatic chords in the violins that represent the sweet Elizabeth, and later the not-so-sweet Elsa Lancaster; and the *staccato* unisons in angular rhythmic array that indicate peril when the bride upsets her groom.

Korngold worked a similar magic for the emerging genre of period adventure films. *The Adventures of Robin Hood* not only saved his life; it provided a template for all future heroic-themed movies. A four-plus minute cue accompanying the fight at Gisbourne's castle and Robin's subsequent escape supplies plenty of atmosphere and one or two moments of Mickey Mouse. The best of the latter is when Robin (Errol Flynn) runs to jump on his horse, and the action is given a roll on a kettledrum followed by a cymbal crash. The general sense of the music is of almost directionless fury and even confusion, the better to convey the clash of Robin with the forces of King John. These ideas seem commonplace now, but in 1938 such complex orchestral maneuvering was fresh, and *The Adventures of Robin Hood* won Korngold the first-ever Oscar specifically for best musical score, the prize before that having been given to the sound designer for best overall sound, including music.

By the end of the 1930s, then, film music had taken shape as a major contributor to the artistic nature of film, at least in Hollywood. It may be true that producers were, for the most part, ignorant of music's technical aspects, but all recognized the importance of music to their final product. None was more aware of music's role than David O. Selznick. In a letter to conductor Walter Damrosch, Selznick once bragged, "I don't think there is another producer in Hollywood that devotes ten per cent as much time to the score as I do—and it may interest you to know that I was the first producer to use dramatic scores."

A brag it was, but it was also true. It was Selznick who had encouraged Steiner to pull out all the stops on *King Kong* in 1933. Now, in 1939, he undertook the project that was to cement his fame as one of the greatest shapers of Hollywood: *Gone with the Wind*. Filming for MGM's mega-movie of Margaret Mitchell's novel began in January 1939, and in March, Selznick sent a memo to Warner Bros. asking to borrow Steiner, then under contract to that studio. Selznick wanted the music to include actual songs of the Civil War era, and had reams of sheet music ordered for Steiner to use in his score. But the use of ready-mades rankled Steiner, who felt that when an audience recognized a piece of music, it distracted them from the film. As it turned out, a fair amount of music from the time was used, from "Dixie" and "Marching Through Georgia" to "Maryland, My Maryland" (to the melody more widely known as "O Christmas Tree"), "When Johnny Comes Marching Home," and a variety of Irish jigs and reels. Something called the "Chicken Reel" is heard during a literal chicken chase. Generally, these period songs are referenced fleetingly, giving an impression of Civil War ambiance without dominating the scene. Steiner also used several songs by Stephen Foster, America's first writer of popular songs. Some are well known, such as "Old Folks at Home," but several are obscure. One of the better-known Foster songs is used in a diegetic context (as a part of the action, not underscoring) when Prissy sings "Old Kentucky Home."

Steiner's music opens with an overture, heard before the film begins. The title music slides immediately into a rendition of "Dixie" and then, as the name of the movie fills the screen, one enormous word at a time, we hear "Tara's Theme," music meant to evoke the O'Hara land but more generally associated with the film itself. "Tara's Theme" is the first major example of a big melody that the public ended up associating with the movie as kind of sonic nametag. Sometimes with words, sometimes without, these melodies are slow to medium in tempo, broad in their rhythmic conception (as opposed to "busy"), and usually rangy, meaning that they don't move simply from one note in a scale to the next, but leap about, from one extreme of a range to another. "Tara's Theme" begins with a boldly ascending octave, steps down politely, then throws us the same ascending octave, this time with a still more polite step-down. Then it pushes up yet a third ascending octave (on different, higher notes), offset by a somewhat less polite step-down. Finally, the melody repeats exactly as at the opening, except that at the end, the last gesture reaches up to the highest note of all, bringing the melody to a heroic climax. As the first great movie theme, "Tara's

Theme" set a standard for the future. Particularly important in such pieces are their beginnings, which must settle into the listener's ears with such finality that, whenever they are heard again, memory rushes to meet the whole. Think of the first two notes of "Tara's Theme," but also the first two of Maurice Jarre's theme for *Lawrence of Arabia* (a descending perfect fourth) and, most famously of all, the opening pair of John Williams's theme for *Star Wars* (an ascending perfect fifth) and the entire melodies will show up, invited or not.

"Tara's Theme" promises an epic ahead, and of course the film delivers. As the titles end and we see Scarlett surrounded by beaus, Steiner gives us playful music to accompany Scarlett's flirtations. There's a brief, music-less moment before we hear "Irish" music that accompanies the appearance of Scarlett's father. As Scarlett and Mr. O'Hara talk, the music continues—true mood music without any Mickey Mousing, a victory for Selznick! As the talk turns to the land, the plantation called Tara, "Tara's Theme" emerges full-blown for the first time, underscoring the majesty of the famous tableau that profiles Scarlett and her father against a glowing sunset. From now on, the music will be nearly nonstop: three hours of it, composed and recorded in four months. In the heyday of RKO, Steiner had pumped out music for as many as twenty-plus movies a year, but those were shorter features, throwaways that needed little attention, and many of them included stock music—music previously written and recorded to fit a range of standard-issue action scenes or dramatic situations. But *Gone with the Wind* was an epic of massive proportions that demanded a certain consistency of style amid a wide dramatic range of scenes, and on top of that, Steiner was working at the same time on another major release, *Intermezzo*. Aided by music director Tom Forbes and a fleet of more than a dozen orchestrators, however, Steiner pulled it off, barely in time for the movie's December 1939 opening. (The role of the orchestrator will be discussed in a "Spotlight" feature following chapter 3.)

Steiner might not have made the deadline, save for a certain incident. Selznick, worried that Steiner's music would hold up the premiere, arranged behind the composer's back for Herbert Stothart, an MGM contract musician known largely for his arrangements of the Nelson Eddy/Jeanette MacDonald screen musicals, to compose additional cues. The story goes that Stothart got drunk one night in a Hollywood night club and bragged loudly about his new job. Word got to

Steiner, and suddenly his pace on the *Gone with the Wind* soundtrack picked up considerable speed. But Stothart had the last laugh for, incredible as it now seems, Steiner's standard-setting music for *Gone with the Wind* did not win that year's Oscar for best score. It went instead to Stothart's incidental music and arrangements for *The Wizard of Oz*, which consisted of little more than arrangements of, and a few background cues in between, the Harold Arlen/Yip Harburg songs. This stands as an early example of the Motion Picture Association's failure to understand what film music is or how it works.

Gone with the Wind was the most important Hollywood film score up to that time, and one of two (with *King Kong*) Steiner scores to make the American Film Institute's Top 25. Its rich orchestration, the subtle use of borrowed materials, the majestic "Tara's Theme," and, most of all, Steiner's aesthetic of providing support for the screen action and atmosphere earn the movie a well-deserved second place on that list, right behind *Star Wars* and just ahead of *Lawrence of Arabia*. (All three of the top listings boast those distinctively broad, memorable themes.) From that moment on, film composers aspired to achieve the kind of unity of music with image that Steiner achieved. The future would bring clones of Steiner's approach, cheap imitations of it, and some genuine innovations along its lines.

Steiner continued to compose music for film into his seventies, with later credits including *Treasure of the Sierra Madre* (1948) and *The Searchers* (1956). His legacy of telling audiences how to feel through music was so widely known—and in some cases, feared—that it is referenced in a famous story about actress Bette Davis. Davis, shooting a scene with director William Wyler in which she quietly descended a staircase, and aware that Wyler had hired Steiner to compose the music, said to Wyler: "I want to come down these stairs alone—not with Max Steiner!"

Spotlight:
Spotting and the Click Track

Directors' desire to control the placement of music gave birth to spotting, and the need for a precise coordination of image and music generated the click track. Spotting is the process in which a director and a composer go through the edited film, with all in place except the music, and spot the places for the music to go. In theory, either artist may suggest this spot or that. In actuality, the director calls the shots. It's been said countless times that film is the director's medium and, while this fact may not be necessary to the art of cinema per se—one can imagine a film in which the writer and the composer, say, dictate frame-to-frame content, with the director's role no more than the blocking of actors and the assemblage of the final product according to the wishes of writer and composer—but in fact, that is how it inevitably turns out.

The director's musical sense, then, is vital to his or her finished product. The director's relationship with the composer is also important, and it is no accident that many directors, once they find a composer with whom communication is easy and results are more or less understood in advance, stick with him. Spotting means agreeing on the sort of music that must be created after the fact to fit the already edited image. Of course, there are exceptions, especially among art films. The whole point of Godfrey Reggio's *Koyaanisqatsi* and *Powaqqatsi* was the creation of mesmerizing images to match the phasing repetitions of Phillip Glass's music, so the visual edit actually followed the musical one. Examples among commercial films, though, are rare. Sergio Leone encouraged Ennio Morricone to compose his distinctive scores for *Once Upon a Time in the West* and *Once Upon a Time in America* in advance, then cut his film to match the music. John Williams's music for the finale of *E.T. The Extraterrestrial* was composed before the final edit, with director Steven Spielberg using his composer-partner's unerring sense of dramatic timing to create rhythmically identical visuals after the fact. In a handful of recent cases, composers have been asked by directors to create music in advance based on the story and characters: Hans Zimmer for Terrence Malick's *The Thin Red Line* (1999); Zimmer again for Christopher Nolan's *Inception* (2010); and Gustavo Santaolalla for Ang Lee's *Brokeback Mountain* (2005). The latter won an Oscar.

But the vast majority of films continue to be scored in the usual manner, after everything else—including the visual edit—has been completed, and following a spotting session between director and composer (and sometimes, a nosy producer or two). This requires a click track in order to coordinate the precise time in seconds on the screen with the beats per minute of the music. Musical time is measured in beats or counts per minute. Film length is measured in frames, of which there are, in standard sound film usage, twenty-four per second. So when, say, a director wants music for a certain scene of precisely 732 frames, and the music required is a moderate-tempo piece of 80 beats per minute, the composer does a quick computation: 732 frames divided by 24 comes out to 30.5 seconds. At eighty beats per minute (bpm), the composer will need just a hair under forty-one counts of music. To make sure this is what comes out, the composer (assuming the composer is also conducting) listens to a click track set to eighty bpm and leads the orchestra precisely at that tempo. If he has composed a cue of forty-one beats—with the last count cut just a little short—the fit should be perfect.

Some fits need to be more snug than others. Max Steiner's Mickey Mouse cues for *King Kong* needed to land exactly as the great ape made this motion or that. Other scenes in other films of varying aesthetics will not require this frame-by-frame precision. And in fact, the decision whether to land a note or not is an artistic decision of the first water. I once observed a group of students at the 2005 ASCAP film-scoring workshop in New York respond to an assignment in which they were requested to write a cue for a scene from a TV movie about the Manson family. The movie's actual music had been stripped out, so the young composers could do whatever they wished with what (if I remember correctly) was a scene of about a minute and forty-five seconds in which the "family" members tear around a house they have broken into, gleefully throwing items against the wall and smashing them, staring drug-crazed at the ceiling, and pulling books and knickknacks off the shelves.

No two students treated the scene the same way. Two were polar opposites: one in which every book ripped from the shelf and every smashed item had a corresponding percussion hit or string glissando; and another in which the entire episode came under the musical umbrella of an ironic waltz, untimed to any particular event of the scene, but forming instead a general, macabre musical environment for the act of destruction. Viewing these two versions side by side, I experienced completely different scenes, despite the fact that the visuals were identical. When composers make these sorts of root-sensibility decisions, they occupy, however briefly, an artistic status equal to that of the director.

3

MYSTERIES, THRILLERS, AND FILM NOIR

In this chapter we deal largely with music for a range of genres that emerged with the advent of talking motion pictures. If epic films dealt with the big, brightly lit exteriors of life, then the darker forms of mysteries, thrillers, and horror flicks, and especially the distinctive Hollywood hybrid of crime story and expressionist drama called film noir, represented the dim interiors of sexually repressed motivations and death-anxiety. For the epic, a composer had to muster heroic gestures and clear colors, because when characters in an epic are silent, the music has to take over, as in the famous shot of Tara near the start of *Gone with the Wind*. By contrast, Miklos Rozsa's music for Billy Wilder's *Double Indemnity* (1944) is spare, subtle, and always lurking well behind the dialogue. Only one time in that score does the music jump forward a bit, other than in the opening credits, and that's a Mickey Mouse moment when Barbara Stanwyck hides a revolver under a seat cushion.

Instrumentation plays a role in creating a film's musical character. In general, the brass instruments get more of a workout in mysteries and thrillers than in movies of other genres. Composers call on low brass, in particular, to indicate menace. The saxophone is, for some reason, associated with film noir more than it deserves. Earlier examples of the genre don't feature the sax at all. The kind of urban sexiness mixed with psychological darkness linked to that instrument came in slowly, and by the time of *Taxi Driver* (1975) was exploited to great effect by Bernard Herrmann. Horror films, as might be imagined, employ more Mickey

Mouse cues than other genres, so much so that stock music serves some horror films as well or better than original music. Case in point: George Romero's *Night of the Living Dead* (1968), for which the music is all pre-canned stuff. Romero's decision wasn't just a budget consideration: an actual composer might have added unwelcome emotional dimension to a film that is all about the surface sense of constant terror.

Music for one of the earliest and best-regarded examples of film noir is about neither low brass nor saxophones, but a song. Listening to David Raksin's music for *Laura* (1944), one might get the idea that film noir isn't so *noir* after all. The sumptuous theme dominates, of course, but it takes on many forms, all of them elegant and without a hint of shadow. One listens at first in vain for the dark side of things, and when at last it comes, it sounds more generally sinister than urban-threatening. Perhaps Raksin's theme was just too beautiful to admit anything less than haunting or more than mildly threatening; that, surely, was Raksin's intent. After all, *Laura* is a murder mystery in which the murder victim, apparently the title character, turns out not to have been the title character at all. Voted by AFI one of its Top 20 mystery films of all times, *Laura* is as much a love story as a mystery, because the investigating detective (Dana Andrews) falls in love with the "dead" woman. The presence of an insistent, irresistibly beautiful theme, therefore, was just what director Otto Preminger ordered—or would have ordered, if he had been musically inclined. Fortunately, Preminger left the decision for the kind of music to his composer, and Raksin—at age thirty-two, still young but with plenty of experience under his belt (he was an orchestrator for Charlie Chaplin's *Modern Times* and had recently scored two of the fabled Sherlock Holmes films starring Basil Rathbone)—produced a perfect fit.

It's hard to believe that Raksin's musical theme was not originally composed as a vocal work, but it was not. The famous melody became a full-fledged song only after the film's release, when lyricist Johnny Mercer added words. Mercer's skills were such that it seemed the lyrics and music must have been born together, but in fact the film's theme became so popular as an instrumental that the market virtually demanded a sung version. Since its unveiling in 1945, the Raksin/Mercer "Laura" has consistently been one of the most widely recorded songs in the canon of American classic pop.

Melodies that effective are not random products of some whistling tunesmith. Let's take a look at how Raksin's theme is put together, and how it tells the story of the film even without—especially without—Mercer's words. It begins on what seems to be a remote note. This kind of beginning is characteristic of a certain type of classic popular song; "Cry Me a River" (1955) is another example. Its beginning, like that of "Laura," seems suspended without any ground beneath it. Of course, this is the intent of these songs' respective composers (Arthur Hamilton in the case of "Cry Me a River"), and not some arbitrary matter of "pick a note to start." In "Laura," Raksin begins at a remote tonal spot, not only to suggest a certain mystery at the outset, but to lead the ear through a melodic maze that seems at first to confirm a minor mode, yet will at length—as in thirty-two bars later, at the very end of the song—become major. That seemingly distant note at the start turns out in retrospect to have been the leading tone (the next-to-last step of the scale) of the eventual major key of the song. And this is the story of the movie in musical miniature: We think the title character is dead (the suggested minor, weeping mode), and through a series of unexpected plot twists we become intrigued by her (the chord changes that lead us slowly away from the initially suggested minor key), until at last, we find out she's actually alive (the final resolution to a major key).

Well, it is the story of the movie's first third, at least, and it is that first third of *Laura* that is saturated with Raksin's theme. After that, as the tension of the mystery (who killed the girl thought to be Laura?) builds, Raksin's cues become darker and somewhat more standard-issue, with minor chord strings and brass. This is, in essence, a one-idea score—but what an idea! Raksin would go on to score dozens more films. His music for *The Bad and the Beautiful* (1954) has its vocal admirers, including no less than Stephen Sondheim, but it lacks the mass appeal of the *Laura* theme, with a long-lined structure that is more conceptually oriented than musically intuitive.

There is no sexy, slinky saxophone in *Laura*, which might be considered the iconic film noir masterpiece of the genre's early years. Neither is the saxophone a major player in the cues for Orson Welles's *Touch of Evil* (1958), considered by many the other bookend of classic film noir. So, how did the cliché of the smoky-hot, bluesy sax solo come to be associated with film noir so closely that everyone got the joke when composer Michael Kamen evoked the sound in the guys-with-fedoras scene of Terry Gilliam's *Brazil*, or when radio host Garrison Keillor made such a solo the theme of his genre spoof, "Guy Noir"?

It's a good question, and one for which I can't find a definitive answer. Composer Adolph Deutsch supplied the 1941 *Maltese Falcon*, which could be seen as the launch of the genre, with plenty of tremolo-ing strings and "sinister" chords from the low brass, and when Mary Astor was arrested at the end, she exited not with a saxophone behind her, but to an oboe cue. Miklos Rozsa eschewed the sax for the slippery electronic sound of the theremin in *Lost Weekend* (1945). Max Steiner scored *The Big Sleep* (1946), showing that he could make rising harmonies work to build tension in a detective story just as well as in a Civil War epic. But Humphrey Bogart's Philip Marlowe has no sax sound tagging along behind him, and when love interest Lauren Bacall makes her entrance at a swanky nightspot, a rinky-dink piano accompanies her sway; there's not a sax in sight (or sound).

The saxophone does show up in the film many consider the peak of classic film noir, Billy Wilder's *Sunset Boulevard* (1950), although it is not connected with anything explicitly sexy. The score finds Franz Waxman, a European-born, classically trained composer, completely in charge of the American musical idiom. Following the opening credits—a knot of aggressive minor chords in low strings and brass, prefacing the murder scene that opens the movie—Waxman tosses out a languid, dotted-rhythm motto in the piano, a jazzy riff that might have rolled off the fingers of any nightclub pianist in a relaxing moment. This motive follows the action of Joe Gillis, the writer character played by William Holden, as he tries to pitch a script, beg a loan, and escape a pair of collection agents trying to take his car. When at length the agents spot him and start the inevitable car chase, the orchestra breaks into fairly standard "frantic" music, but over this we hear the piano playing long chromatic runs and crazy repeated notes against the rhythm. Finally, Gillis wheels his car into a driveway to ditch the collectors, the music changes to a slower pace, and the piano becomes almost reflective. Throughout the early part of *Sunset Boulevard*, the piano will provide commentary on Gillis's mental and emotional states.

Of course, Gillis has pulled into the grounds of the mansion belonging to silent film star Norma Desmond, played by Gloria Swanson. The first instrument we hear when Desmond speaks is a flute in its low register, following instantly by strings playing the two-chord motto that will bloom into a silent-film-like romantic tango á la Rudolph Valentino, music that will send shivers up the spine as Swanson proclaims, "All right, Mr. DeMille, I'm ready for my close-up now." That famous moment is still ninety minutes away, but now, when Holden recognizes the woman he's talking to, he says: "You're Norma Desmond. You used to be big," and she says, in a near tie with the "ready for my close-up" line: "I'm still big. It's the pictures that got small." During this exchange, Waxman brings in the saxophone, an alto in high register, squeezing out a snaky little line that just might be the trailhead of the saxophone–film noir relationship we've been looking for. And yet—it's short. The little sax motive will return from time to time, but it is only one musical moment among many, and not necessarily the most striking one. That distinction would probably go either to the Valentino string chords or to the terrifying wheeze of organ music that recurs here and there, prompted by the broken-down instrument in Desmond's museum of a living room.

Gillis decides to stay on when invited by Desmond to collaborate on a script, and as he gazes out from his guest-room window that night, he spies rats in the empty, dilapidated swimming pool and views the bizarre cortege of Desmond and her servant, Max, as they bury her pet monkey in the yard. Waxman makes the most of this, providing a chilling funeral march. The sax shows up here as a macabre timbre, not as an emblem of sex. Gillis has a dream in which he hears organ music, and when he wakes in the middle of the night, Max is playing Bach's famous Toccata and Fugue in D minor on the old broken-down organ. One could hardly wish for a more effective switch from incidental score to diegetic music.

Pyramiding winds (no sax) signal the collection agents taking Gillis's car away, and a drive in Desmond's classic vehicle is accompanied by strings. The sax shows up again about thirty-eight minutes in, to accompany the deluge that sends Gillis from the leaky-roofed guest house to the main building—and closer to the narcissistic nightmare that is Norma Desmond. It is not sexiness per se, but seduction.

A tango band plays for the insane New Year's Eve party-for-two that Desmond throws to show her desire for Gillis. As Gillis leaves the house in disgust, the band is playing Erno Rapee's silent movie-era hit waltz tune, "Diane." (See the chapter on "Theme Songs.") They are still playing it when Gillis returns, hours later! He has attempted escape by hitchhiking to a real New Year's Eve party, but comes back when he hears that Desmond has attempted suicide. The piano at the party is the last time we will hear that instrument—Gillis's instrument. That night, he gives in to Desmond's sick seduction.

Distracted flute music plays as Max drives Desmond and Gillis to a bridge game a few nights later. As Desmond gives Gillis money for cigarettes the sax theme emerges again, this time very prominently, and we start to get the feeling that Waxman is using it as emblematic of selling out. The sax will disappear now until near the film's end, just before Desmond descends the staircase while the cameras—news cameras—are rolling. In between, the strings handle most of the cues, though there is a wonderfully tender musical moment when Gillis almost redeems himself by loving the Betty Schaefer character: Waxman gives a scene between them a reminiscence of the old Joe by inserting a few measures of the now-lost piano music, but this time on the bell-like celesta for greater nostalgia.

It may be that Waxman's *Sunset Boulevard* score is the source of the sexy-sax-equals-film-noir notion, or it may be that the equation is one of those myths that somehow catches on despite a total lack of relationship to facts, as is the case with the belief that Humphrey Bogart says "Play it again, Sam" in *Casablanca*. (He doesn't, though he says something similar). What's far more important is that Waxman here produced a true masterpiece of film scoring, cues that never interfere with the dialogue or visuals, yet enrich the meaning of the whole so thoroughly that without them the film would be immeasurably poorer. In any case, music and film noir went their separate ways in what is generally considered the last great film of the genre's classic period, Welles's *Touch of Evil* (1958).

As with many of Welles's movies after *Citizen Kane*, the final cut of the theatrical release was not in keeping with the director's desires. The music was one of Welles's points of disagreement: namely, that there was too much of it. To supply music for this darkest of dark tales of police corruption, the studio (Universal) had hired young Henry Mancini. Mancini, a former chart writer for the Glenn Miller Orchestra, had paid his dues with six years of toil on Universal "B" flicks and had just broken through to a degree of fame with his theme for the TV detective series, *Peter Gunn*. The jump from a TV detective series to a crime drama on the big screen might seem natural enough, but *Peter Gunn*

was a lighthearted, half-comic series in which the title character's sua-
vity was half the appeal, while *Touch of Evil* addressed the abuse of
police power and the deep corruption not only of politics but of the
human soul itself—hardly related themes. Welles wanted the film's
music to be almost entirely diegetic—particularly the opening sequence
that played out as the main titles rolled. Instead of a theme over the
titles, Welles wanted the sounds coming from the dingy nightclubs of
the border town where a murder is about to take place. This was in
keeping with the film's general aesthetic, a feeling that the action arises
as much from the social, cultural, and political environment as from the
characters themselves.

But Universal insisted on Mancini's "swinging" big-band music—not
unlike his popular *Peter Gunn* theme—to play over the credits and
opening action, and the final release reflected their wishes. A restored
version of the film, which I have not seen, reportedly removes the
Mancini opening-credit music, but one can see even by viewing the
original theatrical release that the diegetic music Welles wanted was by
far the more effective choice. Throughout the film, source music does
much more to tell the story than any of Mancini's cues. The most
effective of the diegetic moments is a player piano in a brothel that is
heard twice, the second time in a poignant context.

By the time of *Touch of Evil*, film noir had indeed grown very dark,
and for roughly the span of a decade and a half, it would essentially
disappear. But when, in 1974, the genre made a brief return, it took the
form of one of the most powerful films in screen history, with music
that many believe should head the list of the all-time greatest cinema
scores.

Chinatown (1974) feels like film noir and plays out like Greek drama. Director Roman Polanski's masterpiece pulls back the veils of power to expose absolute corruption at the deepest levels. Robert Towne's
screenplay negotiates the story of Los Angeles private investigator Jake
Gittes (Jack Nicholson) and his (at first seemingly mundane) encounter
with the city's water department. It's a mystery that begins in cliché,
when Gittes is hired to track a philandering husband, only to end in
hair-raising revelation and tragedy.

The music for such a film would have to do two relatively easy things
and one very hard thing. The two easy things are: cultivate the state of
persistent mystery, and hit the action cues. The hard thing: create a

mood of deep tragedy within the frame of *Chinatown*'s place and time (Los Angeles, 1937) and its unfolding from "detective story" to existential horror show. Jerry Goldsmith's music does the hard thing so well that it is consistently named among the top ten film scores of all time (the AFI ranks it ninth), and was dubbed "the perfect film score" by *Wall Street Journal* critic Terry Teachout.

Goldsmith's score begins by announcing the main credits with a shower of notes from four harps playing at once. The harps soften the edge of what would otherwise be a sharp dissonance, effecting a misty feeling that is underlined by violins softly playing whistling harmonics. A trumpet enters with the main theme, smoky, poignant, and redolent of the 1930s. The theme will return throughout the film, especially at moments when the plot takes one of its many turns. Twelve minutes into the movie, we will hear where Goldsmith may have gotten the idea for it. Gittes is parked on the street, and as he deals with business, the strains of a popular song drift from a bar. It's the Vernon Duke–Ira Gershwin song "I Can't Get Started," which was in fact a huge hit that summer of 1937. Goldsmith's theme bears a resemblance in its shape and its mood, a kind of restrained melancholy.

That melody—and the bluesy color of the trumpet—will haunt the film, accompanying the love scenes and helping to make horribly inevitable the story's shocking ending. Percussive attacks on the harps and/or four pianos, associated with the evil Noah Cross (John Huston), alternate with the theme throughout. Cues are rare and spaced at a distance from each other; in more than two hours of film, there are barely twenty-three minutes of music. The orchestration consists solely of the harps, the pianos, a solo trumpet, and strings. Massed instruments of the same kind are a frequent choice of film composers. Bernard Herrmann used four alto flutes at the start of *Citizen Kane* (1941). The effect of John Williams's two-note shark motive in *Jaws* (1975) relies in no small part on the very large number of double basses that played it. In *Chinatown*, Goldsmith's massed harps and pianos, a dense and resonant jangle of strings, accentuate the confusion and feeling of displacement Gittes experiences as he tries to pierce the arcane mystery in front of him, shrouded in politics, greed, and lust.

Goldsmith composed his extraordinary musical commentary on a subtly powerful drama in only ten days. The reason: *Chinatown* had screened in sneak previews with a completely different score by a young contemporary classical composer, Phillip Lambro, and audiences had walked out halfway through, shaking their heads. Producer Robert Evans believed the problem to be Lambro's busy music, its almost always constant presence evoking 1930s big band and popular songs. (Lambro's music was retained for the trailer, which can be viewed on YouTube. It's decked out in 1930s musical regalia, from a jazzy hi-hat cymbal to sighing strings.) Evans ordered the score dumped and hired Goldsmith to write a new one at lightning speed. The film was rescreened with Goldsmith's music just prior to release—and audiences loved it.

This famous incident is an object lesson in how to score a film. Lambro had quite effectively evoked the 1930s, but *Chinatown* isn't about an era; it's a tragedy about the alliance of evil and power that happens to be set in 1930s Los Angeles. Goldsmith "got" the film, providing music that spoke to its artistic and emotional core, while staying within the stylistic frame of time and place. The story also makes clear something that is all too frequently obscured or ignored: Music is as vitally an important part of the cinematic whole as cinematography and casting. Not just any music will do. Music can greatly strengthen a director's vision. Music can also destroy it.

When Goldsmith returned to the genre in the neo-noir *L.A. Confidential* (1997), he stuck with the trumpet as his main voice, but the theme is not a bluesy song tossed against the timbral rocks of massed harps and pianos. Instead it's a half-elegy, half-blues tune that bears an uncanny resemblance at the outset to the main idea in Leonard Bernstein's score to *On the Waterfront*. Whether this was homage or inadvertent lifting is hard to tell. Musical language is limited and the accepted parameters of film music still more limited, so it may well have been happenstance. Even so, even a casual comparison shows the opening of the two themes to be identical.

✿ ✿ ✿

Bernard Herrmann (1911–1975) holds a place in the hearts of film-music lovers dearer than any composer of his generation, or indeed of any generation. No other film composer has spanned such stylistic distances, working with Orson Welles on what many call the greatest American film of all time, *Citizen Kane* (1941); pioneering the sound of sci-fi in *The Day the Earth Stood Still* (1951); setting a standard for television music in the 1950s; helping to create the greatest body of film from the 1950s in the form of Alfred Hitchcock's *North by Northwest*, *Vertigo*, and *Psycho*; and ending his career with yet another ground-breaker, *Taxi Driver* (1976).

Herrmann could not have chosen a more illustrious start to his career. As music director for Orson Welles's Mercury Theater, he was associated with Welles's early triumphs on stage and radio (he music-supervised the notorious *War of the Worlds* broadcast in 1938). In 1941, Herrmann scored Welles's first feature, a film that a majority of critics over the decades have named the best single contribution to cinema, ever: *Citizen Kane*. Though *Citizen Kane* is not a mystery (except in the broadest sense) and not noir (though its expressionist aesthetic almost qualifies it as such), we are going to address its score here, because most of Herrmann's other music falls under this category, and because *Citizen Kane*, sui generis, doesn't actually belong anywhere else, either.

From the deliberately weird sounds at the start, achieved by four alto flutes in dark cooing, *Citizen Kane* is a very skillful score that more than ably supports this great film. Particularly striking is Herrmann's use of waltzes and other dance forms of the time, as in the marriage montage depicting the progress—or rather regress—of Kane's first marriage. But it's the last two-and-a-half minutes of Herrmann's score for *Citizen Kane* that are as perfect as any cue gets. Kane, the hyper-acquisitive newspaper tycoon, has died in a fit of apoplexy, with the word "Rosebud" on his lips. In Kane's final years, everything he loved—or thought he loved—had gone sour, becoming a pile of thousands of meaningless bits of art and furniture and junk. The camera floats over the expanse of crated debris that is Kane's ugly legacy, and as it does, Herrmann's music reflects the emptiness of Kane's impersonal acquisitions through music that is melodically and harmonically neutral, the sonic equivalent of the indifferent camera. Then, at the moment when a sled enters the frame, the tempo picks up and block chords in the brass signal an imminent threat. But a threat to what? The junk is ordered to be incinerated. What difference could that make, now that Kane is dead?

The music serves the same role here as it does in a horror movie when the ingénue blithely walks into a room she doesn't know contains a monster—it tells us something significant is about to happen. But in a horror film, we know what the music is foretelling: a grisly action of some sort. This is infinitely more mysterious, and it becomes more so as the sled is tossed into the flames. A mid-distance shot shows the sled as it begins to be consumed to the sound of low brass in the minor-mode chromatic language that Herrmann favored, whatever the genre. With the next shot, the camera focuses on the sled's name: "Rosebud." Of course, this is more than a sled going up in flames: it is Kane's youth, his innocence, his very self. This was the sled he was on as a little boy, laughing in carefree abandon at just the moment when a trustee showed up at his family doorstep to tell him he was now a multimillionaire. That last, gleeful sledding was accompanied by some of Herrmann's best "happy" music, twenty seconds of bells and flutes in crisp eighth notes, overlaid by violins in their highest register. It's incredibly brief, yet unforgettable, because it is the only time the music signals innocence. After little Kane ("Charlie") is told he is being taken away from his simple, poor parents by train, we see the sled abandoned and covered by snow as a train whistle blows in the background. We'll hear that train whistle again, or its musical imitation, in the final chords of the film's score, as "Rosebud" and Kane's lost innocence evaporate.

The most famous music in *Citizen Kane* is not this perfect final cue, but a bit of diegetic music supposedly from an opera called *Salammbo*. In the story of the film, Kane has married a talentless, would-be opera singer, and in scenes that are increasingly distressing, she is given lessons by a teacher who can barely contain his displeasure. She is to make her debut in an opera called *Salammbo*, apparently adapted from a Flaubert novel of the same name. In 1941 there were already two operatic works based on Flaubert's novel, both from the previous century: a complete, and completely unknown opera by Ernest Reyer, and an unfinished trunk of a piece by the famous Russian master, Modest Mussorgsky. Rather than use excerpts from either, Herrmann wrote his own aria in nineteenth-century style, "Ah, Cruelle," to a French text by John Houseman, yet another member of Welles's fabled Mercury Theatre personnel. We hear Kane's hapless bride rehearse it and sing it, and as we do, we have every reason to accept it as an actual piece of repertoire. Indeed, that's what the aria eventually became: a concert work performed and recorded by such fabled sopranos as Eileen Farrell and Kiri Te Kanawa. Its last note, a high D above high C, is a killer, but it fits Houseman's text, which metaphorically calls for the singer's faithless lover to stab her in the heart: *"Prete-moi ton epee! Frappe!"* ("Ready your sword for me! Strike!") It is on the last syllable that the high D occurs.

Following *Citizen Kane*, Herrmann signed on to Welles's next film, *The Magnificent Ambersons*, an ill-fated venture that was hacked to pieces when studio executives cut three reels of Welles's work and, with it, much of Herrmann's music. The composer demanded his name be withdrawn from the credits. It was not.

We'll address Herrmann's next significant score, *The Day the Earth Stood Still*, in the chapter on science fiction. For now, we fast-forward to one of the most famous director-composer collaborations in cinema history, that of Herrmann with Alfred Hitchcock. Herrmann scored seven Hitchcock films: *The Trouble with Harry* (1955), the remake of *The Man Who Knew Too Much* (1956), *The Wrong Man* (1956), *Vertigo* (1958), *North by Northwest* (1959), *Psycho* (1960), and *Marnie* (1964). He also served as sound consultant to *The Birds* (1963), which contained electronically generated bird sounds, but no music.

Hitchcock met Herrmann when the director's composer from a previous film introduced the men. A prior commitment meant that the previous composer could not work on Hitchcock's next project—why not try Herrmann? That project, and the Hitchcock-Herrmann collaboration, was *The Trouble with Harry* (1955), a black comedy about a misplaced corpse. Herrmann met the challenge of this very odd tale with a busy main idea of scurrying low woodwinds—instant hilarity—and a four-note "dead man" motive that outlined the so-called Devil's interval of the augmented fourth. There were also numerous Mickey Mouse cues, as when a distracted reader trips over the dead man. The music delighted Hitchcock, and the *Harry* score remained his personal favorite of his collaborations with Herrmann.

Herrmann next scored the 1956 remake of Hitchcock's *The Man Who Knew Too Much*. Jimmy Stewart and Doris Day played the tourist couple in Morocco who witness an assassination and find out, well, too much for their own good. Herrmann's cues took a back seat to a previously composed symphonic work by Arthur Benjamin, which served as part of the climax of the plot, and to the song "Que Sera, Sera" as sung by Doris Day. Hitchcock's next film was *The Wrong Man*, featuring Henry Fonda as a jazz bass player and Herrmann cues that are apt, though hardly remarkable. What came next, however, constituted the three Hitchcock films that culminate the decade, his career, and in a way, the very genre of the thriller.

For many years, the film that topped the list of all-time greats at *Sight & Sound* magazine, a British film critics journal, was *Citizen Kane*. But in 2012, that sterling name among great works of cinema was replaced by Hitchcock's *Vertigo*. Not many people stopped to notice that the two films had almost nothing in common except the name of their composer: Bernard Herrmann.

It is widely asserted that Herrmann based his *Vertigo* score on the famous "Prelude and Love-Death" from Wagner's music-drama, *Tristan und Isolde*. It is not so much that it resembles that famous work on the surface—though the three-note descending motive that dominates much of *Vertigo* can indeed be found in the Wagner, and its key center (E minor) is the same—but that Herrmann adopted Wagner's aesthetic of never-ending melody. This is roughly the idea that music can be extended for a long time (in theory, forever) if a cadence is avoided. A cadence is simply an endpoint, a place at which the harmonies of a musical thought conclude, the way a sentence concludes with a period at the end. In *Tristan und Isolde,* Wagner created the illusion of a suspended-animation universe by constantly delaying the period, as it were, at last employing it only after a very long time in which anticipation has built and built . . . and built. Herrmann does something similar in *Vertigo*, though not at Wagner's great length. He creates a sense of tension by not allowing the music to conclude, save at two very important dramatic spots: the first kiss shared by the Jimmy Stewart and Kim Novak characters, and the actual end of the movie.

Vertigo begins with a famous spiraling graphic over which the opening credits are displayed. Herrmann underscores this with music in a dizzying three-beat pattern, harps and flutes predominating. Periodically this swirling is blasted by brass chords, and eventually we hear the three-note descending motive, which might almost be called the gravity motive, pulling downward as it does in the manner of someone plagued with the condition named in the film's title. In the opening sequence, we see why: Scotty (Jimmy Stewart) is a police detective who was forced to resign when a bout of acrophobia—the fear of heights—caused the death of a fellow law enforcement officer.

A love theme enters the score when Scotty first sees Madeleine (Kim Novak), the wife of a friend who has asked Scotty to come out of retirement in order to track Madeleine's strange ramblings. It starts with clarinets in deep, chalumeau register, pulsing a gentle ostinato over which we hear strings play a simple lyrical phrase. Before you know it, clarinet and strings have switched roles—a subtle musical hint, perhaps, as to what is to come? This is a long, evocative cue that follows Madeleine out of the restaurant, into the streets of San Francisco, and down to the mission, where we hear a hint of organ music that could be diegetic but is probably simply a tip-of-the-hat to the location. Madeleine roams the grounds, coming eventually to view the gravestone of Carlotta Valdes, a mysterious figure from the previous century whom, it will turn out, Madeleine thinks herself to have been in a previous life. As Madeleine views the headstone we hear a bell toll, and a bass clarinet intones a chant-like figure. There is a brief lack of music as the scene changes from the mission to the museum, where Madeleine sits spellbound at the sight of Carlotta Valdes's portrait.

Cues of this length are now, as of 2016, very rare. This one goes on, minute after minute, with only brief pauses, establishing over its length the following in musical terms, since there is little or no dialogue: Scotty's infatuation with Madeleine; Madeleine's obsession with the persona of Carlotta; and the air of mystery that surrounds both Madeleine's peregrinations and Scotty's assignment to track her. We go instantly into another cue, essentially an extension of the previous one, a series of chords over a pedal-point ostinato in the harp. Herrmann's music will lead us from scene to mysterious scene until at last, to the scream of French horns and scrambling strings, Madeleine throws herself into San Francisco Bay.

After Scotty rescues Madeleine, there comes a brief scene at his apartment in which Herrmann moves the harmony relentlessly from one key to another, as if it will never come to rest—Wagner's unending melody. But in a subsequent exterior shot, beneath a tree, as Scotty tries harder and harder to understand who Carlotta is and why Madeleine confuses herself with Carlotta, the restlessness at last comes down to a handful of chords that finally land perfectly on the first clear harmonic cadence of the score—at the very moment that Scotty and Madeleine kiss. This is Mickey Mouse scoring taken to the level of the sublime, a musical manipulation that helps tell the story in wordless sound. Throughout the remainder of the film, Herrmann's music continues to support Hitchcock's storytelling, right down to the second big harmonic cadence, at the film's tragic close.

As treasured as *Vertigo* is today, it failed to impress the critics in 1958, and registered disappointment at the box office as well. The following year brought Hitchcock's *North by Northwest*, perhaps the quintessential movie of the 1950s. The plot concerns the Cold War, and for much of the film, it's nearly impossible to tell exactly what's happening or why—much like the Cold War itself. Most of Herrmann's music for *North by Northwest* is of his busy variety. The main theme is a scurrying, three-count, tight-fisted grouping of rhythmic motives that will later be broken up and manipulated as the film progresses. Herrmann said he based the rhythmic nature of these ideas on the Spanish fandango, a rapid, whirling dance form, and though there is nothing even vaguely Spanish about the film, somehow it works. A softer theme, signaling the presence of the beautiful Eva Marie Saint, gives us a plangent melody that descends delicately via oboe, switching halfway down to a clarinet. The sinister rhythmic motives from the fandango theme become at one point an almost merry-go-round tune, and this is not inappropriate, as the characters are caught on the carousel of Cold War politics. This also fits the dual nature of *North by Northwest*, which can be read as either drama or comedy.

Musically, the most effective moment is the end in which, as Cary Grant is reaching for a desperate Eva Marie Saint on the face of Mount Rushmore, the scene suddenly changes to him reaching to lift her into their train-compartment bed. This instant shift would not have worked nearly so well without Herrmann's music to take the emotions from terror (dissonant chords) to joy (the beautiful theme). It is one of film music's strange facts that the most iconic scene in *North by Northwest*—the crop-duster chasing Cary Grant's character through the fields—is wholly without music. An absence of music is also a musical choice, but one only very rarely employed in such action-packed episodes as the crop-duster chase. Hitchcock would expand this choice to the entirety of his 1963 film, *The Birds*, which contains not a note of non-diegetic music, only electronically produced birdsongs.

We next come to the score for which Herrmann is best known among the general public, and one that contains the twenty-five seconds of music that comprise not only the composer's most famous moment, but arguably the most famous moment in all of film-music history: *Psycho* (1960). The screeching strings of Herrmann's shower scene music are rivaled only by John Williams's two-note shark motive in *Jaws* as the ultimate film-music icon. Yet the shower scene music would not work at all were it not set up perfectly by Herrmann in the form of everything that comes before. *Psycho* is a case of a composer spotting a climax musically, and then shaping the preceding music so as to lead up to it.

The choice of instrumentation is essential to a composer's creation. One cannot write for, say, the saxophone and rhythm section in the same way one writes for full orchestra. Instruments carry with them their own potentials and their own limitations, as well as preconceived baggage. Most people think "sax," for example, and link it to jazzy seduction of some sort. But such associations aside, instrumentation is the color of music, the equivalent of a visual artist's choice of palette. For his most famous score, Herrmann chose an orchestra of only strings. That's right: Herrmann's music for *Psycho*, Alfred Hitchcock's devastatingly violent 1960 horror film, consists entirely of instruments from the violin family.

In the mind of the everyday non-musician, of course, there's nothing particularly scary about bowed strings. The strings cliché, in fact, conjures the opposite: massed strings are silky, smooth, comfortable, and peaceful. A string orchestra is Mantovani conducting sweet old songs, all of them slow. And it's true that strings can sound sweet and peaceful and absurdly cushiony when a composer or arranger writes sweet, peaceful, cushiony music for them. But when a composer of skill wants those same strings to screech or howl or moan or complain, they will do so. Instrumentation makes a difference on the surface of music, but if there's any depth beneath that surface, it's because the composer knew what to do with that instrumentation.

Why did Herrmann employ strings alone? Before trying to answer the question, consider a Herrmann score that went in the opposite direction: *The Day the Earth Stood Still*. That instrumentation includes two theremins, the slip-slidey electronic instruments played when the hands of the performer control pitch and volume by simply moving in mid-air; prepared piano, a piano in which pieces of wood, rubber, and/ or metal are placed between the strings for unusual color effects; and electrically amplified strings and electric organs and guitar, multiple

harps, brass, and percussion. This kitchen-sink orchestration is the opposite of the strings-only score to *Psycho*, not only because of the star-
tling presence of wildly different colors, but the fact that most of these
colors were alien to the ears of America moviegoers in the early 1950s.
And "alien" here is the operative term, given the movie's theme of
visitation and warning from another planet. Herrmann knew that music
to accompany a giant robot and his humanoid-but-spooky pal could not
be given to a set of instruments associated with the everyday. Music for
aliens had to be, well . . . alien.

But *Psycho* concerned phenomena all too familiar. Greed, obsession, and violence are, unfortunately, never far from the human experience. Strings are intimate and ordinary and pliable—even emotionally
neutral in a sense, the way a flute (which is "pretty") and a trumpet
(which signals masculinity) cannot be. They are also neutral in terms of
color. In other words, their timbre does not amplify dissonances. It's
well known among composers and arrangers that a dissonance in the
strings does not have the effect of the same dissonance played by, say,
brass or woodwinds. It's not that the dissonance is somehow less dissonant, but that it is more clenched and implosive than, say, brass dissonance, which might be called "in-your-face." Brass and woodwinds,
instruments of intense tonal color, are extroverts. String timbre, by
contrast, is an inward sound, and dissonance in strings is all the scarier
for being interior. Of course, this fits the psychological horror of *Psycho*
to a proverbial "T." The shower scene in particular typifies what might
be called Rule No. 1 in film-music composition: write the feelings of the
characters, not just the action on the screen. When we hear the music
of the shower scene, it is not only the strings we hear scream—it's Janet
Leigh's true voice, the inner scream of her emotional terror.

Of course, it didn't hurt that Herrmann had already composed a
string-orchestra work that magically suited the mood of *Psycho*. Herrmann's String Sinfonietta of 1936 contains movements that match almost exactly some of *Psycho*'s cues. The recycling of concert music for
film, and vice versa, is common practice among composers with feet in
both cinema and the symphonic world.

Following *Psycho*, Hitchcock turned to Daphne du Maurier's tale of
nature gone wrong, *The Birds* (1963). For this, the great director opted
for no music at all in the normal sense, but rather a combination of
natural and electronically produced bird sounds. This unique and whol-

ly right decision will be discussed in chapter 9, "Ambient Music, No Music, and Ready-Mades."

The Birds was Hitchcock's last universally acclaimed movie. From then on, mixed reviews and a declining box office signaled that the great era of his filmmaking was behind him. In 1964 came *Marnie*, a psychological thriller with aspects of classic mystery starring Sean Connery and Tippi Hedren, whom Hitchcock had just discovered and cast in *The Birds*. For the last time, Herrmann supplied a musical score. But studio execs complained that the film score, some of Herrmann's most conservative and purely symphonic music, was not in sync with the changing times. The Beatles had landed in America, and the sound of music was changing. Hitchcock, who took trends with a seriousness unbecoming to a genius, apparently agreed, for with his next project, *Torn Curtain*, he insisted on a theme song in the pop mode. Famously, Herrmann protested, saying, "But Hitch, you're not a pop director." Not one to have his orders contradicted, Hitchcock fired Herrmann and commissioned a last-minute replacement score from John Addison. Addison dutifully added a little theme song, though it was a rather old-fashioned waltz to complement a distinctly vanilla background score. Hitchcock not only never hired Herrmann again, but refused to talk to him.

Before we leave the subject of Hitchcock, we need to backpedal and look at two pre-Herrmann films of some musical interest: *Spellbound* (1945) and *Notorious* (1949).

We know *Spellbound* is going to be music-heavy because it comes with an overture, designed to be heard prior to the opening credits and intended to set the mood. The composer is no less than Miklos Rozsa, and his overture at first indicates anything but the psychological thriller we are about to experience. There is light, skipping music that obviates anything "heavy" at all, but then we hear the main theme, one of the grandest composed for film up to that time, and one of the greatest ever. With the opening credits comes another surprise: we hear the theremin, the electronic instrument recently invented by a Soviet expatriate (who was later revealed to have been a double agent for the Soviet Union—a Hitchcock plot that never got filmed!). The distinctive sound of the theremin was used twice that year by Rozsa for the first times in movie history. The other film was *Lost Weekend*, a story of alcoholism. In that film, the theremin attends a bender, but in *Spellbound*, it ushers Gregory Peck in and out of his dream states as he sits relating his visions to the beautiful psychoanalyst, Ingrid Bergman. The theme—which Hitchcock reportedly disliked, dismissing it as "schmaltz"—was there, of course, for the inevitable love interest between Peck and Bergman. It showed that Rozsa could craft a Rachmaninoff-ish melody to rival that of Max Steiner's *Gone with the Wind*.

Notorious counts as one of very few times the talents of Roy Webb were given full reign. Webb, an American-born musician, was an aide to Max Steiner during the era of *King Kong*, before striking out on his own as an RKO house composer/arranger. B movies were largely his fate, but in 1949 a studio disagreement led to Hitchcock not getting the composer of his choice, Dmitri Tiomkin. Webb, the studio default, turned in a deft and subtle score that compares with some of the best that Herrmann would someday turn in. Ironically, it was Herrmann who helped keep Webb in his usual role of studio hack, and all because of personal pique. In 1946, Webb had dutifully supplied a different ending to the score for Orson Welles's *The Magnificent Ambersons* when RKO cut the film down to size from Welles's original vision. This so outraged Herrmann that he demanded his name be removed from the credits, then made the squashing of Webb's career a lifelong vendetta.

But he couldn't stop *Notorious* from happening. The story concerns a German woman (Ingrid Bergman) pressed into service by U.S. intelligence (personified by Cary Grant) to spy on a postwar Nazi operation, headed by Claude Rains, whom she marries in order to get closer and gain better information. Webb's music dances us back and forth between the darkness of the spy world and the lightness of the inevitable love story that blooms between Grant and Bergman. In one cue of more than six minutes, mostly over silent action, Webb takes us from Rains's naïve belief in his wife's innocence and down into the dank wine cellar where his belief unwinds on the discovery of a clue among the bottles. From there we follow Rains's darkening thoughts, thanks to Webb's continuing cue, as he makes a dawn confession of his discovery to his overbearing mother. It is all done by the canny manipulation of a gesture, heard immediately in the opening credits, of a sustained note followed by a number of shorter notes in triplet deployment. The most common form of Webb's variation on this opening idea is the love theme, but in our six-plus-minute cue it is instead aptly distorted to end with a sinister sound, the musical negation of the actual love theme—

which does not belong to Rains and Bergman, but to Bergman and Grant. Thus, Webb tells us two things at the same time: the sinister fate that probably awaits Ingrid Bergman, and something of the love that sustains her.

Classically trained composers (and Webb and all the other film composers of that generation were classically trained) were strongly aware of the power of related musical ideas. The "denied love theme" of the cue just referenced is but one instance. It's not that the moviegoer is aware of it and consciously sitting and thinking, "Oh, the love theme has just shown up in a darkened form," but that this fact works on the listener despite being unconscious of it. Such is the power of music in film. It takes a canny composer and, what is much more, a savvy director to make it happen.

Hitchcock was decades finding his perfect musical soulmate in Herrmann and, as we have seen, the match ended in divorce. Herrmann soldiered on, however, scoring many films before his death in 1975. His last turned out to be one of his best. From Welles's *Touch of Evil* to Martin Scorcese's *Taxi Driver* (1976) is the distance of a generation and a drastically altered sensibility. If 1959's *Touch of Evil* can be said to have concluded the golden age of film noir, and if 1974's *Chinatown* brought it back in revival form, then *Taxi Driver* is the nightmare that film noir experienced while it slept. *Touch of Evil* and *Chinatown* both boasted good guys to offset the bad, but *Taxi Driver* knows only the emptiness that inhabits everyone, and will not permit of good or evil, only darkness. This is painted in tones when Herrmann shifts obsessively between crescendos on two neighboring minor chords while the title character, Travis, played with legendary mastery by Robert De Niro, drives desperate people around a vulgar and dirty cityscape.

Herrmann chose to bring the slinky sax sound back for one last appearance in *Taxi Driver,* but it's not there to titillate. It's there to mock what once was—or perhaps never was, only imagined. The sax solos belong to the New York City of myth, the great urban playground for adults that existed only in old movies. This is doubly true when Travis sees the Cybill Shepherd character, his idealized vision of white-clad womanhood amid a sea of trash. The sexy cliché of the sax as Travis's voice-over goes on about her purity reveals his real intent, which will later become grotesquely obvious when he chooses to take

Ms. Innocence to a porn theater. Travis is a sick man without any sense of propriety, and the sax music underlines that for us.

It's fitting that Herrmann, who started his film-composing career with one masterpiece, *Citizen Kane*, went out on another, *Taxi Driver*. Scorcese dedicated the film to Herrmann's memory when the composer died prior to release.

We turn lastly to a film score that stands virtually alone among others. Director Carol Reed made one of the most fateful, brave, and perfect decisions in film-music history when he chose not to lard his comedy-spiked, lean film noir of human corruption and folly with luxurious waltzes. *The Third Man* (1949) takes place in Vienna, a city associated with more great musicians than any in Europe. Haydn, Mozart, and Beethoven constitute what is called the first Viennese school, a classic sound known to every symphony concertgoer. The twentieth-century composers Arnold Schoenberg, Alban Berg, and Anton Webern added a second Viennese school of contrasting character. Their dissonant, acerbic sound defined much of modern music.

But of all music associated with Vienna, none comes more readily to mind than the waltz. Every New Year's Eve, American television transmits concerts from Vienna featuring the music of the Strauss family and others, with titles like *The Emperor Waltz, Tales of the Vienna Woods*, and of course, *The Beautiful Blue Danube*. But how could any of this possibly be made to fit the depressing sensibility of post–World War II Vienna, with its bombed-out buildings and decimated population? Of course, it couldn't. What to do to represent this Vienna, and not that of whipped cream and waltzes? An original score was the obvious answer, but by whom? And how might its sound suggest the environment of the story?

Reed was at a party in Vienna, where he was scouting locations, when he found his answer. An unknown musician named Anton Karas was providing the music for the party on a jangly folk instrument called the zither. Something about it alerted Reed that this was what he was looking for. It was one of those intuitive decisions that has no basis in rational thought, though when at last it is thought out, it makes perfect sense. *The Third Man*, shot in black and white, takes place among the darkest corners of the human mind as well as the darkest corners of postwar Vienna. The monochromatic zither was therefore apt, adding a sense of the exotic but also of the secretive. Furthermore, the instrument's shaky tone somehow suggested something of the nerve-shattered, postwar sensibility.

Karas's zither-only score is neither subtle nor complex. There is a main theme (which caught on and became a popular hit), a Harry Lime theme, and a number of fairly obvious cues, including a diminished-chord tremolo at the first sight of the notorious Lime. The score's effectiveness is in its very obviousness. It becomes a companion that walks with us through the film, sharing our reactions to the characters and events. Never again, to my knowledge, did a director hire a party musician with no movie experience to compose for the screen. Karas never scored another film.

Spotlight: Orchestrators

Music is typically the last major ingredient to be created for a movie, and the requirement of writing a lot of music in a short time means that film composers often use orchestrators. The role of the orchestrator is often misunderstood by the general public to be bigger than it actually is.

Orchestration is the craft of assigning parts to an orchestra. In a more global sense, it is the art of shaping the total color of a piece—what the flutes will play and when, what the trombones and violas will be doing, and so forth, determining the weight and surface of a piece. Orchestration is not the creation of harmonies or the shaping of form. A piece played on the piano or via computer as a MIDI mock-up will be the same piece of music after an orchestrator has finished with it (provided he has not exceeded the limits of his assignment) except that the colors—and therefore the impact—of the piece will feel different. A very rough analogy would be colorizing a black-and-white film, with the obvious difference that the black-and-white film is already a finished product and the colorization amounts to a violation. The original black-and-white film will have the same frame-by-frame motion as the colorized version, the actors will say the same things in the same way, and the content of the two movies will be identical. But the impact will feel different because color has now changed the way we see the movie.

One widespread myth has it that a film composer writes nothing more than a single melody line that is then given to orchestrators who flesh out the harmonies and vary the content of the melody to fill in the scenes. If such a "composer" were to exist, he would not be a composer at all in any actual sense, for he would have turned the act of scoring over to real composers after giving them a basic idea. No, film composers do not write just one line of music and then let others do the real work. In most cases, a film composer creates a sketch—a detailed score on multiple staves (usually more than the typical two of a piano score) with indications for what instruments should play which parts. For example, a sketch might start out with a harmonized melody line labeled "saxophones" and then add some chords marked "strings." The orchestrator's job would be to assign the grouping of saxophones for the opening, giving range-appropriate lines to the alto sax, the tenor sax, and so on, followed by voicing the strings, with assignments of the different parts to first and second violins, violas, cellos, and double basses. The orchestrator will then assemble a final score from which parts will be extracted, printed, and handed out to the members of the orchestra. The job of the orchestrator is obviously important to the final product. But it is essentially a technical skill, and only secondarily a creative act. Once in a while, an orchestrator's decision to, say, double a viola line with clarinets will amount to a creative decision, but generally the orchestrator fulfills the composer's intentions.

Some composers refused to use orchestrators, doing all the work themselves, down to the assignment of instrumental groupings. Bernard Herrmann and Ennio Morricone belong to this club. Other composers have formed associations with orchestrators that are so close professionally, the orchestrator could, figuratively speaking, finish the composer's musical sentence. Composer Jerry Goldsmith and orchestrator Arthur Morton were one such team. Another was the partnership of composer John Williams with orchestrator Herbert W. Spencer. Spencer was Williams's orchestrator throughout the early and middle years of the composer's spectacular career, and worked with him on such major scores as the Star Wars films, *E.T. The Extraterrestrial*, and the Indiana Jones franchise.

The importance of a good orchestrator whose skill at realizing the composer's intents cannot be overstressed, and yet it should always be remembered that the orchestrator makes a minimal difference in the final product when the composer is truly doing his job. A case in point: Spencer died in 1992, but there has been no substantial change in the sound of a John Williams score. The Star Wars prequels and the first two Harry Potter films did not offer a radically different John Williams to the public, but the same John Williams, without noticeable alteration. The essence of music lies in the employment of harmonic language, the manipulation of rhythms, and the gestures that define melody, as well as to some extent the choice of instrumentation. But the voicing of the various instrumental choirs and the details of, say, whether the celesta is doubled at the octave by the piano or not make relatively little difference in what we identify as a composer's sound. Orchestrators supply an essential skill that is necessary to realizing the composer's vision; but again, if the composer has truly composed and not just whistled a melody into a recording device, that vision belongs wholly to the composer.

4

THE EPIC, THE EXOTIC, AND WAR

Cinema deals inherently in spatial relationships among its actors and between the actors and their environment. This bends in two directions: the intimate and the epic. A camera in the hands of an able director can zoom in to uncomfortable closeness, all the better to show the sweat on the face of a liar, or the vulnerability in the eyes of a lover. It can also zoom out to embrace the surrounding landscape, placing the parties of a scene in a context vaster than any stage.

Live theater puts an audience in close proximity to the actors, and yet at a comfortable distance from them as well. Within the context of this middle distance, the spatial relationships among actors on a stage vary widely depending on the individual perspectives of audience members, and are therefore of relatively little artistic significance. On the other hand, the audience for a film is united in its view of the on-screen relationships among actors: everyone sees the same close-up, the same wide-angle shot, the same perspective on every scene. This is part of what makes film primarily a visual (as opposed to verbal) medium. Its tensions and resolutions are created at root by the director's ability to suggest emotions via scenic composition. That places an extra demand on the film composer in the sense that an intimate scene can be easily overwhelmed by the wrong music, while an epic scene requires exact emotional equivalency to the relationship of the actors with the surrounding visuals. Failing these demands, the music can come off as mere filler or, worse yet, unwanted exaggeration of the director's intent.

Saving intimate drama for the next chapter, we'll here focus on three different, yet related genres in a discussion of how film composers have handled the musical demands of the epic and the exotic: war films and historical dramas. There is great overlap between the two. *Patton* is obviously a war film, but its subject gives it historical significance as well. *Ben-Hur* is epic fiction situated in a pseudo-biblical timeframe, qualifying it as historical, at least for Hollywood. David Lean made the middle-mature years of his career exclusively about World War I: *Lawrence of Arabia*, *Dr. Zhivago*, and *Ryan's Daughter* all take place during the years of the "Great War," albeit in different geographic locales: *Zhivago* in Russia, *Ryan's Daughter* in Ireland, and *Lawrence*, naturally, on the Arabian peninsula. Each of them qualify as historical dramas, and all of them contain elements of martial conflict, yet only *Lawrence* qualifies (barely) as a war film per se, since it alone contains extended battle scenes. The same composer scored all three, and his success with two of them and failure with the third supply a lesson in the limits of music's ability to evoke feelings not directly etched on the screen.

But let's start with a historically based film that sparked one of the finest scores ever composed for the cinema: *The Lion in Winter* (1968). Not precisely a traditional epic, *The Lion in Winter* nonetheless contains scenes that seem to come directly out of medieval myth-making: a queen sails up the river to her castle, a royal feast commences in a grand hall, the King and Queen of England greet the King of France, and so on. But while James Goldman's screenplay treats of royal personages, it also puts into their mouths the stuff of everyday family bickering; King Henry II (Peter O'Toole) and Eleanor of Aquitaine (Katharine Hepburn) are not idealized figures, but a husband and wife groping for power over each other and their children. For instance, as they enter the grand hall for a feast, their frozen faces smile to the gentry while their conversation is all about who has whom by the vitals. Goldman's script was adapted from his play of the same name, so most scenes are sparsely peopled and dialogue-intense. With lines like "You spare the rod, Henry, and you'll spoil our children," and "It's 1138 and we're all barbarians," the script might qualify as a kitchen-sink costume drama with a thick overlay of ironic postmodernism. What's a composer to do? How to score a film that crosses so many genres without settling for an eclectic grab-bag of cues?

The genius of John Barry's answer to this challenge was in his having grasped that, while the characters shift from monarchs to mundanities, *they are always epic inside.* Even when the grand hall Eleanor and Henry enter is dirty and thick with dogs scrounging bones, even when they reduce themselves to the lowest domestic common denominators, Goldman's Henry and Eleanor—like their sons Richard, John, and Geoffrey—are always fighting world-changing battles in their souls. Barry understood that, in a true epic, characters are always larger than their context.

The film's main title sets the musical character of a strongly unified, yet varied score. After a blast of herald trumpets, it settles into a square pulsing of bass instruments, over which the trumpets sound what will become a familiar, sixteen-note theme based on the opening fanfare. Dark and modal, this evokes both a medieval sensibility (through the lens of Hollywood, of course) and a sense of forbidding power. Halfway through, voices enter, singing in chant style over and against the orchestral fabric. The text is Latin, as befits the twelfth century, and the message is brutal. Translated, the final lines read: "A day of narrow anguish/And bitter sorrowing." Even without knowing Latin, people hearing this music know not to expect a romantic comedy.

Choral singing will play an important role in the score. This is a true rarity in film music, which almost always eschews singing, except in source music. *The Lion in Winter* takes place at Christmas (though it is hardly what one would call a "Christmas movie"), and Barry composed three Christmas songs to enhance the mood. Each has a lyric by Goldman, and each one is in a different language appropriate to the time and setting: Latin, English, and French. The one in English, "The Christmas Wine," is slyly sexual, alluding to Henry's affair with the young Alais (pronounced "Alice"). Here are the opening lines: "The Christmas wine is in the vault/The Christmas coals are red./I'll spend my day the lover's way/Unwrapping all my gifts in bed." The most purely beautiful of Barry's cues is "Chinon/Eleanor's Arrival," which once again includes choral singing. As Queen Eleanor, released by Henry from prison for the Christmas holidays, sits regally on her barge, approaching the magnificent castle at Chinon, France, Henry runs along the riverbank, mad with anticipation. The music will not bow to his hilarity, but maintains a lofty, almost ethereal beauty of herald trumpets blanketed by strings, a musical mood that is nearly a definition of "majesty." The Latin words are a simple greeting to "Eleanor, Queen of the English."

The other cues in *The Lion in Winter* are in the main elaborations of the sixteen-note main theme, with added measures of intense dissonance at those moments especially rife with tension. One, named simply "God damn you," unleashes in salvos of clenched brass utterances and dissonant strings the rage felt by Henry at the fate he must face. The final cue is a little masterpiece of transition. The cue takes its name, "We're jungle creatures," from Eleanor, who utters those words in the morose conclusion that she and her family are no better than, and no different from, the most primitive and desperate of entities. The cue begins with three plaintive notes from a wordless choir, music of sad resignation that fleetly changes to music of quiet hope, taking the listener/viewer from the confines of the Chinon castle back to the river and to Eleanor's barge, where she waves goodbye to Henry—the last time these two epoch-making individuals will ever see each other.

Barry won a well-deserved Oscar for *The Lion in Winter*, which is unique among his scores. Known primarily for his music for the early James Bond films and for *Out of Africa* (1992), Barry never again composed anything to match this unique contribution to the legacy of film music. No other cinematic score known to this writer makes as much use of choral resources as *Lion*, and few others achieve the kind of unity of expression with script and direction that Barry's music achieves. Barry may have felt a certain affinity with the material. It's notable that he scored two other movies with Goldman scripts: *They Might Be Giants* and *Robin and Marian*. The latter contains a beautifully crafted love theme that stands with the best of such cues, but neither one climbs anywhere near the level of *Lion*.

The Roman Empire supplied Hollywood with more than its share of excuses to stage deadly spectacles like gladiatorial combat and chariot races. The greatest example of the latter is, of course, *Ben-Hur* (1959), with music by Miklos Rozsa. As noted in earlier chapters, the Hungarian-born Rozsa came out of the early blossoming of classically trained composers who dominated Hollywood scores in the 1930s and 1940s. He was first associated with the genre of the thriller or suspense film (*Double Indemnity*, 1944; *Spellbound*, 1945), but in 1951 he accepted the job of scoring *Quo Vadis,* a sword-and-sandal Roman Empire epic with a religious twist. He single-handedly created a musical style to match the film genre, using choir (anticipating Barry's extensive use of choral singers in *The Lion in Winter*) and employing Mediterranean rhythms for "native" scenes—an almost unheard of thing at the time. Of course, there was also a broadly romantic theme, in keeping with the expectations of audiences brought up on the essential nineteenth-century language of film music. But Rozsa was an exceptionally gifted composer and the big theme for *Quo Vadis* (1951) is subtle, admitting of all kinds of variations throughout the film as the characters change. Most of all, Rozsa came up with the "Roman March," a medium-tempo, four-beat processional made of pounding drums and herald trumpets. Of course, this was nothing like what real Roman music must have sounded like, but to paraphrase what Richard Rodgers said about his "Siamese" music for *The King and I*, if Rozsa had included actual sounds of Roman music in his score, moviegoers would have run screaming out of the theater.

The artistic and popular success of the *Quo Vadis* score—it was one of the first soundtracks to be released as a commercial recording—meant that studio executives now clamored to get Rozsa for their historical epics instead of their thrillers. In quick succession came *Ivanhoe* (1952), *Julius Caesar* (1953), *The Knights of the Round Table* (1953), and *Valley of the Kings* (1954), though the latter concerns history as experienced by modern anthropologists. The mixture of ancient and medieval periods in this lineup was not the point: to Hollywood producers of the time, anything before the eighteenth century was simply "a long time ago." In 1959, Rozsa's output for this genre reached its pinnacle with *Ben-Hur*. Another Roman Empire–era spectacle with an overlay of Christian theology, *Ben-Hur* was the biggest sword-and-sandal epic of them all. Starring Charlton Heston as the imperial true-believer-turned-Christian, this mega-blockbuster gave Rozsa the opportunity to nail down the genre, and to do that he got out his best hammers. While in some ways *Quo Vadis* is the superior score—it was certainly the more innovative—Rozsa's *Ben-Hur* music essentializes the genre and gives it its best overall representation. The love theme has all the earmarks of the expected romantic-era melody, but is flecked with intervals here and there that suggest the film's Middle Eastern setting. The "Roman March" is truly the quintessence of the genre: herald trumpets that echo each other and draw closer together rhythmically to form a striking fanfare. Other historical epics awaited Rozsa, including *El Cid* and *King of Kings*, both from 1961, but *Ben-Hur* was never bested.

Rozsa was one of the greatest of Hollywood's composers, and the last of the founding generation of classically trained movie musicians. Like Korngold, he also composed for the concert hall and, also like Korngold, he composed a violin concerto of breadth and great beauty. Unlike the violin concerto of his elder colleague, however, Rozsa's Violin Concerto has yet to enter the concert hall. That's a shame, as the work is a real stunner. A bit of it can be heard masquerading as Sherlock Holmes's violin concerto in one of Rozsa's later scores, Billy Wilder's *The Private Life of Sherlock Holmes* (1970), a film which, by the way, has epic grandeur within the confines of a detective story, in part due to Rozsa's often plaintive score.

❋ ❋ ❋

The epic always has a touch of melancholy to it. Melancholy resides in the love theme for *Ben-Hur*, and we will hear it most strikingly in the main theme for *Lawrence of Arabia*. Often, the melancholy theme for an epic will feature a melody that drops, then yearns upward, often to drop again. The shape of the melody is a quiet struggle against gravity. This is literally the case in one of the most memorable movie themes of the 1950s, the "whistling" tune Dimitri Tiomkin wrote for *The High and the Mighty* (1954). This wistful theme accompanies the tale of an airliner doomed to crash before it is saved by the copilot, played by John Wayne. Air travel was still rare enough in 1954 to qualify as exotic, and so the highly chromatic, broad melody Tiomkin wrote was a perfect fit, falling and rising in alternate measures, creating a sense of wonder tinged with longing.

The descriptive term "epic" has such a definite feel to it that "epic poetry" even got its own muse in Greek antiquity. Calliope was her name (after whom was named the garish circus organ), one of nine muses that provided inspiration to the poets of the Greek city-states. Unlike Erato (muse of love poetry) or Euterpe (muse of lyric poetry), Calliope summoned everything writ large. The characters in a love poem might be any two fools in love, and the subjects of a lyric poem need not have any significance beyond themselves. But the characters in an epic poem must change the world, must be the Napoleon-onhorseback that startled Hegel into the consciousness of world-spirit at work in history. War is the most common backdrop for such art, whether the art be poetry, painting, or film.

"War film" usually means a movie about a modern war, "modern" here indicating World War I and after. World War II, the closest thing we have to a black-and-white war, is by far the most "popular" of conflicts in Hollywood war movies. This shifts as time flows. In 1910, D. W. Griffith's *The Fugitive*, about the American Civil War, was considered a war film, because the Civil War was less than half a century in the past. But by the time of the Civil War movie *Glory* in 1989, "war film" no longer fit the bill: it was a historical film. The clear-cut good and bad of World War II (to most people, at least) meant composers of war-story scores might indulge in hyperbolic heroic gestures with impunity. The trick was to make the heroic gestures fresh, not hackneyed. In the early decades of film, most composers failed at this.

Cliché was king in movies such as *Sands of Iwo Jima* (1949), the John Wayne vehicle about U.S. Marines in the famous battle in the Pacific Theater of World War II. Victor Young's music juggles the famous Marine's Hymn with a pouty love theme to no exact effect. Young exploits the opening, upward-reaching gesture of the Marine's Hymn for masculine effect, and softens things with the sweeping theme whenever a woman or the thought of a woman enters the picture. Young also scored *The Flying Tigers* (1942), another John Wayne advertisement for combat. Without a Marine's Hymn to fall back on, Young came up with his own ham-fisted theme to contrast with the obligatory softer melody. To this he added the additional cliché of frequent "Asian" music moments using the pentatonic scale. These examples are typical of their time, when individual characters in war movies were dissolved into the overall boil of patriotism and nationalist gestures.

As the clichés wore thin over the years, war movies started at last to take on more sophistication, and along with better scripts and less propagandistic content came superior music. Two prime examples of this progress were *The Guns of Navarone* (1961, music by Dimitri Tiomkin) and *The Great Escape* (1963, music by Elmer Bernstein). But a sea-change in American sensibility, and especially in the public's attitude toward war, marked a true shift in the way war films were made and war-film scores composed. The keystone score was Jerry Goldsmith's music for *Patton* (1970). The forty-year-old Goldsmith, a Rozsa protégé, had just rattled the world of movie music with his avant-garde-ish 1968 score for *Planet of the Apes* (see chapter 8), and now he would help alter the expectations of audiences for "war movie" music. Instead of the standard opposition of a masculine, aggressive theme balanced by a sweeping, romantic secondary theme, Goldsmith came up with a bright, quickstep military march counterpointed by organ chords and punctuated by echoing trumpet triplets (a single triplet run through an echoplex—a device he'd used in *Planet of the Apes*). These three elements formed a musical portrait of General George Patton: the march was all polished brass buttons, Patton's public persona; the organ was an amazingly effective reminder of the spiritual dimension of Patton's character; and the echoing trumpets, said to be a somewhat literal reference to Patton's belief in reincarnation, signified the historical importance of the title character. *Patton* changed the focus of the genre from broad-spectrum patriotism to individual lives and emotions, and Goldsmith's music was key to that progression.

Only one entry in AFI's Top 25 film scores qualifies as music for a war movie, and even it is more bio-epic than war story: *Lawrence of Arabia*. Director David Lean's focus was not on battle scenes (though there were quite a few), but on the troubled genius of T. E. Lawrence, the English officer who turned Bedouins into a fighting force against the Turks in World War I. Maurice Jarre, a French composer relatively new to the world of film, was brought on board by producer Sam Spiegel when his first choice, Malcolm Arnold, had a falling out with Lean. Arnold had scored (and won an Oscar for) Lean's *Bridge on the River Kwai* (1957), yet another war film that wasn't about battle but (in this case) about the psychology of prisoners of war. *Bridge on the River Kwai* used and made popular the pre-composed "Colonel Bogey March," a piece from 1914, written by British Army bandmaster Kenneth Alford. Arnold, a respected composer of music for the concert hall, composed his own counterpoint to "Colonel Bogey," and supplied numerous effective cues throughout the film. But when the time came to score *Lawrence of Arabia,* Arnold was literally suicidal, having attempted twice to take his life in the wake of a disastrous divorce. The details of his falling out with Lean are unavailable, but the composer's instability almost certainly contributed.

When Lean told Spiegel that Arnold was out, Spiegel's initial idea was to employ multiple composers. But when one of those composers,

the Frenchman Jarre, submitted the lonely sounding, romantically harmonized theme that has since become world-famous, Spiegel was impressed and hired him to score the entire movie. Jarre was given six
weeks to complete the job on a film nearly three-and-a-half hours long.
He reportedly worked in four-hour stretches, with brief periods of sleep
in between. Jarre had become a musician relatively late in life, beginning as a percussion student at age fifteen. In his twenties, he landed a
position with a Paris theater that gave him hands-on experience match-
ing dramatic dialogue to appropriate musical cues. After twelve years at
this day job, Jarre struck out as a freelancer. *Lawrence of Arabia* (1962)
was only his fourth movie score. He was thirty-eight years old on the
film's release, which was one of two breakthrough movies for Jarre that
year. The other, *The Longest Day*, was a World War II sprawl of an all-
star movie that more or less concluded the good guy/bad guy paradigm
in Hollywood movies, and for which Jarre supplied a far less ambitious
score, one long on snare drums and allusions to Beethoven's Fifth Symphony, and which anyway took a back seat to a Paul Anka–authored
pop-song-cum-march played during the credits.

The music for *Lawrence of Arabia* richly deserves its third-place
position in AFI's list of Top 25 film scores. Jarre did not settle for
merely a main theme, even though that theme, in its expansiveness and
songfulness, is unforgettable upon one hearing, and even though that
theme is a perfect match for both the desert vistas of Lean's visuals and
the isolation of the title character's psyche. The cues range in emotional
impact from thorny, menacing dissonances to eerie soundscapes made
all the more eerie by the use of electronic sounds. Jarre had studied and
played an early electronic instrument, the ondes Martenot, with its
inventor, and he put it to effective use in *Lawrence* at such moments as
the long, solitary walk Lawrence takes in the desert to meditate on how
to take the port town of Aqaba. It's unclear who was responsible for
inclusion of yet another Alford march, "The Voice of the Guns," but one
might guess that either Lean or Spiegel saw the opportunity for another
hit like "Colonel Bogey." That didn't happen, but "Voice of the Guns,"
which might have stood out like the proverbial sore thumb, was actually
very much at home as the terribly, terribly British martial music that
welcomes Lawrence back to regular army life after crossing the Sinai.

The score to *Lawrence of Arabia* has been re-recorded for commercial release on compact disc, presumably to take advantage of the many

technological advances after 1962, but for sheer excitement nothing matches the original soundtrack, performed by the London Philharmonic Orchestra and conducted by . . . whom, exactly? Pressings of the soundtrack LP from 1962 credit the esteemed English conductor, Sir Adrian Boult, but later re-issues state clearly, "composed and conducted by Maurice Jarre." What happened? Boult had been unable to time the cues to fit the frames, so Jarre was forced to take over, but Boult's name (he was a well-known classical conductor at the time) remained on the LP. Only with the CD release was the conducting credit given to Jarre. The neophyte did a magnificent job of bringing out the subtleties of his score, the breadth of its emotions, the wild colors of the orchestration, and the punch and savor of its Straussian harmonies. The recording remains one of perhaps a dozen or so soundtracks that can be listened to as a purely symphonic performance, without finding the inevitable throwaway track. There are no throwaways in this score.

In the early 1960s, it was still expected for epic films—and *Lawrence* has rightly been called the epic of all epics—to provide overtures, four- or five-minute pieces to be played prior to the film's beginning, with the intent of warming up the audience to the tone and feeling of the coming several hours. Jarre's overture to *Lawrence* is arguably the finest such piece ever composed. Good percussionist that he was, Jarre begins things on the timpani, which sounds a seven-note rhythm that will recur throughout the film as a kind of head motive for the appearance of the Arab tribes in battle regalia. We then very briefly hear, backed by the continuing timpani, some of the aggressive brass music later associated with the "brigands," the guns-for-hire that will earn the contempt of the nobler Arab participants. Suddenly we slide into strings playing the main theme, the melody's initial plunge downward repeated after a turnaround on a triplet figure. These opening measures are themselves repeated, and then we hear what really amounts to a bridge, a middle section of the theme that flirts with another idea, only to return yet again, and for the last time, to the initial idea. This is essentially a popular song form: AABA, where "A" is the main part of a song and "B" is the bridge. So much for the "exotic" appeal of the theme—its form is pure Tin Pan Alley! The otherworldly beauty of the main theme is interrupted by the "Voice of the Guns," which shortly goes into clever counterpoint with the main theme. We then return to the rhythmic head motive, the music of the brigands, and a flash of Middle Eastern–inflected orchestral glory to bring things to an end.

Of course, this end does nothing but signal a beginning. Now come the opening credits, which used to be the one and only place that actors, writers, tech people, and others got any mention whatsoever. Final credits were a thing of the future. And the credits were snug then, too. Instead of the nine or ten minutes now occupied by final credits in a typical major release of the twenty-first century, those for the 1962 mega-epic *Lawrence* came in at under two minutes. For this, Jarre supplied chipper music for a spring day in rural England—the day the real Lawrence was killed in a motorcycle accident, and the exact incident with which Lean chose to begin his film. The main theme is also touched upon a couple times. In fact, it is heard at the very end, when the music fades out and we fade in on Peter O'Toole, as the title character, racing down a country road on the fated motorcycle.

Some of the film's cues weave the main theme in and out, but there are cues that go wide of the lyric melody's contemplative sensibility. The most compelling of these is "Arrival at Auda's Camp." As Lean's camera pans the desert mountain lair that is home to Auda's tribe, the Howitat, Jarre's music contributes massive, sonorous block chords to match the substance of those mountains. Then the music erupts into mad, whirling figures to accompany the bursting-in of Auda and his guests, Lawrence and the dreaded enemy tribe, the Harif, who are now made welcome as possible allies in the war against the Ottomans. Another cue, called "The Anvil of the Sun," hits the listener over the head with knotty orchestral chords that are as apt a sonic equivalent to the oppression of a desert sun as one might wish. This comes immediately before one of the film's most triumphant moments: the return of Gasim to the camp. In the nocturnal trek across the dreaded Nefud desert, Gasim has fallen asleep and slipped from his camel. He would be left to broil in the heat except that Lawrence ventures back into the desert, under the glare of the deadly sun, to rescue him. Against all odds, Lawrence succeeds, and when he enters the camp, a dusty, weary man, but alive and with Gasim, the music breaks into ecstatic measures. It's a rhythmically enhanced version of the bridge to the main theme, and nothing could be more appropriate. The bridge of a melody is always the most striving and the most poignant, due to its yearning to return to the "A" subject. It serves here to underscore Lawrence's longing to impress and to fit in—somewhere.

Jarre won an Oscar for *Lawrence of Arabia*, but he also won the booby prize of having to work the rest of his life in the shadow of an impossibly successful, even spectacular, beginning. He went on to score many other successful films—*Witness* and *The Man Who Would Be King* are but two—and to win two more Oscars, but Jarre was always "the composer of *Lawrence of Arabia*," just as Rachmaninoff was always the composer of the Second Piano Concerto. The music Jarre wrote for Lean's epic, in a short time and without a great deal of previous film experience, shows what can happen when the right sensibilities meet up. *Lawrence* is not only epic, it's exotic in an almost storybook way, and Jarre's music is storybook music, something close to Richard Strauss or Nikolai Rimsky-Korsakov in the way it colors everything around it. If the impossible task of movie music is to be both unnoticed and indispensable—and that is the job, to be sure—then *Lawrence* falls much closer to the indispensable side of things than the unnoticed side. As you watch *Lawrence of Arabia*, it is impossible not to notice the music, and yet, somehow, the music is so perfectly allied with the visuals and the characters that one might more accurately say that it's impossible not to notice the whole—visuals, dialogue, and music—as they blend together to tell the extraordinary story of a history-changing man who loved his life and hated himself.

Jarre composed three more scores for Lean films, and two of them won Oscars: *Doctor Zhivago* (1965) and *A Passage to India* (1984). *Dr. Zhivago* is known for its main theme, to which words were given under the title, "Somewhere, My Love," producing one of the biggest hit songs of the mid-1960s. It is larded with Russian folk-song clones and balalaikas, as befits the historical frame—the Russian Revolution and the early years of the Soviet Union. One strains to hear the "Internationale" in some form but it is absent, waiting, perhaps, to be used in grand romantic style in Warren Beatty's later and much different film about the Russian Revolution, *Reds* (1981). Familiar Jarre gestures can be heard in *A Passage to India*—the main subject is very close to the theme song from *Ryan's Daughter*, about which more below—and everything is done up in expert orchestration, which by this time had become one of Jarre's best things. To my ears, the old originality had faded, however, and Jarre's Oscar for *Passage* was mostly about nostalgia.

Though I hate to conclude a discussion of Jarre with one of the weakest director-composer collaborations in a major film, *Ryan's Daughter* provides us with a perfect example of how music can damage a film irreparably. Critics agreed that Lean's movie about a young Irish girl, her staid older husband, and the dark young German officer who becomes her lover was a failure, but none noticed the music's role in this debacle. Indeed, critics came down on everything else, including Robert Bolt's script and Lean's obsession with wide camera angles. If I had all the money in the world, one of the things I would do is this: strip Jarre's music out of the soundtrack and replace it with a better, more apt score. On re-release, I predict such an enterprise would be lauded, for Jarre's music does the one thing a movie score should never do: play to the exteriors of the film. That is, nothing in Jarre's music tells us anything about the characters in *Ryan's Daughter*. Instead, we are given "Irish music," and faux-Irish at that, along with "scenic" music of the most obvious kind.

Here is the story of a young woman grasping at life without guidance, blinded by her own passions and in love with urges she mistakes for people—and we get thin musical gruel. The critics were wrong about Bolt's script: it is a masterpiece of storytelling. It has something to say about desire, society, and love, and it says it in an original voice. And while there are the usual "look at that landscape!" moments in Lean's direction, he sticks pretty close to the characters, who are played by an exemplary cast headed by Robert Mitchum and Sarah Miles. But music is a potent part of any film that employs it, and while the right music can elevate the on-screen action to great heights, the wrong music can pull it down. Jarre's main theme, which is supposed to be an "Irish song," has all the earmarks of a Victorian British music-hall tune, as the composer all but admitted when he made a virtual copy of it into the theme for English characters in *A Passage to India*. But, much worse than that, this music doesn't stick to the characters; it slides off of them and settles into a different place altogether. It is the epitome of calling attention to itself. Jarre had enormous talent as a young composer, but as he grew older, that talent seemed to grow thinner and thinner.

Of course, standing at the head of the great line of epic Hollywood movies is *Gone with the Wind*, handled in an earlier chapter because it is more than even "epic" can describe: it is sui generis. Ever since the unparalleled success of that 1939 epoch-maker, the epic and exotic in movies—whether historical, spectacular, martial, or a combination of the three—has always been Hollywood stock-in-trade. Film composers have helped shape the feeling of such films by playing to the characters more than to the scenery, as the best scores in the genre testify. Our overview of epic-film composing has brought us to the cusp of the 1970s, when the composer who did more than any other to put new life into the old style of grand, symphonic film music began his career in earnest. But we will deal with the John Williams phenomenon in chapter 8 on science fiction and fantasy.

Shortly before Williams's arrival, though, came a dark twist in the road for the very meaning of "epic." What kind of music do you provide for a film that glorifies the lives of gritty, materialistic, murderous mobsters, whose exterior existence shouts "glory" but whose inner lives mutely mouth the word "emptiness"? That was one composer's challenge in 1972. His answer had to do with exploiting the difference/closeness between diegetic music—music from a source in the film, "heard" by the characters—and non-diegetic, or background music, heard only by the audience.

Nino Rota (1911–1979) was born in Milan and quickly established himself as a child prodigy. By age fifteen he had composed an oratorio and an opera, both of which received critical and popular acclaim. He studied in Italy, and then at the Curtis Institute in Philadelphia (1930–1932) with Rosario Scalero, who also taught American composers Samuel Barber and Gian Carlo Menotti. He began to work in film in the 1940s, and his subsequent output was vast: a complete list of Rota movie scores is more than 150 entries long. He formed an association with the great Italian film director Federico Fellini, scoring all of his films from *The White Sheik* (1952) to *The Orchestra Rehearsal* (1979), but first came to the attention of American moviegoers with his elegiac score to Franco Zeffirelli's *Romeo and Juliet* (1968). The main theme for *Romeo and Juliet*, altered to give it a bridge, became a hit song as "A Time for Us." When Francis Ford Coppola was looking around for someone to score his ambitious adaptation of Mario Puzo's novel, *The Godfather*, Rota was an obvious choice. As a native Italian, he could command the sound Coppola wanted, and as a film composer with decades of experience working beside one of the globe's greatest directors, he was "film savvy." The latter is as important, if not more so, than being able to compose music appropriate to a scene. A good composer can match a mood or an atmosphere, but it takes a film-savvy composer to grasp what a director is up to, to understand the rhythm of a film and how to complement it in musical terms, and—perhaps the single most important knack a film composer can have—when not to supply music.

The Godfather (1972) opens with a lone trumpet playing a plaintive fourteen-note theme that immediately impresses itself on our memory. Unaccompanied, it hangs there in space like an incomplete thought. This is sometimes called "The Immigrant" theme. It will come back only rarely, and when it does, we will feel it the way we feel an unpleasant reminder of our own mortality. At length, Rota's score will reveal a total of three themes. The haunting trumpet idea is the main theme, while a second, much more ominous idea makes its first entrance in connection with the assassination attempt on Don Corleone. A third theme, an ecstatic love song, is heard only when Michael is in hiding in Sicily, and is associated with Michael's brief, doomed first marriage to Apollonia. Like Rota's theme for Romeo and Juliet, this was given a set of lyrics and released as a pop song: "Speak Softly, Love."

It is a very spare score. Rota saves cues for moments of extreme dramatic tension, such as the famous scene in which the Hollywood producer awakes in bed with the severed head of his beloved stallion. This cue, a wildly distorted restatement of the main theme, is barely heard above the producer's screaming, but it is felt at the deepest level. But what is most remarkable about the score is that almost all of The Godfather's first thirty minutes, following the opening, haunting trumpet tune, is filled with diegetic music. The scene is the wedding of Don Corleone's daughter. We hear band music, we hear Italian folk songs, we hear crooner Johnny Fontane sing something called "I Have One Heart," an actual popular song from 1945. When the don dances with his daughter, at about twenty-six minutes in, we even hear "The Immigrant" played as diegetic: the band accompanies their dance as if the theme is an actual "ready-made" song. It has become the "Godfather Waltz." One ninety-second cue for the wedding band is not an Italian folk song at all: it's faux-Italian folk song composed by the director's father, Carmine Coppola, listed in the credits for "additional music." Coppola pere would also contribute honky-tonk piano music for a transition during the mob "war."

Director Coppola did not do this accidentally. He is stressing the importance of environment—culture, traditions, economic and political situations—to the story's unfolding. The Corleone family and the other mob families portrayed in *The Godfather* are no ideal forms of humanity; they are products of the belief systems in which they were raised and the material conditions in which they find themselves. With diegetic music such a major part of the film's concept, Rota could not but draw on that concept. It's notable that two cues establishing new city locales—Los Angeles for the visit to the hapless Hollywood producer, then Las Vegas when Michael goes there to talk with Moe Greene—are nearly diegetic themselves. No, the actors don't "hear" the cues. But both skate the thin ice of cliché to present a kind of cartoon-music appropriate to the time and place: "swinging" music for Los Angeles (actually an arrangement of a Tommy Dorsey hit of the day, "Manhattan Serenade"), and "sexy" music for Las Vegas. It's exactly the sort of music the characters might have heard in a nightclub in either city.

But the magical—one might say black magical, given the subject—moment is the incredible series of shots that make up the climax of *The Godfather*: the hits on all the various dons that occur while Michael is standing in as godfather to his nephew. In a stroke of genius, Rota does not use the orchestra, but starts with the diegetic and then expands it into background commentary. The source is the church organ. When we hear it, the organ music at first is holy and fit for Michael's famous line renouncing the "devil and all his works." But what Rota does with it in the cue called "The Baptism" is one of film music's greatest scenes of pure genius. Instead of interjecting additional ideas, or bringing in other instruments, Rota develops the holy music into something truly satanic. We, the audience, don't even notice the change from the church diegetic music to the background commentary, because the two elide perfectly. As one after another of the dons falls to Michael's plan, the camera goes back and forth between their deaths and Michael's hypocritical presence at the church, and as this happens, the organ music grows from blessed to damned. The organ has always been a dichotomous instrument, signifying the church and its tenets, but also containing a strangely alien character. "The monster never breathes," said Stravinsky, explaining why he never wrote for the organ. Rota puts this breathless aspect of the organ, this monstrous inhumanity, to perfect use in "The Baptism."

The score for *The Godfather* was nominated for an Oscar, but the nomination was withdrawn when it was discovered that Rota had recycled the main theme from an earlier film. This violated the Academy's stipulation that, to be eligible, a score needs to be "written expressly for the motion picture." A consolation prize of sorts arrived two years later when the Oscar was awarded for the score to *Godfather II*, composed by Rota and father Coppola (now fully credited as co-composer). That score is fuller, more romantic (in keeping with the highly romanticized depiction of the rise of the Corleone family) and more movie-ish, but it does not approach the original *Godfather* music for its innovative conflation of diegetic and non-diegetic, a concept that helped make *The Godfather* one of the best films of all time.

Sometimes, a film composer invents a sound so distinctive that it becomes unmistakably his. When this happens, any film touched by that composer takes on an identity linked to that sound. Our dictum—that music should be necessary but unnoticed—would seem to forbid this. After all, what's more noticeable than a musical style that shouts the composer's name? But sometimes a distinctive musical style also shouts the mood of the direction and the screenplay's theme. So it was with Ennio Morricone's music for *The Mission* (1986), cues made of percussive accents, Catholic vocalizing, climbing strings, Native American rhythms, an evocative oboe melody that links perfectly to one of the main characters, and still more. The layering is thick but transparent due to Morricone's command of counterpoint. The oboe melody goes along, and from nowhere the sound of what might be a Native American work song or chant flows in over the top. Did we mention the effortless flute melody that symbolizes the deep friendship between the Irons and De Niro characters? With a simple guitar accompaniment, this beauty grows from one key into the outstretched arms of another, which then releases it back to its parent tonality. Morricone's *The Mission* sounds like nothing else—least of all like the composer's most famous music, for the trilogy of spaghetti Westerns made by Sergio Leone.

Of course, it is all in keeping with the content and meaning of the film. The rich layering of different kinds of music and sonic impulses relates directly to the richness of the story and its characters: in eighteenth-century South America, a priest (Jeremy Irons) starts a mission with the help of a reformed murderer (Robert De Niro). Robert Bolt's screenplay pits church against state—the latter in the form of a power-hungry church, ironically—in what at length turns out to be a tragic tale, but one also overflowing with redemption. Power meets powerlessness, Europe meets Native America, and love meets greed in this unique film, and Morricone was the perfect choice to give it a unique score as well. Among many other features, the song of the Native Americans (called "River" in the soundtrack) is an unforgettable reimagining of music untouched by European influences.

Sensibilities change over decades, and with them change artistic aims and tastes. Terrence Malick's *The Thin Red Line* (1998) is a war epic that bears virtually no resemblance to *Patton* or *Lawrence of Arabia*. Those two focused on the martial mind in the midst of war, the "complete warrior" that was Patton and the reluctant messiah that was Lawrence. *The Thin Red Line* focused on a single life—that of an army private—in the midst of death at the World War II battle of Guadalcanal in the Pacific. It was only appropriate that the music be handled differently, and Malick—early in his career a composer as well as a filmmaker—came up with a radical plan. He asked composer Hans Zimmer to compose music before shooting began, then played the music back over loudspeakers during filming to put himself in the mood of the subject. Much of Zimmer's music was not used in the final film, and some was added from other, previously composed sources, including Fauré's Requiem and Charles Ives's *The Unanswered Question.*

The most distinctive thing on the final soundtrack was the inclusion of Pacific Islanders' choral music. More than any of the other music, it speaks to the condition of Private Wick, the man who chases down his own death, the better to know life. Malick's blend of local sources, previously composed classical music, and original music composed prior to shooting stands as a potential model for future film music.

5

COWBOYS AND SUPERHEROES

The sound of the Western was distinctive from the start: jagged rhythms, like the bumpy ride of a stage coach; main themes sounded by the brass in manly fashion; secondary themes, usually carried by strings, more genteel and feminine. The main title music of the iconic *Stagecoach* (1930) has it all: the strings create a bed of rushing sixteenth notes while the trumpets blast a theme based on a folk song. To bolster this, trombones echo the theme in imitation. At length, this gives way to a brief allusion to "I Dream of Jeannie with the Light Brown Hair," the feminine balance, but even this is accented by trumpet calls in the distance. At last, we hear the greatest cliché in the genre and possibly in all of moviedom music: The four-beat tom-tom rhythm of "Indian" music.

The music credits for director John Ford's first masterpiece go out of their way to note that the score is "based on American folk songs," and name no less than five people as having adapted these for studio orchestra: Richard Hageman, Franke Harling, Louis Gruenberg, John Leipold, and Leo Shuken. In most reference texts, Hageman gets the major credit, perhaps because he went on to score several Ford features all by himself, including the first two of the cavalry trilogy: *Fort Apache* (1948) and *She Wore a Yellow Ribbon* (1949). (Victor Young provided a much more involved and varied score for the third of them, *Rio Grande*, in 1950, abetted by songs sung by a male vocal group, the Sons of the Pioneers.) The cues are fairly redundant—we hear that opening brass theme quite a lot—and used mostly to fill in for a lack of dialogue when, for example, the coach is seen traveling through the desert.

These basic elements—the masculine rhythms and brassy main theme, the feminine counter-theme, the use of folk music or faux folk music—were the hallmarks of the Western movie score, and it is likely that audiences even expected to hear these things in a John Wayne or Randolph Scott feature, just as they would expect to see a good guy, a bad guy, a helpless lady from back East, and a gunfight. The next scores we will consider represent an exception to this rule (Dimitri Tiomkin's music for *High Noon*), the Western score's peak (Jerome Moross's *The Big Country*, Elmer Bernstein's *The Magnificent Seven*, and Alfred Newman's *How the West Was Won*), and its shattering (Ennio Morricone's *The Good, The Bad and the Ugly*).

Fred Zinnemann's *High Noon* (1952) is generally not even considered a Western, though it takes place in the Old West and stars Gary Cooper as a tired but duty-bound town sheriff. (Someone once remarked to Zinnemann, apropos of this, that it was too bad he'd never directed a Western, to which Zinnemann replied, "But I did. It was called *Oklahoma!*") The reason is that the plot does not revolve around a gunfight (though there is one, and a spectacular one at that) but around the issues of pacifism and marital allegiance. In the film, the Cooper character is about to step down from his position as sheriff to marry a Quaker girl—and who wouldn't, when she looked like Grace Kelly! But just as he and she are about to wed, a bad guy—yes, there's a bad guy—the sheriff had put in jail years before is released, and the news arrives that he is coming back to town to kill the sheriff and raise general hell. The sheriff feels obliged to stay and fight, causing a rift with his beautiful, pacifist bride-to-be. The tension caused by this moral dilemma—and not safeguarding the stagecoach gold or even killing this particular bad guy—forms the real crux of the film, and that is not a traditional Western.

The music had to be different to reflect this. Russian American composer Tiomkin had already scored a number of Westerns, including *Duel in the Sun* (1946) and *Red River* (1948), so he knew well how to write gunfight music, anticipating ever-so-slightly the next move, and hitting, Mickey Mouse style, the shots and their impacts; he knew as well how to craft a typically masculine Western theme. The one for *Duel in the Sun*, for example, was a magisterial tune of great sweep, all within the harmonic confines of what could have been an American folk song. But this non-Western needed something a little off-center, and what Tiomkin did was a stroke of genius. Instead of just a theme, he gave the tale a song, "The Ballad of High Noon (Do Not Forsake Me, O My Darling)," with original music couched in the language of a cowboy tune. The lyric, by Ned Washington, is as rustic and as country as anything you might imagine. The version issued for popular radio consumption is fairly cleaned up, but the movie version, sung over the opening credits by Tex Ritter in his best ol' boy style, ends with the words, "I won't be leavin'/Until I shoot Frank Miller dead"—Miller being, of course, Mr. Bad Guy.

The music, however, is more than a simple cowboy tune. It maintains a strict three-chord harmonic structure (with a handful of secondary chords along the way) that places it firmly in that tradition, but the melody ranges far from its opening notes, and the bridge offers a sudden shift to a different rhythm, suggesting the advance of the clock's hands toward the fatal time of day when the train carrying Frank Miller and his henchmen arrives. The tune, minus its lyrics, saturates the action, no matter whether that action concerns Cooper and Kelly, or Cooper's character and the young boy who shames the adults by volunteering to fight when they run away. And this works, because it reminds us at all moments that the theme of this film is courage: the courage to stick to one's principles and, even more challenging, the courage to abandon principles when they conflict with the overpowering presence of love.

Tiomkin devised the melody so that its various phrases neatly excerpt to form motives that can be manipulated like little cells. He uses this to utmost effect in the last twelve minutes of the film, which is decked with music throughout. Those last minutes consist, of course, of the gunfight between Cooper and the bad guys, followed immediately by Cooper and Kelly leaving town for a presumably happy future together. The music is non-stop, and except for a few measures of grim, menacing, minor chords, is made up entirely of phrases from the song. These are broken up and scattered throughout the gunfight, but when the conflagration is over, the song returns whole, with words, to see the happy couple off on their journey.

The film many (including the AFI) consider the greatest Western ever made, John Ford's *The Searchers* (1956), boasts a score by Max

Steiner, who at sixty-eight still had the chops. (Three years later, age seventy-one, he would write the pop hit, "Theme from A Summer Place.") The cues are expertly spotted. For example, when the Indian attack on the cabin is about to take place, we hear a subtle, sustained high note in the violins that fades only when we are sure that the attack is imminent. The music drops out as the people in the cabin realize with fear what is about to happen, and picks up—this time with a *low* sustained note in cellos and double basses—at the moment just before little Debbie is kidnapped. Steiner was the right composer for the job, as opposed to the journeyman Hageman or the effusive Victor Young, who was busy that year with his last and most famous score, the exotic-sounding *Around the World in 80 Days*. Steiner knew how properly to restrain his musical impulses at moments of intense drama, but also managed to orchestrate a sweeping theme to match the grandeur of Ford's famous landscapes.

Jerome Moross was a Brooklyn-born, classically trained composer who penned ballet scores, chamber music, and the award-winning musical, *The Golden Apple* (1954). More than thirty years after his death in 1983, his distinctive music commands a large and vocal fan base. Moross's contributions to film music are few, but important. In 1955, he contributed music to some episodes of the television Western series, *Gunsmoke,* and it was perhaps that credit that nabbed him the gig of scoring *The Big Country* (1958), a sprawling Western spectacular starring Gregory Peck. The directors expected a distinctively Western score, and they got it. The theme is the epitome of Western-movie, big-sky melancholy, sweeping in its range and longing in its character. This is not achieved willy-nilly. Moross shaped the theme so as to orient harmonically to a IV–I progression at its most fundamental. The difference between this and the V–I orientation of many, if not most, typical song harmonies is vital, because IV–I is less stable than V–I for acoustic reasons too complicated to go into here; IV–I is the more common relationship in folk songs. The important thing is that the result is a feeling of restlessness that is in perfect keeping with the feel of the movie.

Moross did something else remarkable: the score consists almost entirely of variations and permutations on his theme. A cue that needs fast action will speed up the theme's harmonic progression, a sprightly variation will serve as the cue for a "cute" bit, and so on. This is done subtly, unlike in Tiomkin's gunfight music in *High Noon,* where the moviegoer is always aware of the song itself. Moross hides the theme, allowing it to show through almost subconsciously. Though *The Big Country* was not one of the three Westerns in AFI's list of Top 25 scores (these are *High Noon, The Magnificent Seven,* and *How the West Was Won*), a case can be made that it was by far the most sophisticated, if not the outright best, Western score ever composed.

We next come to arguably the most famous Western score ever written, Elmer Bernstein's music for *The Magnificent Seven* (1960). John Sturges's Old West take on Kurosawa's *The Seven Samurai* needed music that could *underline* the tension more than emphasize the conflict, and Bernstein provided one of the most tension-infused scores in movie history. But it is the main theme that most people remember, and with good reason: it encapsulates the feeling of the Western, summarizes the very genre in its craggy rhythms for brass, overlain by a sweeping, desert-vista heroic melody in strings. The intervals of the melody are wide. This has psychological impact. Narrow intervals evoke mystery or even danger. The minor second, the smallest interval in the tonal language, was used to enormous effect both by John Williams to grip the audience with fear in *Jaws,* and by Howard Shore in *The Lord of the Rings* trilogy, to veil the power of the One Ring. Bernstein's *Magnificent Seven* theme, on the other hand, gives us (following the famous nine-note rhythmic intro) a modestly rising minor third that aims toward the distinctively yearning sound of the rising perfect fifth a couple of bars later. The rest unfolds lyrically and freely, always with the rhythmic motive beneath, ready to break out—and in fact it does at the end. The masculine rhythmic support for the free lyricism of the feminine string theme is a clear yet subtle telling of the film's subject: the protection of a humble village by the courageous self-sacrifice of a handful of gunmen.

The Magnificent Seven score, and especially its vigorous theme, came to be nearly synonymous with Western movie music. So familiar was it to the public at large as late as the 1980s, that when a character in an episode of the comedy series *Cheers* began to sing the nine-note rhythmic motive, another character began to sing the theme over it, and everyone in the bar—as, presumably, everyone in the audience—not only knew it was *The Magnificent Seven,* but identified it with Western movies and even the West itself. It's not that Elmer Bernstein had a special affinity for Westerns. Of all the major Hollywood composers, he probably spanned the greatest range of genres. In the years just before and after *The Magnificent Seven*, for example, Bernstein provided an iconic jazz-idiom score for *The Man with the Golden Arm* (see "Spotlight: Jazz in Film Music"), definitive biblical-epic music for *The Ten Commandments*, vivid adventure music for *The Great Escape*, and, in one of the most intimate and exactly mated dramatic scores ever penned, the music for *To Kill a Mockingbird*. Later in life, he would virtually corner the market on comedy scores, starting with *Animal House* and continuing through the *Ghostbusters* franchise.

Despite its popularity, the music for *The Magnificent Seven* has a curious history outside the film itself. The soundtrack was not released with the movie, so it had to wait until the Phoenix Symphony and conductor James Sedares produced a note-for-note reproduction of the score in 1994 for people to hear the music by itself. (That orchestra has continued its association with the composer. In 2016, it unveiled a concert package, intended for licensing, that consisted of clips from Bernstein's films with live orchestral music.) But there was an odd exception: in England, a young musician with a rock 'n' roll band did a cover of the theme, which hit big both in the United Kingdom and the United States. The young musician's name was John Barry, who would go on to make film scores of his own. The cover—by "The John Barry Seven"—is a strange little two-minute take that gives the melody to an electric guitar and is backed by a standard drum beat.

If *The Magnificent Seven* was the peak of the Hollywood Western-movie music tradition, Alfred Newman's music for *How the West Was Won* (1962) concluded it. Newman (1900–1970) was the best-known American-born member of Hollywood film music's first generation, the generation that gave us the European imports Max Steiner, Erich Wolfgang Korngold, and Franz Waxman. Newman scored more than two hundred films, including *Wuthering Heights*, *The Song of Bernadette*, *All About Eve*, and *The Diary of Anne Frank*. He was nominated for an Oscar forty-three times—making him the third most nominated person in Academy history, right behind John Williams and Walt Disney. He took home nine Oscar statuettes.

Newman also founded something of a film-music dynasty. His son David Newman has scored such films as *Tarzan* and the Scooby-Doo movies, while son Thomas Newman has credits that range from

American Beauty (1999) to *Finding Nemo* (2003) to *The Help* (2011). When illness kept Steven Spielberg's usual choice of composer (John Williams) from scoring *Bridge of Spies* (2015), it was Thomas Newman whom Spielberg called on. Alfred Newman's daughter, Maria Newman, is a widely commissioned classical composer, though her film catalog is limited to a library of vintage silent films she has scored after the fact. Finally, Alfred's nephew is Randy Newman, known primarily for his Oscar-nominated (and sometimes Oscar-winning) songs for the *Toy Story* franchise and other animated films, but who is also an underused background-music composer. His theme for Barry Levinson's *The Natural* (1984) is majestic in its grandeur.

Like Max Steiner, Alfred Newman cut his musical teeth on orchestrating Broadway shows in New York before moving West when the talkies opened opportunities for composers. (His affinity for musicals would continue in his film work, including the orchestrations for movie versions of Broadway hits such as *South Pacific* in 1958 and *Camelot* in 1967.) In 1931, Newman assisted Charlie Chaplin in realizing the director's score for *City Lights*, and scored *Street Scene* on his own. *Street Scene* introduced a theme that the composer recycled throughout his career, using it in various guises in numerous films, including 1953's *How to Marry a Millionaire.*

AFI's choice of *How the West Was Won* as Newman's sole top-twenty-five selection is somewhat ironic, as it was the first Western the composer had ever scored—at age sixty-two! (He would compose only one more Western, *Nevada Smith*, in 1967.) And yet the choice is apt. In 1962, Newman had just come off a twenty-year-stint as music director for 20th Century Fox, a studio that, during his tenure, produced very little in the way of first-rate films. Furthermore, a large part of his job as music director had been administrative, and probably deflected him from his best creative work. But now he was free to compose a score that was huge in its scope, for a studio (MGM) that was once again hitting its stride. *How the West Was Won* is a compilation of several stories that serve to tell the tale of the settling of the western United States. The "West" changes throughout the progress of the film, from Ohio to the plains to the southwestern desert to California. Along the way, we encounter mountain men, the Civil War, and a bandito's attempted train robbery. The sweep of it must have appealed to the newly freed composer, who stepped up to the challenge with an array of cues that goes way beyond the accepted "cowboy" music.

Newman's music for *How the West Was Won* begins with the last of the great film overtures. The idea of a piece of music that precedes the movie, heard over a blank screen, was borrowed from the live theater, where overtures have always been in style for musicals and even for some background music to straight plays. The original score for *Birth of a Nation* had included an overture, and the tradition continued to apply to many major releases throughout the silent era. Its persistence faltered with the coming of the talkies, though 1962 saw not one, but two great ones: Newman's for *How the West Was Won*, and Maurice Jarre's for *Lawrence of Arabia*.

For his overture, Newman turned for choral assistance to his longtime working partner, Ken Darby, and assembled an amazing medley of American folk songs. It opens with some strains from the faith-infused "I Am Bound for the Promised Land," sung by a studio chorus and backed by orchestra. This song bears a resemblance to Newman's main theme, which will show up in the main title music, and one assumes Newman did this consciously, forging a link in the listener's ear between the quest for the "promised land" and the film's central idea. Then comes a lush and quite acceptable choral arrangement of "Shenandoah," perhaps the most beautiful and most recognizable of America's folk songs, and then, two real surprises: folk songs that are anything but pretty or optimistic. The studio singers handle the first of them— "Endless Prairie," a woeful plaint about the ugly stretches of nothing that can sometimes seem to comprise the U.S. Midwest. The next one is a master stroke. Newman and Darby decided to ask some real folk singers to contribute their version of a work song and interpolate it into the overture. It's a harsh look at the strength and endurance that was needed to cross the prairie. The words concern getting a wagon out of a rut by whipping the oxen: "I pop that whip and I drink the blood/ I watch those leaders take the mud." Not what one would expect to hear at a "cowboy" movie.

The main title that follows does not surrender the intensity of what we have just heard. A series of syncopated tutti blasts from the orchestra signal that this is, indeed, a Western, and then comes Newman's main theme, a striding, masculine melody etched in hard, angular intervals. At length, it segues into "The Promised Land," which it resembles more than slightly, and then back into the main theme. From that point on, Newman's score maintains its power to express what is on the screen and yet remain true to the sound of the American West. Especially striking is Newman's use of the tender Western ballad, "He's Gone Away," to underscore a young man's leaving for the army. Newman's first Western was also his undoubted masterpiece, and the music to *How the West Was Won* deserves a place on every Top 25 or Top 50 list of Hollywood music scores.

The Magnificent Seven and *How the West Was Won* culminated the combination of craggy brass, syncopated percussion, folk-song allusions, and the arching melancholy melody that had come down through the decades to signify the Western. It was left to an Italian composer to engineer a massive alteration of that sound.

Composer Ennio Morricone and film director Sergio Leone had been school buddies, so when Leone started his series of what would come to be called "spaghetti Westerns"—movies set in the American Old West but filmed in Europe by an Italian company—it was only natural that he called on Morricone to score them. The look of Leone's Westerns did not match the California exteriors of traditional Westerns. Filmed in desolate stretches of southern Spain, they evoked an emptiness that dominated all three movies of the series: *A Fistful of Dollars* (1964), *For a Few Dollars More* (1965), and *The Good, the Bad and the Ugly* (1966). The trilogy's hero was played by Clint Eastwood with a cynicism that would have shocked Randolph Scott, and the rest of the characters looked less like the well-coiffed figures in something like *The Searchers* than a gang of ruffians from a bad neighborhood. Clearly, the music could not be standard issue.

Working closely with Leone, Morricone shaped a score that did sonically what Leone's direction did visually: Create a gritty environment of dirty, dusty danger wrapped in heatstroke. The composer translated into orchestration the coyote calls, whistling wind, and gunshots that might form the sound-effects track of such a setting, adding a chorus of grunting human voices that emulate the plodding tread across the barren landscape. The instrumental sound in the forefront is electric guitar—this is the mid-1960s, after all—and the end of the theme brings in overlapping, military-style trumpets to backdrop the story's Civil War timeframe. The theme opens with the faux coyote call, a pair of rapidly alternating notes a perfect fourth apart, and goes on at length to grow into a full-blooded theme of a fairly standard harmonic structure. It is the opening that sticks with you, though, and it is the coyote call that everyone thinks of when they think of spaghetti Western music.

Some have said that Morricone changed the sound of the Western score, but in fact, subsequent Westerns for the most part did nothing to expand on Morricone's innovations. The sound of the Dollars trilogy scores is sui generis, a unique contribution to the film music repertoire that has not been so much developed as occasionally imitated, as Morricone himself imitated it at the request of director Quentin Tarantino in *The Hateful Eight* (2016), the score that at long last won Morricone an Oscar.

While the particulars of the trilogy scores have to do with picking up on the set's environment, the more specific musical elements include percussive accents, the inclusion of chorus used as an instrument, and the layering of musical ideas—all of which figure in Morricone's AFI-rated score to *The Mission* (1986). (For more on this, see the previous chapter on epics.) But lest one limit perspective on Morricone's music to these stylistic characteristics, consider the theme to *Cinema Paradiso* (1988), a very non-percussive theme that unfolds in harmonic luxury so vast that you start to think Morricone may have had Michel LeGrand (*The Picasso Summer*, *The Thomas Crown Affair*) as a model, conscious or otherwise.

In recent years, music for Westerns has for the most part settled into standard good guy–bad guy cues, minus the references to folk music and plus (occasionally) the edge of modern rock and pop. As of this writing (April 2016), it remains to be seen what sort of music will make up the soundtrack for the remake of *The Magnificent Seven*, set for release in September 2016, but the trailers suggest a rock 'n' roll feel. Only Morricone can imitate Morricone and get away with it, so individual was the sound of the Dollars trilogy. The genre itself has faded to the point where the release of a Western is an unusual event, not the weekly occurrence it was during the 1940s, '50s, and even somewhat into the '60s. In 1952, the year *High Noon* was released, more than seventy-five Westerns made their way to the silver screen. By 1962, the year of *How the West Was Won*, the number had dwindled to twenty-one. The year 1972 saw a return of sorts, with forty-four Westerns released, but by 1982 this resurgence was over, and only thirteen Westerns saw light of day. The number has hovered around one release per month ever since. The popularity of the old Western is not difficult to understand. There was a threat—a bad guy—and an answer to that threat in the form of a reluctant sheriff or a rogue gunman whose abilities were often way beyond the expected; you could even call them superhuman. The seven men who defended that little village against brigands were magnificent indeed, holding off hordes of thuggish invaders against all odds. This appetite to see good guys with immense powers fight bad guys, despite being ridiculously outnumbered, did not fade with the Western, but showed up in heightened colors as the superhero flick.

Batman, Spider-Man, Superman, and even Ant-Man need music to go with their superhuman feats. A whole new generation of film composers quite naturally grew up around them, with Danny Elfman leading that pack.

Danny Elfman began his musical career in 1976 as lead singer and songwriter for new wave band Oingo Boingo, a role he continued throughout the band's many stylistic changes, until its retirement in 1995. For the last ten years of fronting Oingo Boingo, Elfman somehow managed to balance the demands of the band with a newfound career of film composer. This unexpectedly began in 1985, when director Tim Burton asked him to score *Pee-Wee's Big Adventure*. Elfman was initially doubtful that he could manage it, as he was not formally trained, but he didn't have far to go to find someone to help: Oingo Boingo lead guitarist Steve Bartek had the training that allowed him to coach Elfman in matters such as orchestration and notation. After *Pee-Wee's Big Adventure*, Elfman went on to score *Beetlejuice* (1988) and *Scrooged* (1988), but when Burton invited him to score *Batman*, he was once more plagued by doubt. This was a bigger, more "serious" project than the others, and the orchestration would almost certainly take on a John Williams–sized nature. This time Elfman not only engaged Bartek's help, but also that of Shirley Walker, one of very few women composers in cinema.

Walker, a skilled orchestrator, had co-composed with Carmine Coppola the music for *The Black Stallion* (1979) and co-composed with Richard Band the score to *Ghoulies* (1985). (She also had racked up many episodes of the TV series *Falcon Crest*.) That Walker was kept in "second place" to male film composers and not given a solo credit until

1992's *Memoirs of an Invisible Man* is an unexplored example of male privilege, and perhaps emblematic of the industry's pro-male bias in general. At any rate, while her name was kept behind the scenes, her skills were well known and respected, so it's reasonable that Elfman turned to her for guidance. It's also reasonable to assume that a great deal of the romantic-style orchestration that makes the score to *Batman* so effective is hers.

Burton chose a two-pronged score for *Batman*. In addition to the majestic Elfman–Walker symphonic music, he asked Prince to come up with songs to fit some of the scenes. Prince ended up writing an entire album's worth of originals, which was eventually released on its own. Six of the songs were used in *Batman*: "The Future," "Vicki Waiting," "Electric Chair," "Partyman," "Trust," and "Scandalous." This combination of traditional and pop music was an inspiration. The result is a soundtrack that evokes the heroic, both in the old sense that movies had held up cowboys as heroes, and the contemporary sense of bringing that heroism to bear on "real" life as it's lived in the American urban jungle. Since then, superhero movies typically use this contrast in their soundtracks. In *Batman*, the pop half of the score provides context, while mood is most important in the Elfman half of things. Orchestral cues are less oriented to action than to the situation, whether dramatic, romantic, comical, or other circumstances.

Elfman has gone on to score an amazing number of movies and TV shows, ranging wildly in genre. His theme for *The Simpsons* is probably the most frequently heard music on television. A few of his big-screen credits include *Edward Scissorhands* (1990), *Batman Returns* (1992), *Mars Attacks!* (1996), *Sleepy Hollow* (1999), *Spy Kids* (2001), *Big Fish* (2003), *The Kingdom* (2007), *Mr. Peabody and Sherman* (2014), and *Fifty Shades of Grey* (2015). But it is Elfman's second foray into the universe of superheroes for which he is perhaps best known. The Spider-Man franchise, beginning in 2002, provided Elfman with the opportunity to fully explore his capabilities.

The main title music for the first film, *Spider-Man*, opens with a high, sustained note on the violins that quickly spins out a scurrying rhythmic pattern like the web of the movie's title character. This expands into a massive symphonic statement that depends for its effect on the sheer weight of the orchestration. As the percussion lays down a beat that is almost ska in its pattern of accents, brass choirs swell with the main theme, and strings and winds do sonic embroidery around them. Between the first *Batman* and the first *Spider-Man*, Elfman essentially defined the genre as cognate with the overwhelming sonic power of the orchestra. Big-boned brass choirs (sometime abetted by vocal choirs as well) proclaiming anthem-like tunes over driving rhythms overwhelm listeners, assuring them that the superhero they see on the screen really has a limitless store of sound to match his limitless abilities. If you are looking for subtlety in a typical superhero score, you are looking in the wrong place. Even rhythmic subtleties are out the window. Drive, big sound, and plain themes that repeat certain melodic tropes are the stuff of the genre. Melancholy of the sort that shows up in the Western is strictly out.

This aesthetic remains true from composer to composer. Just when you think that Christophe Beck's music for *Ant-Man* (2013) will be a little different, opening as it does with a quieter musical idea, it strides directly into a rhythmically redundant and aggressive pattern that does not let the ears escape. *Avengers: Age of Ultron* (2015), with score credits shared by Elfman and Brian Tyler, gives us a similar beginning and change-up, though this time at least the theme has a little more range to it, and includes a bridge passage that provides a brief respite from the onslaught of the steady 4/4 beat and the tutti orchestral mass that it carries. The insistence of common meter in superhero films, which supports relentlessly an unrelieved procession of orchestral block chords, bypasses the ears and goes directly for the neural pathways. Let's call it the Wall of Sound, a kind of musical equivalent to CGI. CGI cheats the eye by filling in gaps with computer-generated imagery. The Wall of Sound fills in the gaps between the beats with notes that could almost be any notes, since most of them move away from their key center very little, if at all, and consist of melodies that stay insistently within the given diatonic (simple) harmony.

This is to be expected, given the aesthetic of the genre itself. Unlike Westerns, superhero movies remain essentially live comic books. The music needs to be simple, outlining and insisting on the beat, soaking the listener in sound the way the screen soaks him in hyperactive visuals. Every genre needs to be defined, and the definition of heavy, insistent, relentless Wall of Sound defines the superhero genre. Even Hans Zimmer, who clearly has a command of a breadth of musical expression (*The Thin Red Line* is the very model of a score crafted to reflect the visuals), gave into the Wall of Sound in the theme for *The Dark Knight* (2008). While the Zimmer/James Newton Howard music for the Batman movies of the Christopher Nolan franchise have, overall, more varied and interesting cues than scores for *Iron Man*, *Spider-Man*, and *Ant-Man*, the main credits for *The Dark Knight* sound almost like a parody of the Wall of Sound. One imagines Zimmer cynically saying to himself, "Well, if this is what they want . . ." There is almost nothing to this five-minute chunk of sound besides a repeating beat pattern. The Wall of Sound is so ubiquitous that when something vaguely interesting is introduced to vary it—as Alan Silvestri does in his layered theme for *The Avengers*—it stands out prominently from the bunch.

The truth to be reminded of here is that the composer is at the mercy of the director and the producers. The very talented James Horner, whose premature death in 2015 was a loss to film music, affords a case in point. His music for James Cameron's *Avatar* (2009) is nearly a superhero score translated into the realm of fantasy. The film's action-driven nature demands this. But his score for Ron Howard's *A Beautiful Mind* (2001) is a masterpiece of invention that uses musical concepts to mirror the themes of the film. There is the computer-like generation of data sounds, symbolizing the lead character's genius-level mathematics, but well beyond this is the manipulation of harmonies to miraculously "slip" and go in directions other than expected, a depiction in music of the character's evolving madness. And underlying it all is warm and original love music, depicting the extraordinary devotion of that character's wife. But without Howard's understanding and treatment of the subject—without, in other words, a film that is in all other departments strong and expressive and subtle—there will be no room for music that is strong, expressive, and subtle. In most superhero movies, there is room only for the Wall of Sound.

Our old dictum that good movie music must be both indispensable and unnoticed applies here. The film is the thing, not the music. The composers who dutifully manufacture superhero music are filling their job descriptions. Their music is indispensable because without it, the CGI splendor of the visuals would not have an aural partner to hold its hand. It is unnoticed because it blends in so effortlessly with the aesthetic of the movie in which, in some sense, *everything* is background—story, characters, dialogue, visuals, and music. The only foreground is the comic-book feel of the whole.

This makes us challenge one-half of our dictum. Yes, music must be indispensable to a film or else, why have any at all? But is it really so terrible that we notice Elmer Bernstein's theme for *The Magnificent Seven*, so much so that we come away humming it? A film is a whole made of script, acting, cinematography, and other parts and, of course, it must all hang together in order to work. But truth be told, any viewer of almost any movie will notice individual filmic elements from time to time. We can't help but notice the sweep of cinematography in *Lawrence of Arabia*, and that isn't a bad thing. So, why should it be a bad thing if we also notice the sweep of Maurice Jarre's music? It's hard not to be riveted by a stellar performance or a clever script. This does not detract from the film as a whole, but gives the experience texture. A strongly profiled melody can lend a film character and at the same time be lifted from the film and exist on its own as a piece of music. Cinema is a complicated art, and at just over a century old, it has yet to be completely understood.

6

DRAMA

To Kill a Mockingbird starts out with the most unlikely opening credits. At first, over the Universal Pictures logo, we hear single notes on a piano sounding what seems to be the final phrase of a melody we haven't heard yet in its entirety. This is replaced by the sound of Scout, the little girl and narrator of the story, tunelessly singing a little thing that more or less resembles what's to come: a gentle melody in a medium-tempo, three-beat meter that opens with a rising, five-note gesture that will become a motive for later manipulation. As this simple, open melody plays in full strings and winds, we see Scout's hands going through the stuff of childhood: jacks and marbles, pens and crayons. At last, she picks up these crayons and begins to color a picture of a mockingbird, the story's symbol of innocence. Along with the visuals, Elmer Bernstein's music for the titles has effectively established the following: the centrality of innocence in the coming story; the atmospheric nostalgia of the film's tone; and even—by way of that half-heard piano melody in the first measures—the unfinished nature story, a morality tale that will have an implied resonance far beyond the action of the film.

Of all the divisions made in this book by genre, that of drama is perhaps the most nebulous. There is drama and there is *drama*. As a generalization, this includes kitchen-sink pieces like *Marty*, domestic tales with life lessons (such as *To Kill a Mockingbird*), social-sexual commentary (*Who's Afraid of Virginia Wolff?*), traditional Shakespearean tragedies, and even the black comedies of more recent vintage and popularity, such as many films by Wes Anderson and Joel and Ethan

Coen. Regarding music, they have this in common: more than comedies or Westerns or thrillers, they depend on exposition. Whether it's a relationship between characters or the factual foundation of the plot, a drama somehow needs to spend a little more time relating the background of its story.

For the composer scoring a dramatic film, this can sometimes mean maintaining a viewer's involvement through a series of quick expository scenes. This occurs in *To Kill a Mockingbird*, when the story takes us from a scene in which Scout and her brother Jim accompany their lawyer father, Atticus, in their car to the home of a man he is defending, and from there back to Scout's home and to bed. It takes more than five minutes and not much happens, but what does happen is critical to the story. We discover that Robinson, the man Atticus is defending, is black. While Atticus goes into the house to talk with Mrs. Robinson, Scout and Jim stay in the car. They quietly begin to befriend the Robinson children, when a crazed-looking white man approaches them threateningly. Jim asks one of the Robinson children to go into the house and get their father, and shortly Atticus emerges and the crazy man withdraws, but not before shouting a racial epithet. It seems that Atticus is not very popular for defending a black man in this time and space. Back home on the porch, Scout asleep in his arms, Atticus explains to Jim that there is ugliness in the world that he wishes he could protect his children from.

That's not a lot to happen in five minutes of screen time, but it is critical, not just to the plot but to the emotions attached to the story: Atticus's decency and his desire to protect his children; the initial joy of the children going with their father, followed by the fear they feel at the approach of the crazed man; and the revelation they begin to experience at the unveiling of racial prejudice. Bernstein accompanies each turn of action and emotion with a shift in the rhythms and harmonies. It begins with a jaunty, Copland-esque sequence for the children and their father. As they pile into the car, Scout and Jim are given the comfortable beat of a medium-four count. Arrival at the Robinson house is laced with woodwinds, in many ways Bernstein's most expressive instruments, as they were Tchaikovsky's. The oboe takes front and center in letting us hear the children's inner feelings as they are approached as friends by the Robinson children. Then the low strings take over with the advance of the crazed man and, at last, after the Robinson kids have run to get Atticus, music of comfort and assurance. The effect is simple and direct; nothing is played out in the music that is not evident on the screen. The music adds nothing, in one sense. In another, it adds the very thing missing in the visuals: clarity and depth of feeling. It takes a specialized skill to be able to do this, and a gift to do it at Bernstein's level.

Notice that after Atticus has returned his children home, and the cue ends, you remember nothing of the music. What is recalled instead is a sequence of feelings, capped by the next cue, in which Jim, left alone as Scout sleeps while Atticus drives the maid home, runs up and down the street in terror, suddenly aware of what dangers there might be in the world. Throughout, Bernstein will keep the music of panic within a certain childlike limit—there is nothing like the screaming violins of *Psycho* here—because *To Kill a Mockingbird* isn't about adult fear, but very specifically the birth of fear in young children. Bernstein not only knew that; he knew how to accommodate that musically.

☼ ☼ ☼

"Drama" covers a lot of aesthetic ground. Dramas come packaged as adventures, romances, coming-of-age pieces, and more. The challenge for the composer is to understand the exact nature of the drama being scored and to settle on a musical language—such as a harmonic vocabulary or an idiom—to match it.

Alex North's music for *A Streetcar Named Desire* (1949) is the finest score ever written for the film adaptation of a stage play, and arguably the best score ever composed for a dramatic film. North met the challenge of creating cues to go with Tennessee Williams's already musical words—musical in the sense that each character has his or her distinctive voice—by giving distinct instrumentation to each strand of the script's manifold meaning. *A Streetcar Named Desire* is about the meeting of brutal, naked predation (in the form of Stanley Kowalski) and ritualized, refined predation (Blanche Dubois). At one time or another, each of the two central predatory figures also becomes prey, twisting the plot like a pretzel and bringing out the ambiguities as well as the vivid contrasts of sexual interplay. North's use of woodwinds traces this interplay in musical colors—flute as feminine, sax as masculine, and clarinet for moments of neutrality or indecision. Strings are there to cull the memories of Blanche's long-dead young husband, and the trumpet stands like a symbol both of New Orleans and of the title itself: desire that, like a streetcar, takes us where it will.

Because this is New Orleans, there is plenty of diegetic music, but North doesn't try to link to it or mimic it in any way. His score is parallel to Williams's script, not to the environment, and there is no mistaking his dramatic intent for local color. The main title opens brashly with a plunging line from the trumpets. The first interval is a descending minor second, a distillation of the blues. As the music continues, there is good reason to believe that we are going to see a drama of strictly human dimensions, as when the violins take up the brassy opening, turning it into a plaint instead of a protest. Over this, briefly, comes a solo trumpet, before the strings lead these ninety seconds of music to an end. Some hot jazz makes its way from a bar as Blanche wends her way to the home of her sister, Stella. The next cue comes at the moment when Blanche and Stella have their first fight. Blanche tells her sister she has lost their family home, and the blues theme from the opening comes back, but gently, because the fight, while animated, is more sad than angry.

Another cue follows almost immediately, and gives an answer to a question asked in chapter 3 on film noir: What was the origin of film noir's sexy sax cue, usually associated with seductive blondes in detective offices? Well, here it is, and there's not a detective in sight, and no murder mystery to come. What's more, the seducer isn't a female at all. The source of the sexy sax cue is a ripped, sweaty Marlon Brando! As Brando strips his shirt off in front of an embarrassingly excited Blanche (Vivien Leigh), the sax lets out a stream of bluesy ecstasy. Somehow, this cue became associated with film noir, a genre only distantly related to the psychological drama *sans* violent crime that is Williams's play. But North doesn't settle for just telling us how sexy Stanley is. He also paints Blanche's response in the counterpoint of a feminine flute line that keeps ascending and ascending against the sax's earthiness—a subtle tonal picture of Blanche's attempt to resist.

North's most skillful and effective cue comes at the film's most famous moment, and indeed helps shape that moment. Stanley has thrown the family radio through a window and causes a huge scene that sends his wife, Stella, and her sister out of the apartment and into sanctuary in an upstairs neighbor's place. He is immediately remorseful, and runs out into the courtyard yelling, "Stella! Hey Stella!" At first, we hear clarinet, a neutral sound that meanders around desperately in need, like those famous cries of "Stella!" But the sax soon takes over, and then goes wild as the camera shifts to Stella's face in the apartment above. We see Stella's anger transform into a fiery desire, and as she descends the staircase, we hear the feminine flute once more, but this time, instead of climbing out of the way, it wraps itself around the sax cue and leads unflinchingly to a passionate kiss, with all instruments blending ecstatically. This is film composing of the first water, in which the music tells us what is happening in perfect accord with the visuals and the actors' demeanors.

Remembering that the best film scores are both unobtrusive and indispensable, North's music fulfills these paradoxical requirements with flourish. We don't so much hear his music as feel it, feel it in accord with the characters and their action. And yet, without it, those characters and their actions would not be the same.

Our next example of a score to a drama, which incidentally also features Marlon Brando, comprises some of the best music ever written for a film. In fact, of all the scores in the AFI Top 25, the music by Leonard Bernstein (no relation to Elmer) for *On the Waterfront* (1954) is probably the best music, as music, on the list. It is the only one that survives as a symphonic suite played in classical concerts by symphony orchestras. But as film music, its success is mixed, for the very reason that it makes itself heard, puts itself forward in a way that—at moments at least—deflect our attention from the whole. To understand this, and to understand a little better when music cues work well and when they don't, we'll examine the film and Bernstein's cues, one scene at a time.

Bernstein's score captures with an almost savage intensity the main elements of the story: the brutal life of a working man on the docks, the sinister presence of deadly power, and the transformational potential of love. Yet it sometimes moves the musical statements of these things to the foreground of the movie. Bernstein even wrung his hands over the genre's priorities in a fantasy dialogue that takes place in "Upper Dubbing, California." Published in Bernstein's first book, *The Joy of Music*, the dialogue finds the composer wearily acquiescing to the fact that film is not a musical form per se, but nonetheless lodging the complaint that one of his score's best moments had been usurped by "one of Marlon Brando's grunts." An extensive look at Bernstein's cues provides a lesson in what works and what doesn't in the world of the film composer, whose frustrating job it is to be the musical voice of the director and the writer.

Even as the familiar lady-with-the-torch Columbia Pictures logo hits the black-and-white screen, a forlorn, unaccompanied horn announces a theme. Taking a shape typical of early Bernstein melodies, the theme pushes upward, falls and climbs again, falls and climbs yet again, this time higher and, as it climbs it slips from minor into major by the most unlikely of means: a blue note. A blue note is an altered pitch, a flattened note where a flattened note is unexpected. It comes from the blues. Blue notes don't replace their non-flattened or natural counterparts; they exist side-by-side with them, creating an ambiguity of expression. Bernstein will exploit this ambiguity as a device to convey the subtle emotions of the characters in the film.

Bernstein's twenty-four-note theme takes less than thirty seconds to play, and in that half-minute, it establishes the emotional premise of striving impeded by exterior obstacles. As the main title credits continue to roll, the theme repeats in woodwinds, with muted brass in close imitation. The first scene lights up the screen, and we are thrown into the world of life on the docks. Men of obvious power, men in suits with expensive overcoats, walk past the ships to their cars, and one of them slaps Marlon Brando's character on the shoulder and says, "You take it from here, slugger." Brando, dressed in flannels and clearly not one of them, walks away, and the setting shifts to the streets of Manhattan.

The action seems almost banal, yet Bernstein's music—a muscled knot of percussion overlaid by incisive, two-note jabs from an alto saxophone—overflows with drama. We'll call the quick, two-note jabbing idea the "stabbing motive." It will expand to a three-note version and beyond, but it is always as jagged as a boxer's punch, as now it expands into something abrasive and aggressive, like a dark fanfare. We are about to conclude that the music is overkill, that Bernstein has flooded the screen with music that portends tragedy when all that's happening is a friendly slap on the shoulder and a walk along the shore, when we see Brando call up to someone on the top floor of a tenement, "Joey! Joey Doyle!" Something more is up. At length, the terrible truth is revealed: Brando's character, named Terry Malloy, has been sent by the men in suits to lure Joey to the roof of his building. Terry tells Joey he's found one of Joey's birds, one of the pigeons he keeps in coops on the

roof. Terry sends the bird to the roof, Joey follows, and shortly Joey is a
bloody pulp in the street, thrown from the roof by thugs waiting there
for him. Terry has been party to the killing of a man, though he had not
understood, when he agreed to follow instructions from the suits, that
murder was the aim. Now the dark music, which ends as Joey hits the
pavement, makes a kind of horrible sense in retrospect.

Joey had been planning to talk to "the crime commission." His trip to
the roof was insurance that the people he was about to rat out would
not be ratted. These are the union bosses who run the action at the
docks, hiring only those workers who agree to take loans from them at
usurious interest rates, and skimming money off the top of workers'
wages. One of the bosses is Charley Malloy (Rod Steiger), Terry's
brother, second in power only to Johnny Friendly (Lee J. Cobb). In
Johnny Friendly's bar, Johnny and Charley try to cheer up Terry, who is
feeling awful about Joey. We learn that Terry is a former boxer, who
once had a shot at a title. Johnny gives Terry fifty dollars and tells him,
"Go get a load on" (i.e., get drunk). Instead, Terry goes back to Joey's
building, and to the rooftop where Joey kept his pigeons.

In one of Bernstein's most sensitive cues, a quiet harp sets the scene
and low-pitched flute and strings flutter like the pigeons. Terry sits,
dejected, next to Joey's coop. An oboe sounds a simple, plaintive, four-
note motive borrowed from the "stabbing" notes of the sax in the opening cue, which extends into a melancholy statement. Terry talks with a
neighborhood kid about the pigeons, but his feelings are in the oboe
cue.

It's Monday morning and laborers throng the docks, looking for a
day's work. The union rep stands before them, handing out chits to the
men he chooses. Work is scarce; most of the hopefuls will be declined.
Terry's is the first name called, and after a few more men are selected,
some laborers start to surreptitiously hand dollar bills to the union rep
as bribes. The laborers begin to clamor and push the union rep, who
throws the remaining chits into the air. Union bosses look on and laugh
as the men fight for a chance to earn a few bucks. Bernstein's cue is a
fortissimo chunk of jagged, rhythmic writing accented by a chime. The
chime is a perfect touch, revealing the pathetic nature of what, on the
surface, is merely a mad scramble.

Someone makes an unlikely entrance: It's Joey Doyle's sister, Edie
(Eva Marie Saint). She's come down to the docks with Father Barry

(Karl Malden), her parish priest, to ask questions about the death of her brother, and to be there with her father, who insists on trying to work that day. ("How else will I pay for the funeral?" he asks.) As Edie grabs for a chit for her father, Terry playfully takes one just out of her grasp and then flirts with her, even inviting a slap that makes him smile. A fellow worker says to him, "Hey, don't you know who that is? That's Joey Doyle's sister?" At this moment, the music should suddenly stop, or at least go instantly quiet. But Bernstein punctuates things with a strident, three-note motive from the brass—a cinematic error, to be sure. Those three notes will later become the first notes of a love theme for Terry and Edie, but here they are woefully misplaced.

Father Barry and Edie decide to hold a meeting in the basement of the church to discuss what's happened. Of course, the mob/union leaders get hold of the info and send Terry to the meeting as a plant. Defeated, Father Barry cedes that the meeting is over, but before a prayer can be offered, a rock crashes through one of the basement windows. The jagged, angry music of the previous cue starts up again, as we see thugs outside the church. To the incessant slicing sound of the violins in rapid unison, the thugs beat the workers from the meeting as they exit.

In a nearby park, Edie and Terry talk. They are about to part ways when Edie says she remembers Terry from school. That she'd remembered him the moment she saw him. This sparks one of Bernstein's loveliest melodies, the love theme. It reaches far—up an octave—and then down, but not as far. Another reach up, to a blue note this time, and down once more. And then, unexpectedly, it soars still higher, and in the harmonies beneath, a chord that was minor becomes major. If this sounds familiar, that's because it's very similar to the shape of the main title theme described above. Similar—yet substantially different. The love theme is more open, more expansive, more embracing than the main theme. Something of the tight little struggle of the opening subject has been released, and the once-imprisoned passion is readying to fly. The conversation stops before it can take off.

The melody gets a second chance in the next scene. Edie wanders to the rooftop and finds Terry and the neighborhood kid there, looking after the pigeons. "You got a second?" Terry asks, and the love theme starts up in the strings. This time, the ending latches on to a certain gesture and suddenly the melody is being repeated . . . a perfect fifth higher. This built-in transposition, or change of key, is a brilliant musical stroke, and it lifts an already beautifully inspiring melody into a place of uncanny spirituality. The message to the listener whose ears are open is clear: This could go on forever, growing and changing and yet always being the same melody. It's a perfect musical picture of the devotion Edie and Terry allude to when they talk about pigeons mating for life. In an opera, this could be an extraordinarily effective duet. Alas, it's a movie and the whole thing doesn't work.

It doesn't work because the music doesn't match the dialogue. "You like beer?" Terry asks. "I don't know," Edie says. "You ever have a glass of beer?" Terry asks. "No," Edie answers. Yes, there is talk of pigeons and how they mate for life and the subtext of mutual interest is clear. But the music is a full-out panorama, not of a subtle little hint at intimacy via aviary biology, but of Devotion Itself, of LOVE in all capital letters. If the characters were saying to each other, "I'll love you until I die, I pledge my everything to you," then the music would be apt.

Edie says yes to a glass of beer, and the music climaxes as Terry releases a pigeon. The talk turns to Joey's murder and Edie says, "Help me if you can, for God's sake." The love theme starts up again, blunted somewhat and more subtle, in bassoon and strings. This time, it's right. It's a short cue, but the moment when Edie touches Terry's cheek and Brando registers something between shame and ecstatic release, the music does its job. Edie tries to escape the back room of the saloon where she and Terry are drinking, but she runs into a drunken wedding party and turns back. Terry finds her and gets her to dance to the wedding party's music—"a pretty tune," Edie calls it. It's the love theme played as a dance tune on muted trumpet, without the interlocking transpositions. A thug shows up to tell Terry to go see the boss, and within moments, members of the crime commission deliver Terry a subpoena. Edie wakes up to Terry's probable involvement in her brother's death and leaves.

Johnny Friendly and Charley Malloy confront Terry and tell him to stop seeing Edie. It seems that a certain Dugan, who was at the church meeting, has sung like the proverbial canary and testified to the crime commission. The next day, Dugan is in the hold of a ship, where the mob thugs arrange for an accident: Dugan is crushed to death by falling cases of whisky. Father Barry makes an impassioned speech over Dugan's body and dares the other men to come forward with the truth about the graft and corruption of their mob-run union. At the conclusion, somber strings intone a sort of requiem over the scene. The next scene is that night, and Edie has come to the roof looking for Terry. She wants to give Joey's jacket to him, but it's clear she's come for much more than that. The love theme is heard the way it probably should have been heard the first time—played unaccompanied, by a single flute. It moves to the strings just in time for Terry and Edie's first kiss. The exact moment of the kiss is underlined by a sudden, dramatic shift in the harmony.

The kiss and the cue fade out and we fade in on the church the next morning. Terry and Father Barry take a walk and Terry tells Father Barry about luring Joey to the roof. Father Barry tells Terry to confess this to Edie, which he does, but it goes badly and she runs away. The entire sequence of Terry and Edie is shot right at the waterfront, and as Terry tries to explain to Edie that he didn't know Joey was going to be murdered, a tugboat lets its steam whistle sound and all Edie can hear is it and some vague words of excuse coming from Terry. To the sound of the "stabbing" motive, Edie runs away. In one of his best cues, Bernstein allows the motive to continue into the next scene, and then soften. It's a transition from the intensity of Terry's confession to the rooftop, where Glover from the crime commission (played by Leif Erickson) has come to confront Terry one more time.

Johnny Friendly confronts Charley on Terry's scheduled upcoming testimony. "Will he be D and D [deaf and dumb] or a pigeon?" Friendly asks. "I wish I knew," Charley answers. Friendly tells Charley to take his brother out for a little talk and, if he doesn't see the light, to "give him the Jerry G." We don't know what the "Jerry G" is, but it doesn't sound good, and Charley says, "I can't do that." The scene ends ambiguously and Charley leaves to a cue of sinister-sounding, pyramiding brass. That night, Charley and Terry have their famous conversation in a cab. Terry tells Charley he doesn't know what he's going to do about the subpoena, and Charley pulls a gun and tells him to take a cushy boss's job on the docks and keep his mouth shut.

This leads to a conversation about Terry's boxing career. Gently, lovingly, Terry expresses to Charley the enormous hurt and disappointment he felt when he had to throw the big fight at the Garden to another boxer just so Charley could win a bet. It was a "one-way ticket to Palookaville," Terry says. "You was my brother, Charley, you shoulda watched out for me a little." Brass introduces a three-note variation on the stabbing motive which moves easily into a hauntingly tragic theme in the strings. "I coulda had class, I coulda been a contender," Terry says, in the most famous quote from the film and, arguably, all of Brando's career. Bernstein's sorrowful music is effective, though perhaps just a little too interesting in and of itself.

Then comes the most awkward cue of them all. Bernstein reintroduces the rushing strings and punctuating brass that accompanied the end of the church meeting scene. This works fine at first, but it continues into the next scene, when Terry goes to Edie's apartment and demands she open the door. We then hear the love theme in angry dress, counterpointed by percussion, first in the strings and then repeated in the trumpets. Terry forces his way in and Edie shouts at him to leave. In an act that today would be actionable as sexual harassment, Terry forces Edie into a kiss, saying, "Edie, you love me." The music now shifts to the stabbing motive, which attempts in sound to equal the edgy passion of Brando's visual ardor, but comes off instead as overly operatic. In fact, by this time, we are beginning to get the idea that Bernstein has conceived of the love scenes in the film as a kind of unsung opera. In opera, a scene of angry lovers, torn apart by circumstance but still passionately, almost violently in love, would be wrapped in precisely this kind of music. In a film, however, it goes overboard.

After the score's most strained moment comes the finest few minutes in Bernstein's one-movie career as a composer of background music for film. Terry is called out of the apartment by voices who say his brother wants to talk to him. He leaves to Edie's protests, and a muted trumpet sounds the stabbing motive, taken up in turn by the strings. It intensifies as Edie leaves to take chase, and builds still further as a truck tries to run over Terry and Edie in an alleyway. Terry thrusts his hand through the glass panel of a locked door, opens it and throws Edie and himself to safety behind it, just as the truck catches up to them. As he does, the truck's headlights fall on the horrifying sight of Charley hanging from a meat hook in the alley. Bernstein's music climaxes in an emotional release that leads directly into the deep, sorrowful string music from Terry and Charley's conversation in the cab. We hear now that the sorrow music is intimately related to the stabbing motive, linking the harsh life on the docks to the tragedy of Terry and Charley's hurtful relationship. As Terry wraps his arms gently around his brother to take him down from his death perch, the sorrow music reaches a height of unspeakable grief. It is a perfectly realized coordination of screen action and dramatic music. And here, Bernstein's music actually covers up for the script's most ridiculous line, when Terry says, "They got Charley." What Terry says is not what Terry feels. What he feels is in the music.

Down on the docks the next day, the union boss says, "Everybody works today" and proceeds to call out the name of every man there—except Terry. The French horn calls out the notes of the opening. Terry walks down to the dockside office occupied by Friendly and the rest of the mob, and yells for Friendly to come out. He does, and their confrontation is understandably heated. "You ratted on us!" Friendly screams. "Maybe from where you're standing but I'm standing over here now. I was ratting on myself all those years and didn't even know it," Terry retorts. Friendly goads Terry into a fight and of course as soon as Terry gets the upper hand, the other mobsters gang up on him and beat him to a bloody pulp. The music of the first dock scene, the bursts of brass and percussion, backdrops the beating.

Edie and Father Barry show up, too late to do anything but minister to Terry. A ship's owner starts to scream for workers, but when Friendly orders the men to work, they refuse, saying, "If Terry works, we work." Tussling with one of the workers, Friendly falls into the water and the men laugh uproariously. To Father Barry's urging, Terry gets up and walks to the ship's hold and into work, his painful walk supported by a transformed main theme. That theme is now triumphant. When Terry enters the hold, the men at last go to work, to the frantic screaming of Johnny Friendly and the climactic sounds of the main theme, briefly and magically intertwined with the love theme; as pure music, this is as good as anything in cinematic scoring gets.

In the final twenty-plus minutes of the film, Bernstein seems to have found his way. The cues are powerful, but restrained. They admirably fit the action and, more than that, the emotions associated with that action. It's as if Bernstein had learned by doing, and as he worked his way through the film, got better at it. Unfortunately, some of the earlier, clumsier cues went uncorrected, and the score, though powerful in and of itself, is flawed by its frequent intrusions. On the Waterfront won eight Oscars, including best picture, Brando for best actor, Kazan for best director, and Schulberg for writing. Bernstein was nominated, but lost to Dimitri Tiomkin's eerie aerial music for *The High and the Mighty*. Had he wished to do so, there's no doubt that Bernstein could have become one of the screen's finest composers of dramatic scores. But he and the form did not mesh well, and Bernstein never scored another movie. His deepest gifts lay elsewhere, as he would soon demonstrate in the groundbreaking musical, *West Side Story*.

It would be easy to blame Leonard Bernstein's classical background for the over-cueing that marks much of *On the Waterfront*. But in fact, other classically trained composers have written film scores and managed more successfully to withhold their operatic and concert impulses. Aaron Copland, the composer of *Appalachian Spring* and other symphonic standards, won an Oscar for his demure cues to *The Heiress* (1949), the last of a series of films he scored. In only one of his films did he write music that warranted transfer to the concert hall, and that was *The Red Pony* (1948), in which the story, told from a child's perspective, called for something somewhat more extroverted. Considering the wealth of writing talent among America's concert composers, it in fact seems odd that more of their talents were not used for the screen. It was well, perhaps, that Oliver Stone discovered the effectiveness of Samuel Barber's Adagio in time to use it for *Platoon*, but why didn't film directors during Barber's lifetime (he died in 1980) think to commission him a score? The Soviet Union made very good use of its concert composers in film, and both Shostakovich and Prokofiev contributed movie music, portions of which also work in the concert hall.

More recent examples of American concert composers' success on the screen include Phillip Glass's perfectly mated music for *The Hours* (2002) and John Corigliano's *The Red Violin* (1998). In *The Hours*, Glass stretched his minimalist aesthetic to embrace the unspoken emotions of a trio of women. In *The Red Violin*, Corigliano made music at once both the star and the support of the dramatic action.

Given that the subject of *The Red Violin* was a mysterious instrument that finds its way into the hands of a series of musicians in a variety of times and locales—including seventeenth-century Italy, nineteenth-century England, and China at the time of the Cultural Revolution—it was only natural that a classical composer with a command of the violin's potential and an understanding of changing musical styles should be hired. In Corigliano the producers also got a man of deep melodic gifts, as is evidenced in "Anna's Theme," the mysterious, haunting melody associated at first with the violin maker's wife, and subsequently with the violin in a range of guises as it travels the world and time. Anna herself only hums the theme, but Corigliano arranged it for violin in era-appropriate styles for the various episodes that follow. The result is a unified story with widely eclectic variations throughout. *The Red Violin* won Corigliano a richly deserved Oscar.

Corigliano had previously scored two other films: *Altered States* (1980) and *Revolution* (1981). The first was a huge success, both for the movie and for Corigliano's music, which captured both the psychedelic and personal aspects of the complex story. I have not seen the second film, nor have many, for *Revolution* was a notorious flop in which Al Pacino, reportedly in a thick Brooklyn accent, attempted to act the role of a soldier in the American Revolution. It's understandable that Corigliano shied away from film scoring in the wake of such a disaster, but what has made him avoid cinema since the acclaim given *The Red Violin*? I can't imagine that Hollywood has not extended him any offers; it must be that Corigliano is just not interested. The composer has been mute on the subject (to the best of my knowledge). But I would imagine that he counts film as just one area among many that fascinate him (he has composed concertos, chamber music, an opera, and symphonies, one of which won the Pulitzer Prize), and that he fears over-specializing. Who knows? Corigliano, now in his seventies, may yet have another film score in him.

The difference between a Copland, Corigliano, or Leonard Bernstein on the one hand, and all the rest on the other, it that someone who identifies as a film-music composer is essentially a film artist who works in music, just as a screenwriter is a film artist who works in words or a cameraman is a film artist who works with lenses; classical composers who occasionally pen something for the cinema are musical artists working in film. Thus, the frustration faced by Leonard Bernstein in scoring *On the Waterfront*. Of course, there are examples of film composers breaking out of film and composing for the concert hall. John Williams is the major example. Williams has amassed a catalog of pieces that, taken on their own and quite apart from his many celebrated film scores, constitute the high-profile career of a classical composer. These include concertos for flute, oboe, clarinet, bassoon, trumpet, horn, tuba, violin, viola, cello, and harp. Were he to add concertos for trombone, double bass, and percussion, Williams would then have written a concerto for every instrument in the orchestra—an astonishing feat for any composer, let alone one with such an extensive, highly esteemed film-music catalog.

For the most part, though, film composers remain film artists, some of them amassing a catalog as impressive for its variety as Williams's concerto lineup. One is Carter Burwell, who, as of April 2016, had scored eighty-eight films—one for each key of the piano—including every Coen brothers film since Joel and Ethan started with *Blood Simple* in 1984 (with the sole exception of *O Brother, Where Art Thou?*). The Coen brothers make films eclectic not only in subject matter, but in style. The sad romantic feel of *Miller's Crossing* (1990) makes one wonder how it possibly came from the same minds that gave us the unforgivingly brutal edge of *No Country for Old Men* (2007). For a composer, this necessitates becoming a sonic chameleon, shape-shifting instrumental resources, harmonic language, rhythmic feeling, and formal framework. The two films above reflect these changing musical identities. Burwell's tiny, but perfect, contribution to *No Country for Old Men* is dealt with elsewhere, but Burwell contributed a much larger and more essential score to a film some (including this writer) consider the Coens' best film yet, *A Serious Man* (2009). It's a drama (or if you will, a very dark comedy), though that term has evolved greatly since the days of *A Streetcar Named Desire* and *To Kill a Mockingbird*. The conflict at hand here is neither sexual nor social, but existential, and it is played out, not so much in external actions of the characters, but in the things that happen to them.

A Serious Man concerns Larry Gopnik, a Jewish physics professor living in the American Midwest in the 1960s. The plot itself is nothing remarkable. In a series of events, his wife leaves him for another man and his university tenure is challenged. Through yet another series of events, his wife returns to him and his tenure is awarded. But the Coens use this as a trampoline on which to bounce the one theme that figures prominently in nearly every film they have ever made: the authentic masculine versus the inauthentic masculine. The masculine is, as such, neither good nor bad. Its role is to take action in the world, and clearly, action per se can be as bad as it is good. Still, above and beyond the "good versus evil" of the actions themselves lies the masculine itself, which is the ability to make decisions about reality and take responsibility for those decisions. This is not a gender issue; think of the symbol of "the eternal Tao" and how in it, masculine (yang) and feminine (yin) enter each other. The authentic masculine can be found in women as well as men, as the Frances McDormand character in *Fargo* attests. It can also be all but absent in men. We see this in the controversial opening to *A Serious Man*.

It has been said that the Coens claim there is no link between the film's prologue, which takes place long ago in a Jewish shtetl (probably in Poland) and is entirely in Yiddish, and the rest of the film. If so, they are being disingenuous, for the theme of the film is set out very clearly in the prologue, and is then developed mercilessly in the main body of the film. As *A Serious Man* begins, we hear a harp (David's instrument, which will become the main color of Burwell's score) plucking simple chords, and over this we hear a violin that could very well be from a klezmer band playing an eight-note theme that reaches up, tentatively falls back, reaches up again, and falls back at last. This is a motive that is halfway to being a full-blooded theme, and its memorable shape will dominate the film with a sense of mystery. How does it do that? Burwell's eight notes divide into two sets of four, with each set shaped the same way: a pick-up note (a note before the first beat) followed by a higher note and then two descending notes. In each pair, the falling notes outline a minor third. The minor third is common in Jewish folk music, but the piling of two on top of one another creates an ambiguity. Where are we at the end? What is the key? This is akin to the way Bernard Herrmann kept delaying harmonic cadence in *Vertigo* (see chapter 3) á la Wagner. But instead of working inside a tonal frame, Burwell lets us float freely. There will be no final assertion of a key center in his score, only elaborations of this de-centeredness.

As Burwell's cue plays, the prologue in the shtetl begins. On a snowy winter's night in the little village, a couple welcomes into their house a man who could be a *dybbuk*, or one of the walking dead in Jewish lore. We say "could be" because, while the husband claims this man to be a living soul, his wife is certain the man in question had actually died three years previously. So certain is she of the visitor's demonic status that she stabs him with an icepick, and he lumbers back into the cold, much to the horror of the husband, who has proclaimed himself a "rational man" without belief in the existence of dybbuks. The mastery of *A Serious Man* is that everything that happens in the film—many years later and a continent away—relates to the theme brought out by this bizarre opening: Is the truth mere correctness? Or is it the result of our interaction with the world? Is it "just there"? Or do we contribute to it? The wife in the prologue has exampled the authentically masculine mold: she has acted in accordance with her belief and taken responsibility for it, creating her truth; her husband has merely cowered in fear over what has happened, fearing it to be incorrect. With a transition to the main body of the film announced by percussive electronic beats that segue into a period song, Jefferson Airplane's "Somebody to Love," we enter an environment completely stripped of the authentic masculine save for two unlikely figures: an ancient rabbi and a boy celebrating his bar mitzvah.

Burwell's three most substantial cues after the opening pin down turning points in the film. In a scene when Larry climbs up on his roof to fix the TV antenna, we hear again the distinctive harp color and the eight-note motive, played now on the piano and expanded slightly into a listless melody. From here, Larry accidentally spies a neighbor woman sunbathing nude in her backyard. Larry is captivated, but will he act? After all, his wife is leaving him and has almost certainly slept with their friend, Sy Abelman, so he is within his moral rights, so far as that goes. And it will later be made clear that he wants this, when he shows up at the woman's door on the pretext of being "neighborly." But Larry is a man who proudly and frequently says, "I haven't done anything," because, well, he doesn't do anything. (Larry says "I didn't do anything" a dozen times during the film.) He accepts things. In mathematical demonstrations before his class, Larry tries to make the case that the truth is a matter of getting the math right, of accepting the answer, so when he is faced with the truth of his desire and the need to make a moral decision, he opts for the default, which is . . . not to do anything. Up on the roof, he sees his potential before him, accompanied by the ambiguous notes of Burwell's theme. To clear the ambiguity, all he has to do is make a decision and take responsibility for it, but something—something in the genes from an ancestor in that shtetl, perhaps—holds him back. The music of the prologue is the music of the roof scene, only slightly altered, merging their meaning in sound.

The next cue is the music's most important moment in the film. Larry and his brother Arthur, who now live together in a seedy motel room after having been kicked out of the house by Larry's wife and her lover, have a middle-of-the-night scene in which Arthur weeps out his despair at having a life as empty as the motel pool. He has been arrested for "sodomy" at a nightclub that is, it is implied, a gay pick-up spot. (This is 1967, and homosexuality is illegal.) In a dream sequence that immediately follows, which at first seems real, we see Larry drive Arthur to a lake on the Canadian border, give him money, put him in a canoe, and send him off to freedom. Larry loves his brother, and will do anything for him. Even though it is only a dream sequence, this scene tells us that, and one way it tells us is through the music. For here again is the eight-note theme, on woodwinds backed once more by harp, but over it is layered for the first and only time a gently rocking melody that's like a cradle song in its simplicity and endearment. If the eight-note idea can't make up its mind, then at least it can frame an embracing melody. His love for his brother is Larry's redemption. The music tells us that.

More than one critic has seen *A Serious Man* as an update of the book of Job. It is true that in the film, as in Job, someone loses everything, then regains it. But Job also gained wisdom from the events that ruined his life, and Larry does not. More to the point, the Coens originally planned the project as a short film centered on what is now the next-to-last sequence: the stoned bar mitzvah of Larry's son, Danny, and Danny's visit to the old rabbi. This is wholly unrelated to anything in Job. And it is the climax of the film, for throughout the story we have seen Danny acting as the film's only representative of the authentic masculine, making decisions and taking responsibility for them. The right or wrong of those decisions—one decision is to buy pot and another is to ransack a teacher's desk—is entirely beside the point. (The Coens are Nietzscheans, and their themes are "beyond good and evil.") So it is only the natural fulfillment of the movie's central idea that the story culminates in Danny's bar mitzvah—his becoming a man. The old rabbi, whom Larry never succeeds in seeing and who is almost certainly a stand-in for God, confirms Danny's manhood in a touching scene.

But it's not over. Things have resolved, but they never stay resolved. And in the last series of shots, a kind of epilogue, it is implied that Larry, at last secure in his marriage and position, may have a serious disease. Even worse, a tornado is about to hit the Hebrew school that Danny attends. The music changes utterly, for here is nature—disease and disaster—making a mockery of all our decisions. Gone are the eight notes, and now the harp does nothing more than support the darkening string chords that lead, with a single, threatening low note on the piano, to the closing credits and Jefferson Airplane singing the moral of the story: "You better find somebody to love."

Why have I spent 1,500 words on the story and thematic aspects of a film that contains only a few minutes of incidental music? To show the role that music can play in explicating a director's intentions, even in a handful of cues. One suspects that the Coens and Burwell spend a great deal of time in the spotting process, and that the Coens very explicitly tell Burwell what they want. Either that, or Burwell owns the most intuitively apt musical mind in the movie business.

As we've seen in Elmer Bernstein's moodily suggestive cues for *To Kill a Mockingbird*, in Alex North's sexual tone-painting in *A Streetcar Named Desire*, Leonard Bernstein's musical stand-in for Joey's feelings in *On the Waterfront*, or Carter Burwell's underlying love of a man for his brother in *A Serious Man*, dramas of every stripe need a little more help than other genres in suggesting musically what's going on beneath the surface action. That doesn't necessarily mean a lot of cues (*On the Waterfront* has many; *A Serious Man*, very few), but it does mean that every cue has something to tell.

❋ ❋ ❋

Sentimentality poses a peculiar dilemma for the film composer. *On Golden Pond* (1981) concerns the Thayers, a relentlessly cute old couple (Henry Fonda and Katharine Hepburn) visiting their cabin in the woods . . . on Golden Pond. Though a retired professor, Norman Thayer is remarkably narrow-minded. When his wife Ethel says she has met a family called the Miglionis, Norman asks sarcastically, "What kind of name is that?" He knows, apparently, because later he says he doesn't want to have dinner with them and "have to eat rigatoni." But Norman has bigger problems than his personal prejudices. Alzheimer's disease has started to eat away at the eighty-year-old's memory. The film concerns the very real issue of aging and its attendant challenges, but the clichés run thick and fast in Ernest Thompson's script. Hard to believe that the AFI counted as the eighty-eighth most memorable movie line Hepburn's comforting words to Norman: "You're my knight in shining armor." The presence of Hepburn and of two Fondas—Jane Fonda plays the couple's daughter—apparently made *On Golden Pond* a favorite with the movie community despite all this.

Somehow, though they are very few in number, Dave Grusin's cues help. It's hard to care about the humorless curmudgeon played by Henry Fonda, but when Grusin accompanies Fonda's walk in the woods with a gentle, medieval-flavored theme played by woodwinds, and then slowly alters this to dissonant confusion as Fonda's Alzheimer's begins to kick in, we experience a bit of the character's terror. And while it's hard to think of a more stereotypical setup than a young boy coming closer to an older man by fishing with him, a cocktail-lounge piano cue pokes some gentle fun and underlines its charm at the same time. Grusin's music sets us up effectively for the story's climax, a boat accident that nearly claims Norman Thayer's life, but also lets us know that everything will be all right. In short, the score lets us in on the conceit of the script: things shouldn't be taken too seriously.

Grusin, eighty-one as of early 2016, is a prodigiously talented pianist, composer, arranger, and conductor whose work has primarily been in TV. Many hundreds of episodes of such series as *Maude, Baretta, Good Times,* and *St. Elsewhere* boasted Grusin music. For film, he supplied the instrumental cues for *The Graduate* (1967), but this took a backseat to the Simon and Garfunkel songs that director Mike Nichols mined to help create a sense of the era. He is the uncredited arranger, orchestrator, or conductor for a number of films, and has scored (with credit) such features as *Havana* (1990), *The Firm* (1993), and *The Milagro Beanfield War* (1988), for which he won an Oscar. In my view, his best score is neither *On Golden Pond* nor his Oscar winner, but the wistful music that helps lift Warren Beatty's *Heaven Can Wait* (1978) from funny and smart to funny and authentically sweet.

On Golden Pond belongs to a subclass of drama that might be called "drama light." No one dies, so it's not a tragedy. But the main thrust of the story is "serious" to a degree, so it's not a comedy. I imagine this sort of thing, especially when layered with sentimentality, to be the hardest form of cinema to treat well musically. A similar film, and one that also has a score in the AFI Top 25, is *Out of Africa* (1985).

John Barry's propensity for melody made the *Out of Africa* soundtrack one of the most beloved of the 1980s. Its shape betrays the composer's fondness for parallel phrases—phrases that repeat immediately after sounding, each iteration mirroring the other. But it is the melodic gesture itself that gives the tune its plangent character: a rise and fall that urges a restlessness in the listener's ear, a restlessness that is at the same time comforting. When the initial phrase plunges, we know that its answer will rise. There is a passage for low flute that shows Barry's understanding of that range of the instrument, a place in the register of the hollow-sounding flute that sounds like a lover's whisper. The tune then goes to other woodwinds: the clarinet via the oboe, so that at least it feels more out-in-the-open—the whisper has become the lover's bold statement. *Out of Africa* trades for its success on the theme alone, and that theme is not even Barry's best. A far more inspired Barry melody is found in *Robin and Marian* (1975), a Richard Lester–directed film of a script by James Goldman, the same man who wrote the script for the film boasting Barry's most masterful score, *The Lion in Winter*. But *Robin and Marian* was a box office failure, primarily because Lester's quirky direction didn't mate well with Goldman's poetic script. *Out of Africa*, by contrast, was a box office smash. Sometimes, the "best music" means simply the music that accompanies the most popular film.

Spotlight:
Jazz in Film Music

Considering its place as an American art music, jazz has had a surprisingly small role to play in American film music. For the most part, what is meant by *jazz* in the context of film music is music in the jazz idiom. Jazz itself is properly a player's art, an improvisation music made in the moment. But certain gestures and procedures have come to be considered jazz-like, and these gestures are usually called simply jazz by most people.

The flagship jazz-idiom film score of the mid-twentieth century—and one that also did contain some actual jazz in it—was that for *The Man with the Golden Arm* (1955), a dark film about drug addiction directed by Otto Preminger and starring Frank Sinatra and Kim Novak. The soundtrack is truly a miracle of film-composing ingenuity. It consists mostly of symphonic jazz (with Copland-esque moments of repose) by Elmer Bernstein. When one thinks of this Bernstein score, and then of the same composer's landmark Western, *The Magnificent Seven*, and then the series of comedies (*Animal House, Ghostbusters*, etc.) at the end of Bernstein's career, one is tempted to bestow on Bernstein some sort of award along the lines of "Composer Best Suited to Sum Up a Genre." His main theme for *The Man with the Golden Arm* thrives in a place between big band and the blues, with the slightest hint of bebop. The feeling is harsh and ultra-urban.

The Sinatra character is a jazz drummer, so rather than just fake some "jazz" drumming from a studio musician, Bernstein got a West

Coast jazz trumpet player/flugelhornist, Shorty Rogers, and his band—featuring drummer Shelly Manne—to contribute to the soundtrack. Rogers and Manne lent the final product a grounding note of realism that is missing from many other urban dramas of the day. Fred Steiner's orchestration helped control the unusual blend of jazz ensemble and studio symphony orchestra.

For his next film, Preminger went one better and hired a jazz musician to compose the score. And not just any jazz musician, but Duke Ellington, who by that time was the genre's senior statesman. *Anatomy of a Murder* (1959) was a courtroom drama set in contemporary urban America, and Preminger must have felt the need for music to match its edge. Ellington's career had faded earlier in the decade, but was brought back in spectacular fashion by an epoch-making appearance by him and his orchestra at the 1956 Newport Jazz Festival. The new Ellington still had swing, but also boasted a more updated vocabulary. This time around, there's no standard orchestral writing to contrast with the jazz, which is the real thing throughout. Ellington makes a cameo appearance at one point, playing piano and fronting a band in a roadhouse café. This diegetic moment links the Ellington sound to the background score.

Ellington went on to score three more films: *Paris Blues* (1961), *Assault on a Queen* (1966), and *Change of Mind* (1969). *Paris Blues* starred Paul Newman and Sidney Poitier as jazz musicians in Paris, so a jazz score was the only possible music. The film also features Louis Armstrong and contains the most amazing jazz (used diegetically) ever committed to celluloid. *Assault on a Queen* returned to the idea of mixing jazz with orchestral music, this time supplied by Nathan Van Cleave. *Change of Mind* was a bizarre attempt to make a point about race relations via a plot that required a white man's brain to be transplanted into a black man's skull. Ellington and his orchestra supplied the only music. None of Ellington's music for film was among his best, and there was almost always some aspect of plot or mood that required a music "other" than the expected. Jazz was a different music for a different kind of film.

Fast-forward four and five decades to Spike Lee and his ongoing collaboration with jazz trumpeter/composer Terence Blanchard. The music for *X* (1992; Lee's Malcolm X bio-flick) is a powerful amalgam of jazz, blues, orchestral music and, tucked away somewhere in the background, the African American tradition of the spiritual. Blanchard's score forms an emotional bridge from the situation of African Americans inside Christian and secular America to the phenomenon of the Nation of Islam. Blanchard's theme for Lee's documentary salute to New Orleans in the wake of the Katrina disaster, *When the Levees Broke* (2006), is as pure a stream of blues trumpet playing as has ever been paired with celluloid. In *Inside Man* (2009), Blanchard showed that his smoky, blues-flecked sound could translate into a mainstream crime drama with an orchestral score.

One of the best ways to get jazz into movies is, as in *Paris Blues*, to make the movie be about jazz musicians. Clint Eastwood's biopic, *Bird* (1998), offered Charlie Parker's solos in the film thanks to Eastwood's insistence. The studio had wanted to re-record all of Parker's music, but Eastwood found a way to isolate the saxophonist's solos from old recordings, enhance them, and then have contemporary musicians record the other parts, leaving the original solos intact. Eastwood, by the way, is an accomplished musician in his own right and a composer. The most prolific composer-director since Chaplin, Eastwood has scored his films *Mystic River, Million Dollar Baby, J. Edgar,* and others.

Other, recent films that included jazz, mostly in diegetic context, include *Whiplash* (2014), about a fictitious young jazz drummer and his tyrannical bandleader, and *Miles Ahead*, the 2016 biopic about trumpeter Miles Davis.

7

THEME SONGS, COMEDIES, AND ROMANTIC COMEDIES

Songs—vocals cast in the popular style of the day—were not a part of the earliest non-musical films. Chaplin's *Modern Times* (1936) featured a richly beautiful melody that we know today as "Smile," but in the film, it is a melody without words. It would become "Smile" only in 1954, when John Turner and Geoffrey Parsons added lyrics and Nat King Cole released it as a hit vocal. A similar thing happened when David Raksin wrote a plangent melody to accentuate the haunting mystery of the film *Laura* in 1944. In the film, no lyrics are heard. Famed songwriter Johnny Mercer added words the following year, producing one of the most widely performed and recorded popular songs in history.

The list of Oscar winners for best original song from the award's inception in 1934 through 1949 contains only songs written for or used in film musicals. The most famous association of a song with a non-musical film prior to the 1950s, that of "As Time Goes By" in *Casablanca* (1942), makes use of a song already written (from 1931 by Herbert Hupfeld). The idea of an original song sung, not by a character in the film as part of a musical, but by an off-screen voice over the credits or (less often) by one of the film's characters as a bit of diegetic music, was not widely utilized until the 1950s. Starting with "Mona Lisa," a Ray Evans–Jay Livingston song written for the drama, *Captain Carey U.S.A.*, directors began to use vocals as themes for their films, quite apart from the incidental scores for those films. *Captain Carey U.S.A.*, for example, has a background score by Hugo Friedhofer that is wholly unrelated to "Mona Lisa," which won the Oscar for best original song for 1950.

The rest of the 1950s made up for lost time on the song front. Suddenly, it seemed, half the films released featured songs with lyrics rather than music themes alone. Some of these were truly groundbreaking and original. Dimitri Tiomkin's music and Ned Washington's words for "The Ballad of High Noon" ("Do Not Forsake Me, O My Darling") are a remarkable integration of mood-setting melody with a lyric that explores the theme of the film. In *High Noon* (1952), Gary Cooper's character must face a gunslinger in the streets of his town and risk losing the love of his bride-to-be (Grace Kelly), or ensure the love of his bride but turn his back on manly honor. Washington's lyrics speak for him, asking the woman he loves not to "forsake" (or abandon) him at such a moment. The song won that year's Oscar for best original song and was later voted number twenty-five on the American Film Institute's list of the 100 best songs ever written for film.

Then there were embarrassments like the theme song for *Marty* (1955). Paddy Chayefsky's big-screen adaptation of his teleplay was a kitchen-sink drama of the first order. The title character (played by Ernest Borgnine, who won the best actor Oscar for it) is a bland mama's boy who must face being a grownup and act to get what he wants from life. It doesn't need a song and, what is worse, it doesn't need the song it got, heard over the opening credits and again at the end. The music, by Harry Warren, is a lilting waltz that might have been better suited as the title music for a romantic comedy—which *Marty* emphatically is not—while the words, by Chayefsky himself (uncredited), make the playwright's tortured title character into a doe-eyed male counterpart of an ingénue. It is almost impossible not to feel the uncomfortable stain of the song throughout the film's opening scenes, despite the perfectly acceptable background score by Roy Webb.

Oscar winners for best song in the 1950s after "Mona Lisa" were:

1951: "In the Cool, Cool, Cool of the Evening" (music by Hoagy Carmichael; lyric by Johnny Mercer) from *Here Comes the Groom*

1952: "The Ballad of High Noon" (see above)

1953: "Secret Love" (music by Sammy Fain, lyric by Paul Francis Webster) from *Calamity Jane*

1954: "Three Coins in the Fountain" (music by Jule Styne, lyric by Sammy Cahn) from *Three Coins in the Fountain*

1955: "Love is a Many-Splendored Thing" (music by Sammy Fain, lyric by Paul Francis Webster) from *Love is a Many-Splendored Thing*

1956: "Whatever Will Be, Will Be (Que Sera, Sera)" (music and lyric by Jay Livingston and Ray Evans) from *The Man Who Knew Too Much*

1957: "All the Way" (music by Jimmy Van Heusen, lyric by Sammy Cahn), from *The Joker Is Wild*

1958: "Gigi" (music by Frederick Loewe, lyric by Alan Jay Lerner) from *Gigi*

1959: "High Hopes" (music by Jimmy Van Heusen, lyric by Sammy Cahn) from *A Hole in the Head*

The list is divided between songs written for musicals and theme songs written for the credits of non-musical films, with theme songs slightly predominating. What the list shows (in addition to the frequent recycling of the same writers) is a growing tendency for theme songs to share their titles with the names of their films. This filled a marketing purpose, because if the song was a hit, it meant automatic advertising for the film over the radio. Someone hearing "Love is a Many-Splendored Thing" repeatedly over the radio was probably more likely to buy a ticket to the film, *Love is a Many-Splendored Thing*. A list of the decade's nominated songs demonstrates this all the more: the films *The Moon is Blue* (1953), *The High and the Mighty* and *Three Coins in the Fountain* (1954), *Unchained* (1955), *Julie*, *Friendly Persuasion*, and *Written on the Wind* (1956), *An Affair to Remember*, *April Love*, and *Wild is the Wind* (1957), *A Certain Smile* (1958), and *The Best of Everything* and *The Hanging Tree* (1959) all boasted eponymous vocals. Though it did not get a nomination, "Theme from A Summer Place" (1959) should also be mentioned, if only because the indefatigable Max Steiner composed it, managing in his seventies to reach out to a changing popular song market and pen a top-ten hit. Not many composers are that versatile that late in life.

It's odd that it took so long for theme songs to catch fire, because 1920s film composer Erno Rapee had already pioneered the idea in his designated scores for silent films. In addition to providing full orchestral accompaniment for particular movies, the music director of Radio

City Music Hall would occasionally collaborate with a lyricist on a vocal work to go with the movie, especially when the subject matter was romance. The most famous of Rapee's songs was "Diane," composed in 1927 as a theme for one of the last of the major silent releases, *Seventh Heaven*. The song helped sell the movie, and was a hit in its own right over several decades. The Nat Shilkret Orchestra was first to record it, and in the 1950s the song underwent a revival when two artists as far apart in their aesthetic as one might imagine covered it: operatic crooner Mario Lanza, and jazz immortal Miles Davis. It's not that original theme songs were absent from movies of the 1930s and '40s, just that they were relatively few in number and did not have the status of near-indispensable that was bestowed on them in the 1950s and '60s.

The tendency for filmmakers to provide identifying songs with their cinematic products accelerated through the 1960s. Leading this charge of memorable melodies was Henry Mancini (1924–1994), whose songs received five Oscar nominations and two wins for best song between 1961 and 1965. The first of the wins, "Moon River" from *Breakfast at Tiffany's* (1961), stands as the paradigm of all movie theme songs. Fourth on AFI's list of the 100 greatest movie songs, it should actually be second after the obvious and perfectly deserving first-place winner, "Over the Rainbow," from the greatest movie musical ever, *The Wizard of Oz* (1939). A deeply flawed list that includes songs from other sources side-by-side with original material, only about half of the AFI's "top movie songs" are actual movie songs. Numbers two and three, for example, were written many years before the movies in which they were used: "As Time Goes By" and "Singing in the Rain." But whether in second place or fourth, "Moon River" is the first *original* song on AFI's list that's not from a musical. A small masterpiece, it richly deserves the distinction.

Based on Truman Capote's novella of the same name, *Breakfast at Tiffany's* told the story of Holly Golightly, a kid from "the sticks" (rural southern America) who's living in Manhattan and affecting the sophistication of a true New Yorker. Despite her urbanite act, Holly inside is still Lula Mae, the scrawny little hillbilly who married an older man at age fourteen and then ran away with nothing in her head but the idea of seeing the world. This uniquely contemporary romantic situation, reflecting Holly's dual nature, called for a song both simple and subtle in the scene where Holly's neighbor and soon-to-be romantic interest,

Paul "Fred" Varjak, discovers her strumming a guitar and singing on the fire escape. Johnny Mercer's lyric is at first more sophisticated than one might think a hick capable of grasping. The title phrase is already a metaphor for Holly's wanderlust and ceaseless roaming in search of *je ne sais quoi*. But as the words unfold, their reference to huckleberries (Mercer was a southern boy himself and recalled picking huckleberries as a child) and especially the phrase "two drifters, off to see the world" capture the character's essence without any hint of self-consciousness.

Mancini once said that composing "Moon River" was the most difficult assignment he ever got "because it had to be simple." But simple is relative, and the music he wrote for Mercer's words is only simple in the way that the answer to a complex equation is simple, once you see how it works. A song's level of sophistication is measured in its harmonies. Millions (not an exaggeration) of wonderful songs have been written using just the three primary chords of the Western diatonic (do, re, mi, and so on) scale. Folk songs going back forever, scads of old popular songs and still more blues and rock 'n' roll classics need nothing more than the chords known as I, IV, and V (the Roman numerals are commonly used) to make their point. But when a composer wants to suggest something a little deeper emotionally, something perhaps beyond the immediate world of sense perception, he or she goes elsewhere on the scale for inspiration, moving away (temporarily) from the security of I–IV–V into related areas. It was especially relevant for Holly's song to roam musically, as Mercer's lyric had cast her (in keeping with Capote's character) as a "drifter." Mancini settled on a three-four meter at a gentle tempo, and dug deep into the key of F to see what he could find.

The first four measures are direct enough, outlining a IV–I relationship with a quick stop at vi (lowercase Roman numerals indicate minor chords). This is idiomatically correct, as most folk songs—and Holly is supposedly singing a song from her young, rural life—employ IV–I changes more often than V–I. The next four measures take us somewhere altogether new, however. We start out with the IV chord, but end up at measure eight with a secondary dominant. A secondary dominant is a chord that suggests a different key from the one the song has been in. It does so by introducing notes from the scale of the new key that do not appear in the old one. Mancini is here turning toward the relative minor of his initial key of F major: D minor. It's a perfect setup for the turn in Mercer's lyric. Until now, the words have been about crossing *Moon River* "in style," a kind of languid, half-awake wishing. But in the third and fourth lines, the longing becomes palpable. The river is a "dream-maker" and a "heartbreaker." Wherever it's going, the singer is going, too. Had Mancini's music stayed firmly in F major, these lines would have been diminished in their meaning. But in D minor, their poignancy is underlined. The line ending with "I'm going your way" has an urgency, because the singer has "travelled" to D minor but by this time is back in F major. The tune then returns to its beginning, but when it reaches "We're after the same rainbow's end," it moves in a slightly different harmonic direction in order to at last bring the melody back securely to F major.

The point is that the right harmonic changes can serve as a kind of tone painting. Thinkers as far back as Plato have noticed that certain musical gestures have corresponding feelings. *Pace* John Cage, nothing here is a matter of chance; it's a matter of how we hear. The human ear hears one note and, by the very nature of how it hears, hears other notes implied. (This in turn corresponds to the overtone series of acoustical physics.) When we assemble all those implications, we have a scale, and depending on where on the scale a melody goes, certain feelings will be evoked. A skillful song composer knows this and employs it in setting a lyric. Mancini was an expert at this aspect of the songwriting art. The very peak of his songwriting skill is shown in yet another movie song from the 1960s, one that was all but ignored by the Academy: "Two for the Road." This extraordinary setting of a Leslie Bricusse lyric evokes the image in the film (*Two for the Road,* 1967) of the main characters (played by Audrey Hepburn and Albert Finney) drifting through Europe and falling in and out of love. The chord changes are so unusual that the song was completely ignored and not even nominated for an Oscar. Today, "Two for the Road" is a favorite of savvy lounge singers who know a beautiful song when they hear it.

"Moon River" almost didn't make it into *Breakfast at Tiffany's*. Paramount Pictures executive Martin Rackin blamed the song for the film's lukewarm reception in previews and called for it to be cut. Audrey Hepburn's response was reportedly "colorful" and the song was left in. It is now nearly impossible to think of the movie and not hear "Moon River." (Ironically, when the soundtrack album was released, Hepburn's performance was not on it.) The song ended up an enormous hit outside the confines of the film, with Andy Williams's recording of it a top-selling single. From then on, producers did not question the presence of a Mancini song.

Mancini's musical background was typical of film composers of the day. Classically trained, he had studied with, of all people, Ernst Krenek, a composer of the so-called twelve-tone school that most music lovers would associate with the more alienating aspects of "modern" music. That Mancini's melodically oriented talent found its bearings under the tutelage of so acerbic a composer testifies to the powerful neutrality of Western musical language. Western music consists essentially of a set of tools that the composer may use as he or she wishes. The nature of the end product is virtually unlimited.

In 1952, a young Mancini joined the music department at Universal Studios (Universal Pictures) and spent the next six years laboring on nearly one hundred movies, usually making anonymous contributions along with other nameless composers to B-movies, the most famous of which was *Creature from the Black Lagoon*. In 1958, Mancini made a leap from cheap horror films to a major feature by no less than Orson Welles. *Touch of Evil* was film noir, and now widely considered the last great example of the genre from its classic era of the 1940s and '50s. That score, and the controversy surrounding Welles's desire for a music-less opening versus the studio's preference for title music, is covered in chapter 9, "Ambient Music, No Music, and Ready-Mades."

Another side of the composer emerged at almost the same time as *Touch of Evil*. Mancini's way with a tune came to the fore when a director asked him to write a theme for his television series about a hip private investigator: *Peter Gunn*. The title character was a jazz lover, so of course the theme had to be jazzy. Not only did Mancini come through with a memorable piece of music in the jazz idiom, the number became a favorite of jazz and pop musicians who continue to cover it today. And yet, it's not so much a melody as it is a repeating bass line of eight notes, overlaid with bluesy brass chords. The series ran from 1958 to 1961, but Mancini's theme lives on and on.

The director of the *Peter Gunn* series was Blake Edwards, and his work with Mancini in television led him to hire the composer for *Breakfast at Tiffany's* in 1961. Then in 1963 came the first of Edwards's incredibly successful Pink Panther films featuring the inimitable Peter Sellers as the hilariously bumbling Inspector Clouseau. Mancini outdid himself, coming up with a jazz-idiom theme that has outdistanced even his *Peter Gunn* theme for sheer popularity. The theme was used in all subsequent Pink Panther movies, up through the present time. It would be impossible to make a Pink Panther film without Mancini's theme, so indelibly imprinted on the ear is the sneaky little melody that somehow embodies both Clouseau's clumsiness and his pretentions to urbanity.

The score for the original *Pink Panther* landed at number 20 in AFI's list of best film scores, the only pure comedy in the Top 25. Like many well-made scores, it consists of two opposing ideas that play off against each other throughout the movie. The first idea is, of course, the famous "Pink Panther Theme." The tune sneaks up on the listener in the most artful manner. Mancini crafted it from a series of two-note phrases that evince the stealth of the creature of the title. And yet—the "Pink Panther" is no actual cat. The term refers instead to a fictional diamond with a precious flaw at the center: a pink discoloration that looks like a leaping panther. The plot revolves around the bumbling Inspector Clouseau (Peter Sellers) and his attempt to determine the identity of the Phantom, a notorious jewel thief out to steal the Pink Panther. But the filmmakers ingeniously decided to create an animated pink panther (the cat, not the jewel) to present the opening credits. Mancini's theme, heard at first as a breathy tenor sax solo, is largely identified with this, but the two-note phrases are easily separated and presented as isolated motives at appropriate times throughout the movie (Mancini clearly intended that when he wrote the theme), so that when the thieves are afoot or other sneakiness is at hand, the two-note bits show up, usually (and most effectively) on a flute in the low register. "The Pink Panther Theme" is strongly related to the "heist" music from *Breakfast at Tiffany's*, which Mancini had written two years previously.

The second element is, unsurprisingly, a song: "It Had Better Be Tonight," heard in the film in its Italian original, "Meglio Stasera," sung seductively by *Playboy* sex bomb Fran Jeffries as she dances around a fireplace at a ski resort in the Italian Alps. It's a sweet tune given punch by a gentle rhumba rhythm, and it works because *The Pink Panther* is as much bedroom farce as it is anything else. The sexiness and sophistication of what would soon come to be called the "jet set" and the machinations of various partners to jump into bed with the partners of other partners was the aesthetic backdrop to the comedy. With a cast that included David Niven, Capucine, Robert Wagner, and Claudia Cardinale, how could it be otherwise? Sellers's slapstick stole the show, though, and a subsequent series of Pink Panther films were made, focusing on Clouseau's distinct lack of sexiness and sophistication. "The Pink Panther Theme" was featured in every one.

"It Had Better Be Tonight" did not enjoy the popularity of "Moon River" or of Mancini and Mercer's 1962 Oscar-winning theme song, "Days of Wine and Roses." Indeed, a sea change was coming in music. When, on a Sunday in February 1964, the Beatles appeared on TV's Ed Sullivan Show, the songwriting game was forever altered. The sort of song melody composed by Mancini used the scales and chords of the tonal system in a way that created tension and release at various points in the song. The Beatles, along with the other bands of the 1960s British Invasion, favored a more modal approach. This simply means that sometimes the melodies and chords of a Beatles song use a scale that is not simply major or minor; these alternative scales are called modes, and their use follows directly from the fact that the guitar, a naturally modal instrument, was rock's instrument of choice. And then there was the rock beat, with its heavy backbeat and so-called square rhythms that replaced the syncopations of jazz-idiom songs. With these changes also came a different way of writing a lyric, an approach less literal and more metaphorical/fanciful.

This influence took a while to transfer to the screen, and as it did, some of the last great movie songs of the fading era were written: "The Shadow of Your Smile" from *The Sandpiper* (1965, music by Johnny Mandel and lyrics by Paul Francis Webster); "Born Free" from *Born Free* (1966, music by John Barry, lyrics by Don Black); "The Windmills of Your Mind" from *The Thomas Crown Affair* (1968, music by Michel Legrand, lyrics by Alan and Marilyn Bergman); and "Raindrops Keep Falling on My Head" from *Butch Cassidy and the Sundance Kid* (1969, music by Burt Bacharach, lyrics by Hal David)—Oscar winners all.

The emergence of the new style was oddly ignored by the Motion Picture Academy. At least one song in the new idiom was clearly deserving of at least a nomination, and yet was totally ignored: "Mrs. Robinson," written by Paul Simon for Mike Nichols's *The Graduate* in 1967. Nichols was fascinated by the duo of Simon and Garfunkel and felt that their sound fit the mood of his unique new film about the values of an ever-changing American culture. He used previously written Simon and Garfunkel songs for much of the film's background score, but also asked Simon (the songwriter of the duo) to come up with something original. Simon submitted two songs that Nichols rejected. Then he came up with "Mrs. Robinson," a song so perfect in its mode of address, in its subject matter and youthful language, that Nichols immediately grabbed it. The result is one of the best songs ever written for the screen, not just in its quality of music and lyrics, but in its capture of something essential in the film. Rarely do film songs accomplish this, and yet, though the song fit all of the Academy's criteria (an original song written expressly for a film), it was ignored come Oscar time. To the Academy establishment, one might reasonably suppose, the song didn't "feel" like a movie song. As a consolation of sorts, "Mrs. Robinson" holds a more-than-justified sixth place in AFI's list of 100 best cinema songs.

The place of theme songs in the scheme of movies has phased in and out since the 1960s, the height of the theme-song craze. The craze was so crazy, in fact, that Alfred Hitchcock, who had a bad habit of biting his nails over current fads, broke relations with Bernard Herrmann over that composer's refusal to add a pop song to his score for *Torn Curtain*. "You're not a pop film director," Herrmann is reported to have said to his rotund collaborator. But it made no difference. Herrmann was out, and never scored a Hitchcock film again.

Since the 1960s, some of the major movie theme songs—songs that have endured beyond their films' releases—include "The Way We Were" from the movie of the same name (1973, music by Marvin Hamlisch and lyrics by Alan and Marilyn Bergman); "What a Feeling" from *Flashdance* (1983, music by Giorgio Moroder and lyrics by Keith Forsey and Irene Cara); "You've Got a Friend in Me" from *Toy Story* (1995, music and lyrics by Randy Newman); and "Skyfall" from the movie of the same name (2012, music and lyrics by Adele and Paul Epworth).

Special mention goes to probably the biggest hit of all movie theme songs since "Moon River": "My Heart Will Go On" from James Cameron's *Titanic* (1997), with music by James Horner and words by Will Jennings. In a replay of the "Moon River" story, Cameron at first rejected the song, and Celine Dion declined to sing it. It took much convincing from Horner and from Dion's husband/manager to make it happen, but the song—perhaps the single biggest hit ballad of the 1990s—was at last included.

* * *

Do comedies need music? We could more broadly ask, "Do movies need music?" And the answer will vary from film to film. Wherever a visual sequence by itself fails to fully hold the emotional water of a scene, music is needed. But of course, such highfalutin things hardly apply to comedy. We don't really need music to tell us the "emotions" of Laurel as he gets hit by Hardy. We probably don't want to know the emotions of Bob Hope as he sees Bing Crosby's face on his wife's baby. It's enough to get the jokes; we don't have to "feel" them. So comedies often simply eliminate music, save for opening or closing credits (*Bringing Up Baby*), or supply a handful of cues that situate the action in a certain time and place. This often means that the film will quickly date. Watch *Fletch* (1985) today, and the then-hip electronic cues will not so much take you back to the 1980s as make you wish you could forget them.

Mel Brooks's comedies frequently utilize the director's own songs. The title song of *Blazing Saddles* (1974) is a particularly hilarious example, and of course the handful of songs in *The Producers* (1968) later bloomed into the full-fledged stage and later film musical of the early twenty-first century. Unsung (literally) in the background for these films was composer John Morris, whose lively cues helped *The Producers* open to the quick start of Max Bialystock's old-lady seductions. Morris's talents were used equally well in *Young Frankenstein* (1974), where his cues evoked the clichés of the horror film while somehow staying funny. Morris's pinnacle, however, was not a Brooks film at all, but Arthur Hiller's 1979 comedy, *The In-Laws*. The opening signals Comedy with a capital C: the ridiculous heist of a U.S. Treasury truck is accompanied by a rising/falling half-step motive owing to Monty Norman's famous James Bond theme, but the knots of woodwinds above are a built-in musical clue that this is no real thriller. The first cue after the credits is a full twenty-five minutes in, a twenty-second blast of full orchestra as a cab swerves in and out of traffic. Then a couple minutes later, the James Bond-ish theme is recalled, followed by wild and goofy chase music as a bad guy clambers down a fire escape after Alan Arkin, firing his revolver. In short, the purpose of Morris's music is to remind us that this is a comedy, not a caper movie. Now, *The In-Laws* barely needs this, which is why the cues are so few. But an out-of-control cab and shots being fired can veer toward serious unless something is there to keep it from doing so. That's the usual purpose of music for comedy. If a romantic angle is added, then a song is generally thrown in as well.

About the same time *The In-Laws* was being made, *National Lampoon's Animal House* (1978) was killing it at the box office. The score, by no less than Elmer Bernstein, represented a new way of approaching music for comedy. Reportedly, when someone "in the industry" questioned director John Landis about his motivation in hiring a composer renowned for his treatment of dramas (*To Kill a Mockingbird*) and Westerns (*The Magnificent Seven*) to write cues for, of all things, a comedy—and a broad, even sophomoric comedy at that—Landis's answer was to the effect that he wanted *Animal House* scored as if it were a straight drama, the better to hone in the comedic associations of plot and character. A score of the John Morris sort might have provided a little campus color and one or two frantic chase-music sorts of cues, but that's it. The result, with Bernstein tracking the characters as closely as he would a serious drama, was a score that exhibited "seriousness" in its gestures, but always with a wry grin. From the opening pan of the campus of Faber College, accompanied by a faux college hymn resembling Brahms's *Academic Festival Overture*—and punctuated uproariously by two timpani strokes at exactly the right (that is, wrong) moment—to the sweet-sad love theme for the doomed couple, to the menacing music when the evil frat house plants the wrong answers to a test, the score sounds like a "real" movie score, and because of this we care a little more about the characters; even the monstrous Otter, with his deceitful womanizing, seems warmer and more likeable when trying a pick-up line to Bernstein's jaunty theme. (Bernstein had some fun with the mess of a climax, a college homecoming parade gone horribly wrong. At one point, the John Belushi character dons the garb of a pirate and leaps around the tops of buildings. Bernstein's short cue for this is from his own 1958 score to *The Buccaneer*, about French pirate Jean Lafitte.)

The success of the humanizing music for *Animal House*'s outrageous cast of characters made Bernstein in demand for comedies for the first time in his career. Between *Animal House* and the composer's death in 2004, Bernstein added such comedies as *Airplane!* and the Ghostbusters series to his usual lineup of more serious fare. Truth be told, however, it takes a composer with an alert sense of humor to write this kind of a score for a comedy. It is not enough to pen a pratfall cue or an obvious snare-drum-kick commentary on an action or a double take. The composer has to work from within the characters and their motivations, just as he would in a serious film, but must treat them lightly. One non-Bernstein comedy score that does this par excellence is Alan Silvestri's music for *Mouse Hunt* (1997). This "criminally underappreciated" comedy, to quote an online fan, features Nathan Lane and Lee Evans as a pair of brothers who inherit a creepy old house and with it, a pesky mouse. Silvestri gives us a main theme for the opening credits that feels like Prokofiev has just met Mickey Mouse and wants him to have better music than that *Steamboat Willie* stuff. Silvestri makes us feel for the crazy Lane and Evans characters and their ridiculous plight. What's more, his music somehow identifies with the mouse itself, becoming a kind of karmic presence that keeps the brothers from throwing away their lives. There's a great deal more here than "Mickey Mouse," indeed.

The Pirates of the Caribbean franchise qualifies as adventure-comedy, more the latter than the former, given Johnny Depp's constant drunken demeanor and slithery character. Probably no other film scores trade on the expectations of cliché than those of Hans Zimmer for the Pirates movies. And that is exactly what is called for. The most fun is to watch for the music to thwart those expectations to comic effect, as near the end of *On Stranger Tides*, when Depp is about to kiss Penelope Cruz and the music builds and builds toward the typical cinematic climax of locked lips—only to stop short as Depp runs away. Most of the music is standard-issue pirate, and of course that is exactly what we need to go along with the patched eyes and dinged cutlasses of the mates who turn this Disney ride into a Disney ride of a movie. Zimmer supplies this.

Or does he? One of the curious things about Zimmer is that when you actually search for his printed sheet music, the names on it are not always his. In fact, the Pirates franchise's best-known tune, its main theme, bears the name of the composer Klaus Badelt. But when you see the films, the credits always state "Music by Hans Zimmer." It would seem that Zimmer maintains a studio along the lines of the great Renaissance painters, whose masterpieces were sometimes completed by students and associates.

Comedies have recently become a dumping ground for the work of the "music supervisor," the agent in charge of lining up previously written pop songs for inclusion in a given film. See, for example, *Zoolander* and its sequel (2001, 2016). As noted earlier, comedies benefit more than serious film from being situated in a certain time, and it is only reasonable to expect songs from the era to do that.

The truth about comedy is that it needs music less than does serious drama, and when it needs it most urgently, it is best supplied with song rather than instrumental cues. The reason for this may lie in the nature of comedy itself. Whereas characters in drama change, characters in comedies do not. Comedy trades on archetypes. The fathers in *The In-Laws* don't change; they are simply stand-ins for the conservative mainstream guy (Alan Arkin) and the nutty crazy guy (Peter Falk). The only thing music in that situation can do is supply some cues to underscore the loonier moments.

❀ ❀ ❀

Before we leave the general discussion of theme songs/comedies/romantic comedies, mention should be made of one of the greatest sources of movie songs in history: James Bond films. The vintage Bond films of the 1960s and '70s certainly qualify as comedies, given their tongue-in-cheek treatment of espionage as a matter of, as one cue for the Bond movie *Thunderball* puts it, "Kiss-Kiss-Bang-Bang." The later Bond films, especially those starring Daniel Craig, have taken a much more serious turn, and yet they have retained their use of theme songs as identifiers.

Almost from the start, each movie of the Bond franchise had to have a song. Only the very first, *Dr. No* (1962), lacked one, and after that they spun out ceaselessly: *From Russia with Love* (1963), *Goldfinger* (1964), *Thunderball* (1965), *You Only Live Twice* (1967), and *Diamonds Are Forever* (1971). All of these films featured songs with music by the same composer working with a variety of lyricists: John Barry. The charm of Barry's melodies, which catch in the craw quite delightfully, contrasted with the relatively uninspired and redundant dramatic cues of those movies, and would suggest that Barry was perhaps more naturally a songwriter than a composer. Further testimony comes from Barry's one-tune score to *Out of Africa* (1985; see chapter 6 on dramas) and his Oscar-winning theme song for *Born Free* (1966), with lyrics by Don Black. (The exception to this is certainly his 1968 Oscar-winning score to *A Lion in Winter*, and even it relies heavily on vocal—mostly choral—music for its effect.) Barry even began his musical life fronting a pop band and playing songs of the day.

Subsequent Bond movies turned to a range of songwriters for their themes, including Paul and Linda McCartney for *Live and Let Die* (1973), Marvin Hamlisch for *The Spy Who Loved Me* (1977), David Arnold working with the ubiquitous Don Black for *The World Is Not Enough* (1999), and Madonna for *Die Another Day* (2002). The most recent foray into Bond themes was made by Adele for 2012's *Casino Royale*. It won her an Oscar.

And yet, underlying all of the Bond songs down the years is a single, four-note idea. Think "James Bond," and you cannot avoid it. To a steady beat of four, the measure is clearly outlined as a note starts on the downbeat, slides up a half-step, then up a half-step again, then down a half-step, only to step down again to the downbeat of the next measure and start the whole little motion all over again. This continues as an electric guitar plays a figure that parallels the slithery motion of the accompaniment. This is the "James Bond Theme," composed by Monty Norman for *Dr. No*. It came to dominate the sound of all consequent James Bond features. In fact, without it, you don't quite have a James Bond film. We hear it as the big eye comes out at the start of every 007 flick, but more than that, we hear it underlining a great deal of every Bond score. For instance, it figures in the very texture of Adele's song. Norman was fired following *Dr. No*, and for a while, John Barry—who was the arranger for that movie—claimed the credit. But Norman had the last laugh. After some legal haggling, his four-note motive and narrow little theme were declared entirely his, and today constitute perhaps the most distinctive brand in the history of film. As of this writing (2016), Norman is still alive and collecting royalties on his unique, brief, indispensable creation.

Spotlight: Animation

Many film composers have enhanced their careers writing for animated films, taking profitable detours into that area. James Horner made his first big splash in 1982 with *Star Trek: The Wrath of Khan*. But that success didn't keep him from penning music to the much more modestly rewarded, but no less demanding, animated features *An American Tail* (1986), which produced a first hit song ("Somewhere Out There") for the man who would someday compose the biggest hit song of any movie, "My Heart Will Go On"; *The Land Before Time* (1986); *An American Tail: Fievel Goes West* (1991); and *We're Back! A Dinosaur's Tale* (1993). It's as if these films refreshed his creative juices with their simple optimism, so that he could deal with the serious live-action stuff, which in Horner's case was often historical in nature: the U.S. Civil War in *Glory* (1989), the liberation of Scotland in *Braveheart* (1995), the near disaster of *Apollo 13* (1995), and of course, *Titanic* (1997). (Horner reportedly composed a score for the remake of *The Magnificent Seven* before his death in a single-engine airplane crash in 2015. As of this writing—May 2016—the film is still months away from release.)

Michael Giacchino is one film composer whose music for animated films seems somehow freer and fresher than his more "serious" scores for live-action features. Giacchino, like many other composers of his generation and younger—he is in his forties as of 2016—has also written a great deal of video-game music, which is as much if not more in affinity with the sensibility of animation than is live-action films. Giacchino's music for *The Incredibles* (2004) is a sweep of jazzy power music, the better to bolster cartoon superheroes. His score to the fanciful Pixar feature about a rodent who aspires to haute cuisine, *Ratatouille* (2007), is even freer—a wild blend of jazzy cues and French sidewalk-cafe allusions that feels as if the the composer is having way too much fun. You can tell when a composer loves the movie he's scoring, and Giacchino was clearly crazy for the tale of an artist who succeeds against all odds, as was the case with *Up* (2010), which won the composer a much-deserved Oscar. In live-action films, Giacchino seems to have suffered the fate of writing for franchises, such as *Mission: Impossible III* (2006), *Star Trek Into Darkness* (2013), *Jurassic World* (2015), and, most spectacularly, *Rogue One* (2016), in which the mantle of John Williams was passed down to the younger composer.

Michael Kamen was an eclectic even among eclectics, and his compositional and arranging talents were employed for everything from ballet scores (for the Alvin Ailey and La Scala companies, among others) to Pink Floyd's album *The Wall*, to scores for the Die Hard and Lethal Weapon movie franchises. He is perhaps best regarded by cinema buffs for his music for Terry Gilliam's future dystopia, *Brazil* (1985), but garnered many more fans as the co-writer of the mega-hit song, "Everything I Do (I Do for You)," written for *Robin Hood: Prince of Thieves* (1991) but more widely known as a song covered by virtually every pop singer on earth since its first release by Canadian pop singer (and the song's co-writer) Bryan Adams. But it is in Brad Bird's *Iron Giant* (1999), one of the most sophisticated and most fully realized animated features ever made, that Kamen commanded his most impressive range. Kamen's cues carefully follow the folds of the narrative and even the moment-to-moment changes of expression on characters' faces. A scene in which the title character—a huge chunk of metal with a heart of gold, as it were—goes berserk when he thinks his friend Hogarth has been killed is accompanied by music of menace that entirely avoids the clichés of musical danger such as diminished chords. Music that suggests the divine accompanies the giant's decision to sacrifice himself for Hogarth, and the final scene of hope vibrates with Kamen's brightly optimistic (but not at all obvious) cue. When *The Iron Giant* is given its full due as a major event in the history of animated features, Kamen's music will have been a big part of that recognition.

Though not a Hollywood composer, the name Joe Hisaishi cannot be left out of any mention of animated-film composers. The composer-king of anime, the Japanese master has made the form his life work and along the way has developed a distinctive style, a vast catalog, and a huge following. His best-known scores are for the films *Princess Mononoke* (1997), *Spirited Away* (2001), and *Howl's Moving Castle* (2004). Hisaishi's shapely melodies and lush orchestrations pay no heed to postmodern concerns, but wrap the listener in unashamedly gorgeous sounds that attract more and more fans every year. Many introductions to Hisaishi's most famous tracks include the use of quartal harmonies—stacked fourths instead of the usual triadic thirds—that essentially announced, "Music by Joe Hisaishi."

8

SCIENCE FICTION AND FANTASY

The very idea of science fiction and fantasy begs for music that is in some way beyond the ordinary. At the very least, a visit from or to another planet seems to call for sounds suggestive of the planet. Of course, the problem arises: what exactly would music on another planet sound like? All the music we know is, by definition, already familiar to us. Writing a Mahlerian or Straussian score to go with a movie about the Old South or a medieval adventure is one thing; making romantic-era European music stand in for the sonic art of Pluto or Sirius is quite another. One way to suggest a musical culture other than our own is to present colors that are different from the day-to-day music-making of us earthlings. We are all used to hearing bows scrape across strings, lips buzz in a brass mouthpiece, and reeds vibrate a column of air. The trick is to eschew these sounds for other sources. Two classic sci-fi film scores stand out in this regard: Bernard Herrmann's for *The Day the Earth Stood Still* (1951), and Jerry Goldsmith's for *Planet of the Apes* (1968).

The genre was still fairly fresh when *The Day the Earth Stood Still* came out. Director Robert Wise took the idea of interplanetary communication to a new level in this tale of human violence and the need for galactic peace. The plot is well known. A humanoid visitor from another planet (Michael Rennie) lands his craft on earth and disappears into the daily life of an American family. His visit is accompanied by an enormous robot with extraordinary powers. At length, the plot reveals to us the human folly of aggression and the inherent goodness brought by a scientific culture capable of interplanetary travel. It may seem naïve now, but at the time, it was a Big Moral Lesson.

Herrmann saw as his greatest responsibility the creation of a sound that said, "I'm here from another planet with an enormous robot, but don't be frightened. All right, be a little frightened." What is more initially alien than the sound of the theremin? The theremin, invented (logically enough) by a man named Leon Theremin, is the only instrument that does not require the player to touch it. The electronic device produces an eerily pure tone in response to a player whose moving hands change the oscillators for frequency (pitch) and amplitude (volume) in relation to two antennae. Its slipping, sliding sound is by now well known, primarily from science fiction films.

It was not, however, at first used in science fiction at all. Miklos Rozsa employed its otherworldliness to convey the blur of alcoholism in *The Lost Weekend* and the Freudian landscape of a dream in *Spellbound*—and both in the same year, 1945. Then the theremin fell off the radar for half a decade, until Herrmann chose a pair of them as the perfect sound for Klaatu and his giant metal pal, Gort. But Herrmann's quest for interplanetary sound did not stop there. He also employed two Hammond organs, a large studio organ, pairs of harps and pianos, three vibraphones, two glockenspiels, three each of trumpets and trombones, and an astonishing four tubas to create a low-pitched mess of notes resembling chaos. Strings—violin, cello, and bass—are said in most references to have been "electric," but as solid-body violins with built-in pickups were not manufactured until the late 1950s, it seems likely that "electric" meant "amplified." In any case, the sound is out-and-out creepy, and the main theme—later used in the pilot episode of the TV series, *Lost in Space*—gets lost itself amid the kaleidoscope of timbres. Herrmann accomplished his goal of creating music that sounded unlike any heard before, and the sound of the theremin became the sonic symbol of moviedom's "outer space."

Planet of the Apes (1968) is a silly movie that can seem to exist solely for the purpose of making us see Charlton Heston nearly naked for two hours. The plot—especially the plot twist at the end—is obvious, and the dialogue is embarrassing. Jerry Goldsmith's music won a place on the AFI list of great scores because it almost single-handedly saves the movie from seeming entirely at home in the present day, and not a future-fantasy at all. While the apes on the planet-of-the-same all speak

English, and the land, air, and water are all clearly those of earth (hmm—wonder why?), the music, at least, takes us to a slightly different place and time.

By 1968 the theremin was old hat, thanks largely to Herrmann's introduction of it in *The Day the Earth Stood Still*. What was an innovator to do? What Goldsmith did was to have brass players blow into their instruments without mouthpieces, ask woodwind players to finger their instruments audibly but without blowing into them, turn things like mixing bowls into percussion instruments, and loop drum parts into an echoplex—a sonic device that echoes sound in ever-diminishing volume and a favorite Goldsmith device (he used it on the trumpet calls in his 1970 score for *Patton*).

Yet what Goldsmith did that makes *Planet of the Apes* such a landmark goes well beyond the employment of unusual colors, or surface timbres. Many of the musical gestures are atonal, even suggesting the use of rows or series. The row or series in twentieth-century music is an assembly of the twelve tones of the chromatic scale (all the notes, white and black, on a keyboard from one name note to the next one an octave away) in a manner that repeats none of them until all are sounded. The result throws off our usual expectation that one note will follow another in a certain pattern. Goldsmith doesn't employ this technique outright in *Planet of the Apes*, but there are a handful of measures, accompanying the most alien of the planet's ways, that suggest it strongly by denying the usual tonal expectations of the listener. There are also passages where the rhythms seem to disconnect from the beat. A beat is a framework or count, as in four beats to the measure or three or two. A rhythm is the pattern of durations (or note values) superimposed over the beat. In 99 percent of music, the two are intricately entwined. At one point in the chase sequence in *Planet of the Apes*, however, a brushes-on-snare drum pattern we would normally associate with 6/8 time (long-short, long-short, etc.) is juxtaposed with a beat pattern completely foreign to it, conveying the same sense one has when stumbling over oneself from running too fast. Goldsmith even makes rhythmic patterns of the sound of an ape and uses that, albeit sparingly, when the ape government flexes its muscles.

Against this alien sound of the ape culture, Goldsmith places the "normal" music of humanity. When the focus is on the Heston character and his colleagues, the music tends more toward the standard music we might expect in a movie. There is even a triumphant major chord when the Heston character first talks to the apes, amazing them with his intelligence.

Goldsmith's score took things about as far as they could go. After *Planet of the Apes*, sagas of outer space would need something altogether different. Sounds indicating alien cultures became almost beside the point. Everyone was onto the trick, after all. What then would come along to give new life to the musical soundtracks of science fiction and fantasy?

INTERLUDE: OF OSCARS AND INNOVATIONS

Two composers of enormous stature were among those nominated for the 2016 Academy Award for best original score. Both were in their eighties, and both still composing at the top of their games. Indeed, the scores for which they were nominated were iconic of their output: Ennio Morricone for Quentin Tarantino's take on spaghetti Westerns, *The Hateful Eight*; and John Williams for the latest in the Star Wars franchise. Morricone's score was a throwback to the landmark rethinking he had done for the Western genre in such films as *The Good, The Bad and the Ugly* (see chapter 5, "Cowboys and Superheroes"). Williams's music continued with unfailing power the "sound" that he had given to the Star Wars films from the very first installment in 1977. Morricone won, which was right, as somehow (in the noble tradition of the Academy getting things wrong) he never before had been awarded a best-score Oscar, while Williams counted four best-score wins plus an Oscar for his orchestrations for the film version of *Fiddler on the Roof*. What was remarkable about those two composers being nominated in the same year, in addition to the artistic power they both still wield in their ninth decades, was that they represented innovators of totally opposite types.

Morricone innovated by going against the nineteenth-century grain of most orchestral soundtracks in his unique scores for Sergio Leone, and eventually in the extraordinary music for *The Mission* (see chapter 4, "The Epic, the Exotic, and War"). Williams went in the opposite direction. As movie music was moving ever-so-gently away from the language of the late romantic symphonists, employing modest avant-garde techniques like Goldsmith's in *Planet of the Apes*, or sounds owing more to rhythm and percussive color á la Morricone, Williams grabbed the falling baton of the symphonist and raised it aloft once more. This was not reaction, but recognition. As a consequence, it is unthinkable to consider the history of movie scores from the 1970s on without Williams's omnipresent talent. The number of blockbuster films over the decades with a Williams score is phenomenal, starting with *Jaws* and the original *Star Wars* . Somehow, Williams has managed to win only five Oscars, but he is the most Oscar-nominated artist of any kind in cinema history, with an astonishing fifty as of 2016.

As noted in chapter 1, Williams's modus operandi is the delivery of music that continues the late nineteenth-century tradition of orchestral music in the form of music for the screen. This is surely no casual decision on Williams's part, but a canny and purposeful one. From the earliest days of the silent era, music played a salient role in the emotional content of the cinematic experience. Also from the beginning, film music was primarily the music of the mid- to late nineteenth century. The classical music used to underlie the silents—such as the music of Chopin, Liszt, and Wagner—inspired the earliest generation of film composers, who were themselves trained in that tradition. As we have seen, people like Max Steiner and Erich Wolfgang Korngold even studied with some of the late masters of romantic-era music, such as Mahler.

A psychological synthesis occurred. Moviegoers came to associate the late nineteenth-century style of music-making with film music's very language. Large choirs of strings, winds, and brass, playing from a chromatic vocabulary with certain melodic gestures inherently suggestive of parallel emotional states, were "movie music." Given some other set of circumstances, "movie music" might have meant jazz and the blues, or folk songs, or gamelan music. But it came to mean classical music of a certain stripe because the earliest suppliers of music for the screen were classically trained musicians, and the late nineteenth and early twentieth centuries were their training ground. Throughout decades this persisted. Max Steiner's scores for *King Kong* and *Gone with the Wind* are Mahlerian/Straussian, and so, with variations, are most of the scores for films in the 1940s and '50s. Even film noir was more given to the luscious strings of David Raksin's *Laura* than to the jazzy riffs of what we now think of as detective music.

Film music, in short, had become a form—a certain set of tools and expectations that identified it as movie music. Any musical form has defining factors which, when musicians stray from them, beg to return. The music that strays is sometimes the most interesting music (though not always), but the music that returns us to the language—to the defining musical factors that make the music a certain kind of music—is often the strongest in its ability to speak to listeners.

An example from rock is case in point. Rock harmonies are fundamentally modal, which follows naturally from the guitar as rock's major instrument. In other words, where "tonal" music (used here only to distinguish it from "modal") uses certain relationships such as a G chord that leads to the home chord of C, rock more typically uses a chord that includes notes not in the key; in our example, for instance, a B-flat chord (and not the G) might precede the home chord of C. It's a different sonic relationship and, therefore, a different feel. (To hear an archetypal example of modal rock harmonies, listen to Cream's "Sunshine of Our Love." Relationships among the chords of that song sound nothing like they do in a mainstream popular song of the same era, such as "The Windmills of My Mind.") Whenever music drifts from that sound, as it did in the 1980s, rock comes back to assert its identity with this harmonic difference. In the early 1990s, it was Nirvana that returned the sound to prominence and confirmed what qualified as rock, in contrast to pop.

In the 1960s and early '70s, a number of cultural, technological, and economic factors started to produce deviations from that form. Popular music changed in the '60s with the influence of rock coming to full flower, and theme songs reached a peak (see chapter 7, "Theme Songs, Comedies, and Romantic Comedies"). Even jazz and classical music had altered their identity. Jazz artists were more avant-garde, while in the concert hall, new compositions took on an atonal edge. These changes sparked parallel changes on screen. Goldsmith's excursion into the avant-garde in *Planet of the Apes* was a prominent example, as were the popular songs that dominated *The Graduate*, the whistling-yodeling-gunfire rhythms of Morricone's *The Good, The Bad and the Ugly*, pop adapted for a Western in *Butch Cassidy and the Sundance Kid*, and the abandonment of original music altogether in *2001: A Space Odyssey*.

What John Williams did was to answer this with a bold and clear re-assertion of movie music as consisting of original scores fashioned in the tradition of chromatic, late nineteenth-century romantic symphonic works. As a strategy, it was an unparalleled success.

The outline of his early career is fairly straightforward. Born in Queens, Williams moved with his family to Los Angeles when he was sixteen. "Johnny Williams," as he was known in his young days, served a long apprenticeship with the film-music industry, working as a studio pianist for senior Hollywood composers such as Henry Mancini and Jerry Goldsmith, orchestrating music by other composers (including Franz Waxman and Alfred Newman), scoring B movies in the 1950s, and enduring the weekly chore of providing music for the TV series *Lost in Space* (1965–1968). Then he orchestrated the 1971 film version of the Broadway hit *Fiddler on the Roof* and won his first Oscar for it. Directors began to notice him. Williams's score for *The Reivers* (1969) was a breakthrough. In 1973 his music for the John Wayne film, *The Cowboys*, got the attention of young director Steven Spielberg, who hired Williams to score *Sugarland Express* (1974). Thus began one of the longest lasting director-composer collaborations in cinematic history. *Jaws* (1975) sealed the Spielberg-Williams partnership, and suddenly John (he had long since dropped "Johnny") Williams was in demand.

We now return you to our feature . . .

✷ ✷ ✷

The music destined to forever change the way we think of scores for sci-fi and fantasy was the work of John Williams. It was Williams who returned movie music to itself in a string of films stretching from the 1970s on, including the Star Wars franchise; *Close Encounters of the Third Kind*; *Superman*; *E.T. The Extraterrestrial*; the Indiana Jones adventures; *Jurassic Park*; and others. Melody is the essence of all Williams's music, serving to express something about the film at hand. The *Star Wars* main theme outlines bold action; contrastingly, the angular delicacy of "Hedwig's Theme" for the Harry Potter films suggests the otherworldly through sudden leaps, accompanied by unexpected harmonies. Of course, they weren't all sci-fi and fantasy. *Home Alone* put Williams's stamp on comedy; *JFK* threw him into "American" music territory, more á la Roy Harris than Aaron Copland; and *Catch Me If*

You Can—in many ways his most interesting score—reminded us of his jazz-playing origins. And of course, *Schindler's List* and *Saving Private Ryan* were historical epics to which Williams brought the appropriate sweep. The transformation he worked on sci-fi and fantasy translated into other genres. But it's significant that his most immediately recognizable work, the music that first made him famous, was in the area most threatened by the changes that had come to Hollywood film scores. Composers before Williams strove to make the aliens sound more alien, and the future sound as different from the present as possible. Williams opted to make the aliens sound more human and the future pretty much like the present, perhaps because he understood that, in the movies, the aliens really are us and the future actually is today. In doing so, he confirmed and reinforced the romantic-era symphonic heritage of film music.

It began in 1975 with *Jaws*, which is hardly sci-fi but certainly not reality. We'll call it soft fantasy: an impossibly huge shark eats people and boats, and drives the market in beach vacations into the sand. The story goes that when Spielberg visited Williams and asked him to play his idea for the shark music, he heard the now-famous two-note motive and said, "That's it?" Williams then explained to the director that the see-sawing half-step, played with increasing speed, would be performed on sixteen double basses in their lowest register, and that this massed weight would produce a threatening effect. The result, as we now know, was a sound you could patent as sinister. The story illustrates several things, chief among them the trust that is required between director and composer to make a good working relationship. Unimpressed by two back-and-forth notes on the piano, Spielberg had to trust Williams's musical knowledge that it would transform, as transform it did, when orchestrated properly. Secondly, it shows the importance of assigning the right notes to the right instruments. The same notes on bassoon or electric bass would not have had the weighted effect—suggesting the deep of the ocean—that it had when played on sixteen double basses. Finally, it shows the genius of coming up with a motive that fits what is happening on the screen. For most of *Jaws*, we don't actually see the shark; we are made aware of its presence through camera angles or movement in the water. Williams knew that he had to capture the threat beneath the water and make audiences squirm every time they heard those two notes.

Jaws is a problematic score in that, as a score, it's perfectly apt, but unremarkable. Listen to it and you will find as much lyrical music as there are cues that shout "danger!" It's those two notes, in basso profundo, that make the whole thing. Never has an entire score gained so much from so little.

With Williams's next film we enter the era of his greatest invention. As we have mentioned, the Williams sound returns to the roots of Hollywood music-making in the romantic era that birthed its first generation of composers. Williams specifically mined one area of music: harmony. But before we get into that fairly long discussion, two observations about Williams.

First, almost from the start of his career, Williams has been slandered by the accusation that he "steals" music from classical composers. These assertions are usually put forward by people who can't tell the difference between similarity of style (such as the deliberate return to late romanticism that we just observed) and actual musical theft. Some of the accusations are hysterical, such as one that finds the "Imperial March" from *The Empire Strikes Back* similar to "Entrance of the Knights" from Prokofiev's ballet score, *Romeo and Juliet.* There is even a video on YouTube that overlays both pieces, letting us hear them at the same time in the poster's hope that we will find them identical or nearly so. Listen to it and it's obvious that the only things the two pieces have in common are meter and tempo. Melodically, Williams's theme sticks to one note insistently before inching upward; Prokofiev's angular melody lurches all over the place, defining a vast tonal space. Harmonies for the two pieces have nothing in common, as is made clear by the musical train wreck that issues from their collision in the YouTube video. The poster, like Williams's slanderers in general, have mistaken incidental things for important things: in this case tempo, and a general sense of an attempt to escape a certain weighted feeling in the gestures, for actual similarity.

Secondly—is it just me, or do many of Williams's themes suggest the titles of their films in the melody? The opening notes of the *Star Wars* theme practically sing "Star WARS, nothing but STAR Wars," and so on, while every time I hear the theme to *Jurassic Park* I find it impossible not to sing in my head, "in Jurassic Park, in Jurassic Park," at a key point. The theme to *Superman* is of particular interest. The old Superman comics used a dialogue that went: "What's that in the sky? Is it a bird? Is it a plane? No, it's Superman!" Listen to Williams's theme and you will hear five notes that very easily could be sung as "What's that in the sky?" followed by a few answering notes, and then the last three, suddenly triumphant notes. If these latter don't all but sing "Superman!" then nothing can. I suspect that Williams is a frustrated songwriter and that this seeps into the shaping of at least some of his themes. Very early in his career, long before *Jaws* or even *The Cowboys*, he wrote a musical that was not successful. And of course, there are plenty of actual songs in the Williams film canon, most famously "Somewhere in My Memory" from *Home Alone* and "Can You Read My Mind?" from *Superman*, though the lyrics for the latter are read, not sung, by the Lois Lane character. But I hear song-type writing in many Williams pieces that have no lyrics.

And now to the meat of the matter: harmony. Music in the traditional Western sense is an intersection of melody, harmony, and rhythm. Timbre and form are also important, but the core of the musical experience for the listener is shaped by the arc of the melody, the character of the rhythm, and the tonal context of the harmony. Harmony is a slightly more challenging concept than the others. Everyone knows what a melody is, and hums or sings one from time to time. Everyone also knows that the melody they hum or sing has a certain rhythm; otherwise, it would be just a succession of pitches without any profile. Melody by definition contains rhythm, and while rhythm can exist by itself, it cries out for some kind of melody.

Harmony is the odd duck. It is not strictly necessary to the making of music—melody and rhythm are quite capable of making a statement on their own—and yet it is the one element that defines Western music. No other music on the globe has ever developed harmony. The fluid melody of the sitar is accompanied by a drone, and the chant of the Native American is supported by a drum beat, but even a simple English folk song has chords to go with it. (Some will argue that they hear music from Bollywood or other international culture outlets that contain harmonies, but they miss the point: music around the world has been Westernized in recent decades.) It's hardly possible to go into what harmony is and how it has functioned without writing another, completely different, book. For our purposes, what is important about harmony is its ability to characterize a musical style. That was the point made above about rock's identification with modal harmonies. Now, the late romantic/film music harmonic language has a distinguishing feature as well: chromaticism.

Chromaticism may best be defined as the compositional mode of borrowing notes from other keys in order to suggest other keys. It is not quite the same as the modal harmony described above in connection with rock. Modal harmony sets up an alternative set of pitches for a key. The guitar progression that goes from B-flat to C, with C as the home key, is using B-flat as an alternative to the G chord. It is not there to suggest the key of B-flat. In chromatic harmony, the B-flat chord would be there precisely to imply the possibility of another key entirely. The purpose of modal harmony is a kind of tonal stability that is different from the stability of standard tonality. The purpose of chromatic harmony is to suggest the connection of one key to another—an "instability," but without negative implications. It's the difference between sitting securely in one's backyard, surrounded by a fence, and sitting in an unfenced backyard with a view of everything surrounding it. If it helps, think of diatonic music (non-chromatic music) as black-and-white, and chromatic music as having hue, exactly as colors of hue are called "chromatic" to contrast them with black and white.

Williams's masterly use of chromatic harmony, combined with a songlike knack for melody, distinguishes his film music and, for that matter, his concert music. Let's see how by looking at famous cues from the three installments of the Star Wars trilogy.

The "Star Wars Main Theme," written for the 1977 original and used since in every film of the franchise, is arguably the single best-known piece of film music ever written. At first, it seems to contradict what we just said about Williams's essentially chromatic language. The opening is as diatonic—and as black-and-white—as one might imagine, and the piece remains a diatonic one, but with important chromatic embellishments. A triplet pick-up leads immediately to the famous rising perfect fifth, then a second triplet sends us up to the higher octave and a descending perfect fourth—the inversion of the rising fifth. We hear this twice, and the effect is that of an echoing fanfare. Then we hear another triplet followed by a longer note, only this is the one that gives us, very briefly, a chromatic reference, before leading back to an exact repetition of what we have just heard.

Then comes the bridge, just as in thirty-two-bar popular song form. (The bridge in a traditional popular song is a middle section that contrasts with the main part of the song, which comes before and after.) It's this little eight-measure interlude that gives us a prominent chromatic embellishment in the form of chords that color the dominant chord of the home key—the D or V chord to the home chord of G. In the next-to-last measure of the bridge comes the real chromatic kicker: a C minor chord instead of the expected C major chord. It's a small change, but exactly the right small change to dress the black-and-white up in a tinted edge. It should also be noted that the triplets don't always come where they are expected—most of them are on the downbeat, rather than an upbeat. What at first seems obvious in Williams's music is actually lined with subtleties that give each piece a highly individual profile.

The "Imperial March" lent a perfectly sinister tone to the greatest sequel ever made, *The Empire Strikes Back* (1980). This is the one that has been accused of being similar to a passage from Prokofiev's *Romeo and Juliet*, though a closer Prokofiev model would be the Soviet composer's "March" from *The Love for Three Oranges*. They share the heavy tread of a slow march and an insistent initial melody that centers around one note. But there the resemblance ends. Williams's piece begins with that one-note melody that changes its harmony on the fourth count of the measure to a chord that is tonally distant from the home key of G minor. (That the "Star Wars Main Theme" and "Imperial March" are on the major and minor sides of the same key center is significant in itself.) It's an E-flat minor chord, the defining middle note of which is a G-flat. This effectively neutralizes the G-natural of the key center, throwing things off in a way that creates the feeling of something being . . . wrong. The first four measures do this, and the answering four measures do something even more to the point: harmonically, the answering phrase "crushes" all opposition to its G minor hegemony. It's a piece of tone painting. At first, the melody dives down an octave and then back up and then down again, but this time by chromatic half-steps to land on a C-sharp minor chord—about as far from G minor as is possible. This landing is in turn answered by the E-flat minor chord that serves as a roundabout way to bring things back to G minor.

What does all this have to do with the film? Harmonic relationships are things that we, raised with Western, harmony-dominated music, feel without thinking about it. You don't have to know a C-sharp minor chord from a Phillips screwdriver to sense what is happening in the

"Imperial March": a sinister, yet unstable force is out to flatten everything in its path. Williams creates this sense by manipulating harmonic expectations in the context of a heavy march.

Williams seemed to become more and more chromatic as the trilogy progressed, culminating in a cue that is one of the most sophisticated ever made for a film: "Luke and Leia" in *The Return of the Jedi* (1983). Detailing what goes on harmonically in this cue would take us beyond my ability to simplify music-theory terms for general understanding. Suffice it to say that the music seems to reveal something new at every turn, just as the Big Reveal in the third film is that Luke and Leia are indeed siblings. As is often the case in highly chromatic music, the defining interval is the half-step—the shortest distance between any two notes. After the first three pick-up notes, the melody lands on a high note that immediately drops a half-step. This will be the central gesture repeated throughout the four-minute, forty-seven-second cue. The cue is a feat of sustained musical interest; it never sags or becomes weak, but maintains a sturdy musical presence.

Throughout all the Star Wars films, various themes will come back again and again as leitmotifs, or "leading motives." These are themes that show up when certain people or ideas enter the script. The most famous of these in the films is "The Force," which forms a nice, upward-yearning melodic arc against a simple but effective harmonic change. It is memorable, and so its return whenever "the force" is mentioned is expected. The use of leitmotifs is rife in film music, and many commentators give it a great deal of importance. It is, of course, very effective to create a musical stamp to go with certain characters or events, and this useful tool goes back at least to "Tara's Theme" in *Gone with the Wind*. (For that matter, as we saw in the chapter on silent film, even Chaplin used this in *City Lights*; a certain theme goes with the Tramp's walk, with the blind flower girl, etc.)

While the leitmotif is indeed a useful tool, the more relevant aspect of composing a film score is the musical vocabulary chosen by the composer, and how he uses it to create those motives and themes. That is what makes the sound of a composer unique, if the composer is good at what he does. It also matters what the composer does with the theme or motive to develop it. The two-note motive so famous in *Jaws*, for example, becomes the bass line of a large cue that goes with the fight between shark and man. To do this, Williams expands the half-step to a whole step at times, while at other times he transposes the half-step motive to different notes.

Williams is the only composer with three films on the AFI Top 25 film scores list. Two of them are, of course, *Jaws* and *Star Wars*. The third is *E.T. The Extraterrestrial*, which we will now consider briefly.

The credits open with a low electronic humming. This throws off our expectations of music, but as a forest scene emerges on the screen we at last hear a veil of strings, and then, suddenly, we hear deep unison strings like an organ stop and we see the ship—a magnificent space-craft, outfitted with spectacular lights. As we view the ship, the music shifts to a chant-like passage, with celesta adding a touch of color and sliding middle-voiced strings infusing the sound with the slightest sense of dislocation. This leads to our first view of the E.T.s, who are awkward little doughy fellows. The sepulchral sound continues while an E.T. waddles among the redwoods, and as this single E.T. pushes his way through the brush, the music becomes more "human," more familiar to modern ears.

But then things get "more human" in a negative way, as a menacing truck roars up into the quietude of the forest, blowing exhaust and making noise. Low woodwinds utter a threatening theme—but immedi-ately a flute adds bright counterpoint. This is more important than one might think, because it reassures the listener that the menace an-nounced by the low woodwinds is not the major sensibility of the film to come. Moviegoers don't like a bait-and-switch. The light-sounding flute makes it clear that the movie will be, essentially, a comedy.

A chase ensues and the music turns more distinctly Williams-ish. Strings oscillate back and forth in a broken-chord pattern while salvos of brass beat out a parade-like figure. The spaceship leaves E.T. behind, and the humans beat it out of there. We are almost nine minutes into the film and no words have been spoken. The entire exposition has been accomplished with visuals, sound effects, and music. More than the other elements, the music has told us what this movie is going to be about.

The famous theme from *E.T.*, sometimes known as the "Flying Theme," is handled very carefully, like a precious commodity that needs to be stretched. It is hinted at, the composer teasing us with its opening, upward-reaching interval time and again, for over an hour, until at last the theme breaks loose at the moment when E.T. uses his powers to make him and Elliott fly on Elliott's bike. It's the perfect example of the power of restraint. If Williams had used the theme earlier, we'd have grown tired of it, or at least used to it, by the time of the flying scene—and the flying scene is arguably the climax of the film's first half, the scene that sets straight just how magical E.T.'s powers are, and which makes clear the not-so-secret secret behind this little masterpiece: that it is a boy's fantasy, with a childhood point of view that will not let go or allow itself to "grow up." All of Spielberg's films owe, in some way, to *Peter Pan* (and not just *Hook*)—even the most adult ones. Goodness triumphs in *Saving Private Ryan* because the hero holds on to a boy-hood vision of the good. That's also true to some extent of *Schindler's List*. One of Spielberg's best—yet almost universally ignored—films addresses precisely the need to hold on to a boy's innocent faith in the face of danger and betrayal: *Empire of the Sun*. Williams's music feeds this vision perfectly. The colors of his particular kind of chromaticism evoke a feeling of adventure—but innocent adventure, filled always with hope, musically embodied in the inevitable and certain return to the home key.

Williams's chromaticism is not quite that of Strauss and Mahler—at least not generally ("Luke and Leia" is a magnificent exception). It more closely resembles the chromatic moves of standard popular songs of the "American Songbook" stripe. Again, the composer's beginnings as a jazz-idiom pianist, and his early flirtation with musical theater, are relevant. In continuing the symphonic tradition of Hollywood film music, then, Williams also went some distance to mate it with its sister, the American popular song. This is shown most strikingly in the harmonic scheme of the *E.T.* theme. But before we get to that, let's look at the opening notes of the melody, where we're going to find something most interesting.

The opening interval is an ascending perfect fifth. If you know the melody, go ahead and sing those notes to yourself—and then stop short, and instead of continuing with the *E.T.* theme, proceed to sing the main theme from *Star Wars* instead. That's right: the opening notes of both themes are the same. And the resemblance doesn't stop there. Where the theme from *Star Wars* next moves up to the root note above the fifth, the *E.T.* theme moves down to the root note below! These two are musical siblings, sharing quite a bit of melodic DNA. Of course, the differences change everything, and allow us to tell one sibling from the other. What's more, the *E.T.* theme is in a broad three, while that of *Stars Wars* maintains a stentorian four. The relationship is not so much heard as it is felt. Listening to the two themes side by side, it would be clear that they were either written by the same composer, or written by two composers whose influences were very similar.

Returning to the harmonies in the *E.T.* theme, we hear almost immediately a shift away from the key of C. After the first two measures described above, an answering phrase expands the opening climbing fifth to a dramatic octave, and with this comes an F-sharp to suggest the key's dominant relation of G. This is a simple "secondary dominant," but it comes much sooner than expected. And then, in the most perfect and completely unexpected move in the whole piece, in the fourth measure we hear yet another climbing interval, and while "only" a sixth, it startles us by showing up right on top of the second one. Then comes yet *another* climbing interval that puts us in the area of F major/D minor, a seventh that takes us to the home note an octave higher. From there we do climb down, but we do not reach C major again until we have passed through A-flat major. The melody is a constant climb up, up and further up, accomplishing neatly the musical picture of a boy and his alien, flying on a bike. And yet, the breathtaking climb only reaches up . . . a single octave, total. The feeling of unmeasurable ascendancy is created by the repositioning of the key center with every move. In other words, the harmonic shift from C to G, then to F/D, and finally to A-flat, make us feel we've gone further than we have. This is the alchemy of chromatic harmony, a magic put frequently to use in classic American songs by the likes of Gershwin, Rodgers, and Porter. It should be noted that Williams likes to balance the chromatic with the diatonic, so that when a theme is asserted diatonic—as it is for the Indiana Jones main theme, for example—chromatic cues will "take us away" from that, as does the "March of the Slave Children" in *Indiana Jones and the Temple of Doom.*

John Williams's place in film music is secure forever, and his influence is undeniable. Love him or hate him, he is not escapable. What I have called his "return of film music to itself" made it possible for late twentieth- and early twenty-first-century film composers to luxuriate unabashedly in the language that gave birth to Steiner, Korngold, Waxman, and Rozsa. One of those composers was Howard Shore.

The universe-grasping effect of Howard Shore's magical and masterful score for *The Lord of the Rings* trilogy lies in the fact that it is almost constant. Barely three minutes go by anywhere in the films that is not accompanied by music. Director Peter Jackson must have understood that J. R. R. Tolkien's text was essentially bardic—poetic in the old sense that ancient poets sang, or rather chanted, their tales. While the modern sensibility would never stand for ten hours of chanted words, cinema audiences had been primed for music as a presence on celluloid for decades. The choice to make the music a constant partner in the storytelling process made Shore's task enormous. It amounted to coming up with ten-plus hours of orchestral musical narrative, parallel to the film's verbal narrative and consonant with the visual splendor of the cinematography. Further, the subject of ancient Celtic myth, of wizards and elves and idyllic village life, almost shouted cliché. The composer would have to transcend the standard-issue musical gestures without straying too far from expectations. This is the work of a lifetime.

Consider the "Shire Theme," which initially appears in the first part of a larger cue called "Concerning Hobbits." It is couched in the repose of D major and never tries to leave it; the Shire, secure and childlike, needs music that is assuredly diatonic—the opposite of Williams's chromatic striving. (In fact, Shore very smartly made most of the score straightforwardly diatonic. The ears, after all, can only take so much moving of the sonic object before it tires. In a two-hour movie with forty minutes' worth of cues, chromatic language can accentuate high points of tension. In nearly constant music over the span of a massive trilogy, it would be exhausting.) The theme proper, crafted as to be lodged in the ear firmly, is followed by a whimsical variation that evokes a villager indolently playing a fiddle tune. This captures the open innocence of the Hobbits perfectly.

The motive that signals the "one ring to rule them all" is sinister without being obvious about it, and owes its mystery to a gesture that grabs onto a half-step, toys with it, and then plunges downward. The prominence of the half-step in portraying danger and/or evil in films would be a study in itself. This is, of course, the same interval that Williams used for his shark.

Shore's music for *The Lord of the Rings* is of sufficient depth and sophistication to warrant a book of its own, and indeed, Doug Adams's *The Music of* The Lord of the Rings *Films* is highly recommended. The score uses the heritage of Steiner and company to create a lasting monument to the form.

The music of science fiction and fantasy began with the quest to "make strange" the sounds of a new planet or its people. It shifted into "space opera" with Williams's reassertion of Hollywood's original film-music symphonic style. And now it seems to have stalled. If such films as *Star Trek: Into Darkness* (2013) and *The Martian* (2015) are typical, the main musical focus is to make the moviegoer feel that she is at home through the lacing of pop songs into the score. Harry Gregson-Williams's stated goal in writing cues for *The Martian* was to suggest the alien feel of the Martian landscape, but the long, sustained notes of his score are more desolate than alien. When the Matt Damon character seeks comfort, he does so through recordings of old pop songs from the home planet. And when young Captain Kirk wakes up after a night's debauch on leave in *Into Darkness*, the music system is playing . . . hip-hop. Ragtime was good for twenty years, rock 'n' roll endured half a century, but hip-hop, apparently, will still be the music of choice among the young more than two thousand years from now. So much for changing musical tastes. You'd think director J. A. Abrams would have asked his composer, the talented and creative Michael Giacchino, to come up with a sound that might conceivably exist two millennia from now, but again, I suspect the idea here is to make people feel comfortable. (Giacchino's cues are very well-done in the space opera mold.)

Film music seems always to be a tug-of-war between convention and innovation, and nowhere is that more obvious than in the scoring of films whose very point is the existence of other worlds.

9

AMBIENT MUSIC, NO MUSIC, AND READY-MADES

Some films need no music, or almost none. Others need a diegetic moment here and there, and that's all. At least two major films—Hitchcock's *The Birds* (1963) and Kubrick's *Full Metal Jacket* (1987)—have used electronic sounds either to form a pseudo-musical set of sound effects, bridging the gap between sound design and "music" (*The Birds*), or to form a musical score that grows effortlessly out of sound effects, bridging that gap from the opposite end, as it were (the second half of *Full Metal Jacket*).

In the earliest days of sound films, when it was not unusual for studio musicians to grind out many dozens of movie scores a year, sometimes those "scores" consisted only of brief opening credits, very brief closing titles, and perhaps a little in between. One of the finest and most hilarious cinema comedies, *Bringing Up Baby* (1938), has no music aside from two arrangements, by music supervisor Roy Webb, of the song that Cary Grant and Katharine Hepburn sing to their pet leopard, "I Can't Give You Anything but Love, Baby"—one over the opening credits, the other at the close.

On reflection, it is in some way almost by chance that Hollywood decided in the long run that background music should be a major part of the cinematic experience. European filmmakers in general have never employed music to the extent that Americans have. It is an aesthetic decision, without a right or a wrong, but one that does affect how moviegoers view films and the expectations they have. The canny filmmaker can play on these expectations, providing music where none might normally occur, or removing it altogether, or blending it so closely with sound effects that it "disappears," or plugging in previously composed pieces, or *ready-mades*.

Hitchcock's *The Birds* (1963) stands as an example of either "no music" or "ambient music," depending on how one wishes to define music. The main titles of this film credit Remi Gassmann and Oskar Sala for "electronic sound production and composition," with Bernard Herrmann as consultant, which suggests music of a sort. But the moviegoer will not come away from the film thinking she has heard any music whatsoever, with the exception of Tippi Hedren's character playing the piano—one of the most effective moments of diegetic music in cinematic history, for reasons we will now explore.

The Birds is a grotesque fantasy in which the plumaged creatures of the title turn against humanity and attack it, swooping down with fierce anger to pluck at its eyes, its hair, its skin, and, when possible, its vital organs. At first glance, there is nothing in the odd story to suggest that this will happen. In the opening scene, Melanie (Hedren) spies hunk lawyer Mitch (Rod Taylor) in a San Francisco pet store specializing in birds. He is there to find a pair of lovebirds for his little sister, and Melanie pretends to work for the store in order to hit on him. He leaves the store, but the suddenly obsessed Melanie runs to the street to get his license plate, has a friend at her rich daddy's newspaper trace it, and then buys and transports two lovebirds to his home in the seaside community of Bodega Bay. Slowly, as the rather obvious love plot unwinds, the feathered population of Bodega Bay begins to do strange things, and before long, the crows and gulls of the area are menacing the human population, even killing a friend of Mitch's family by plucking out his eyes. At length, the birds engage in full-out warfare against the human population.

What is going on? I think the sounds are a clue—sounds that, had a traditional background score been included, would have lost their meaning. The soundtrack pits the bird sounds against artificial, human-made sounds of every kind. This is made clear when Melanie drives to Bodega Bay and her convertible makes an unbearable racket. The car, and the other trappings of human civilization, make us deaf to the natural sounds that slowly emerge on the soundtrack. Of course, the racket is a (seemingly) necessary by-product of the technology we need to be human in the modern sense. And it is far from all just noise. In a key scene early in the film before the birds begin their attacks, Melanie plays the piano in Mitch's house. This might have been a disaster, as we have all seen what happens when a director tells the actor something like, "Just move your hands up and down the instrument," while a different performance—one that doesn't nearly match the motion of the actor's hands—is layered over the top. But Hitchcock's perfectionism made him force Hedren to take an intense three weeks of piano lessons, sufficient for her to be able to play Debussy's First Arabesque. Hedren must have worked very hard, because her performance is fluid, even though the script calls for her to interact with another character as she plays.

I take this to be the key scene of the film, unlocking the meaning of the remainder. It was with Melanie's arrival that the birds began to conspire and, in fact, the townspeople will at one point blame her for having brought calamity down on them. What has this mink-coat-clad, piano-playing, overly coiffed blonde done? What has she done? She has become, in du Maurier's heavily symbolic story, the avatar of human civilization, and civilization, as we all know, depends for its existence on ritually sacrificing nature. Thus the mink coat, the caged lovebirds—and most of all, the Debussy. When, in the last of the several spectacular attack scenes, Melanie is cornered and savaged by a frenzied aviary, we hear a confluence of caws and cries and flapping wings that build up a deadly rhythm of natural power. Of course, the irony is that this symphony of the airborne is completely artificial, pieced together by Gassmann, Sala, and Herrmann. But that doesn't change its meaning, which is to oppose the Debussy, and to represent in sound the things that must be sacrificed so that the Debussy—and the mink and the caged birds and the convertible—can exist. The usual thing said about *The Birds* is that it reminds us of the ugliness of our domination of nature, but it's not so black-and-white. If we did not dominate nature, it would dominate us. The choice between Debussy and the mad rhythms of aviary death, a choice made clear by the film, would have been obscured by a "normal" set of musical cues. (A side note: It's intriguing to observe that Hitchcock once before had opted not to use music, and that choice also involved terror from above—the biplane attack on Cary Grant in *North by Northwest*.)

A lack of background music can offset a piece of diegetic music most effectively, and not just in the symbolic manner of *The Birds*. Music for the films of Joel and Ethan Coen varies wildly from one project to the next, which is certainly appropriate to their eclectic canon. The Coen brothers' composer of choice has been the masterfully skillful Carter Burwell. Burwell has been called the "anti-John Williams," because of his propensity for the intimate and the understated. We deal with some of his scores elsewhere, but it is notable that for one of the Coens' biggest films, they spotted almost no cues for Burwell, whose music is heard in only 16 of the more than 120 minutes of *No Country for Old Men*, and many of those in the end credits. Burwell used a Tibetan singing bowl to suggest the vast emptiness of West Texas, and at one telling moment supplies an example of perfect ambient music. This occurs when the killer Anton Chigurh flips a coin to see if a man will live or die. The sounds include the low hum of a refrigerator in the scene, and Burwell essentially expanded that hum into a cue only barely recognizable as music over and above the sound itself. Prior to the credits, the only music in the film that sounds to the moviegoer "like music" is that of the mariachi band on the south side of the border, near the end of the film. Hearing music at that point has the effect of waking up the viewer to a completely new dimension of reality. The story at that stage of the plot has become a nightmare, and the music provides a real (though temporary) respite from the nightmarishness, all the better to make us feel it more pronouncedly when it returns.

❈ ❈ ❈

The music in Stanley Kubrick's mature films exploded the belief that original scoring was a necessary ingredient in cinema. Until *2001: A Space Odyssey* (1968), it was assumed, in films made in Hollywood and around the world, that finishing a film meant hiring a composer to line the soundtrack with music that fit the action and the dialogue. Indeed, that assumption remains more or less in place today, for the very good reason that few, if any, living film directors can provide the sort of musical sensitivity that Kubrick brought to the table in selecting previously composed music for his films.

Kubrick's early works had been scored in the usual manner; the music for *Spartacus* (Alex North, 1960), *Lolita* (Bob Harris, 1962), and

Dr. Strangelove (Laurie Johnson, 1964) is respectable, if unremarkable. Kubrick initially hired Alex North, his collaborator on *Spartacus* and the composer for films as varied as *Who's Afraid of Virginia Woolf?* and *Cleopatra*, to score *2001* and, as a guide, gave North a temporary track consisting of the music we now associate with the film. North dutifully supplied cues that mirrored this pre-supplied music. You can easily find these on YouTube. The opening of North's score is a fanfare in the fashion of the Strauss on the temp track, complete with low organ pedal. For scenes in which Kubrick used Ligeti's music, North wrote pseudo-avant-garde cues with plenty of choral oohing and aahing. Only after North finished the job did Kubrick make the revolutionary decision to use the temp tracks instead. North said he was "devastated" when he found out his music was not going to be used, and understandably took the position that the use of music by the two Strausses was "too Victorian" for the story.

Whatever the merit of North's case, Kubrick's decision to go with the temp tracks was an enormous gamble that paid off handsomely. One of the compositions he used, "On the Beautiful Blue Danube" by Johann Strauss, Jr., was very well known as a popular ballroom dancing piece and frequent entry on the programs of orchestral pops programs everywhere. Kubrick dared to associate the waltz's lilting grace with the slow-motion actions of a weightless waitress inside a spinning spacecraft. Audiences might easily have rejected this as a ridiculous stretch, but instead, most people got it: the literal weightlessness of the waitress matches the musical lightness of the waltz. Grace is grace, whether found in a dance or in space.

Likewise, audiences may well have walked out on the shimmering-but-brittle dissonance of György Ligeti's music, used primarily during the appearances of the monolith and throughout Dave's long and mysterious trip through space. Ligeti was alive and thriving when *2001* was released in 1968, yet Kubrick failed to secure permission to use the Hungarian-born composer's music. This reportedly infuriated Ligeti, but an agreement was reached, peace was made, and the two even became friends. Kubrick would use other Ligeti pieces (with permission!) in *The Shining* and *Eyes Wide Shut*. The composer accompanied Kubrick's widow to the premiere of the latter film. Ligeti's music features densely packed dissonances that peel off in layers and then re-layer, with an overall effect that might be likened to the "blooming, buzzing confusion" that William James once said must attend a newborn's first encounter with the world. Again, audiences got what Kubrick was doing. Entering a new era was like a birth—noisy and ecstatic.

Most famously, Kubrick employed the opening measures of Richard Strauss's *Also Sprach Zarathustra*: twice in the film's beginning scenes, and again at the very end. Strauss's orchestral tone poem was a musical take on Nietzsche's book of the same name, a meditation on the births and deaths of belief systems, and therefore apt for the film's theme of epochal genesis. The first two uses of *Zarathustra*—a harmonically assertive fanfare featuring organ, brass, and timpani—accompany the opening credits and the ape-men's discovery of tool use, a discovery that catapults them to the next evolutionary level. *Zarathustra* is heard once again at the very end, as the next level is achieved.

Perhaps Kubrick's most inspired use of previously composed music in *2001* is the one least talked about. The Adagio from the ballet, *Gayane*, by Soviet composer Aram Khachaturian is the very picture of loneliness: serene string lines that droop sadly and then rise again, almost reluctantly, against a background of almost palpable silence. It is the perfect music for the scene in which an astronaut jogs the periphery of the craft, alone like no one has even been alone before.

Kubrick added deep insult to real injury when he explained in an interview the reason behind his decision not to use North's score. The decision, he said, had rested on the realization that, no matter how good a film composer might be, he could not be "a Beethoven, a Mozart, or a Brahms." After such a remark, he was almost committed to using previously composed music from then on. One easily imagines any film composer he might have hired deliberately sabotaging the project out of pure revenge!

Fortunately for the director, Kubrick's next film was *A Clockwork Orange* (1972), based on an Anthony Burgess novel in which the music of Beethoven figures prominently. Plenty of excuse there was in this film, then, to use Beethoven instead of Alex North or any other living composer. Kubrick hired Walter Carlos, a genius of synthesized music whose album, *Switched-On Bach* (1968), had presented spectacular readings of works by J. S. Bach, to arrange Beethoven and Rossini for electronic realization, suggesting a futuristic twist to the classics. Carlos also submitted original music for consideration, which Kubrick at first approved, but then mostly left on the proverbial cutting room floor.

Carlos, who transitioned gender about this time and became Wendy Carlos, eventually released a compact disc of her complete (and mostly unused) score.

The music of Beethoven in Kubrick's film, and especially the "glorious Ninth of Ludwig Van" (as lead character Alex puts it), is used in the same way Burgess used it in his novel: to stand as an emblem of the cultural product made possible via the sublimation of violence. The inclination to violence that sends Alex and his "droogs" out into the night in search of men to beat and women to rape is the same inclination that makes Beethoven possible. The difference is one of energy channels. That inclination, undiverted from its initial impulse, results in "the old ultra-violence." But channeled into creative focus, it presses out the great works of art, literature, and music. Beethoven, via Carlos, is there to help us see that, though the most effective piece of audio-visual coordination is arguably the darkly hilarious use of Rossini during a bizarre scene in which Alex and his gang interrupt another gang's act of rape and then fight them in a bloody battle for control. Is this serious? Or just "boys at play"? The Rossini seems to suggest the latter.

With his next film, Kubrick outdid himself in the music department. In one brief, incredible scene, he employed a piece of classical music so deftly as to make the hair stand on end. Listen openly to the slow movement of Schubert's E-flat Major Piano Trio, op. 100, as it is heard in the final minutes of *Barry Lyndon* (1975), and you will hear what I mean. It is one of the most striking confluences of music and film in the history of cinema.

We first hear the Schubert earlier in the film, when the title character is married. It is played as the wedding processional, which would be unremarkable save that the piece has all the earmarks of a funeral march—it's in a minor key (C minor), in a medium-tempo, two-beat meter, and its melodic gestures are solemn. In part, this is simple foreshadowing of the doomed relationship, and rather obvious foreshadowing at that. But at the end, the relationship long in the past, we see Lyndon's former wife and their son, who has engineered the couple's demise; we see the wife sign the okay for a dispensation of money to Lyndon, and two things evidently come over her: grief, and a feeling of being trapped.

At the exact moment that we see the tears come to her eyes, we hear it: the subtlest of changes in the funeral march theme. Previously sounded in the cello, the theme now transfers to the piano and to a higher register, the better to emphasize the tiny but all-important alteration of the melody: what had been an A-flat becomes an A-natural. And that A-natural *hurts*. The technical description for this change is that the melody, previously poised in the natural minor, is now in the melodic minor. That's what the musician's ear hears. The ear of the sensitive listener/viewer hears a strange twist in the soul, a shift from solemnity to irony, the heartbreaking-yet-brittle acknowledgment of the inevitability of the tragedy that has befallen the lovers. A hardness and a finality have entered where once were suppleness and possibility.

This is no arbitrary pairing of music and image. It is a careful act of feeling adequation. Kubrick has found the perfect external aural manifestation of his character's internal experience. It is a hermeneutic act, an interpretation, and as such it is one among a possibly infinite range of choices. Kubrick, or some other director, might have found a similar moment in Haydn, perhaps, or Beethoven, or Salieri or Loewe or Mozart *pere* or Mozart *fils* or anyone else from the approximate era. (Schubert lived long after the action of *Barry Lyndon* takes place; Kubrick's choice is just inside the limits that keep it from being unacceptably anachronistic.) But while the number of possible musical correlations approaches infinity, it must be emphasized that *not just anything is a correlation*. And it is not that the correlations are *limited*, but that some choices will not be correlations at all. There are, perhaps, an infinite or near-infinite number of choices of music correlating to the scene just described, but that doesn't mean that Mozart's *Musical Joke* would have worked just as well as the Schubert trio movement.

In a sense, Kubrick's innovation was a throwback to cinema's first years. Musicians who accompanied the old silent movies used bits of classical music to indicate a hero's bravery or a damsel's distress. Only with Max Steiner and the other classically trained composers of Hollywood's early talkie years did the idea come around that every motion picture deserved its very own music. But Kubrick's musical choices in the films just discussed are no ordinary "accompaniments" to the scenes. The Schubert in *Barry Lyndon* and the Ligeti in *2001* are not mood pieces—they are exact commentaries. They have intellectual and thematic content as well as emotional importance. The thick layers of Ligeti's music as Dave hurtles through space are an emblem of the unknown dimensions ahead. The conflation of Rossini and rape in *A*

Clockwork Orange produces a horrifying irony. But in his next two films, *The Shining* and *Full Metal Jacket*, Kubrick took a different tack. For *The Shining* (1980), Kubrick turned again to Carlos, who by this time had transgendered to Wendy Carlos, and who was working with producer Rachel Elkind as a creative partner. Carlos and Elkind together worked out a number of cues, many of which were not used because they were written for parts of the film Kubrick later cut. Their final contribution amounted to the opening credits plus filler, while the real star of the soundtrack was the gripping, dissonance-laden music of contemporary Polish composer Krzysztof Penderecki. (One uncredited piece by Ligeti and some Bartok were also used.) Between the Penderecki excerpts and Kubrick's employment of big-band pieces to suggest the bygone era of the famous hotel, *The Shining* soundtrack created the sense of a haunted past and a chaotic present—a perfect musical representation of the film's story, though lacking in the thematic details of the music for *2001* or *Barry Lyndon*.

Full Metal Jacket (1987) divides neatly into two halves: in the first, the Marines' training on Parris Island ends in a tragic double death; in the second, the Marines in Vietnam are eventually forced to commit an atrocity in order to survive. The music soundtrack alternates between popular songs of the day and brief, mostly percussive synthesizer cues. The original cues are credited to "Abigail Meade," but their composer's actual name was Vivian Kubrick—the director's twenty-seven-year-old daughter. (Daughter Kubrick's career has comprised a smorgasbord of cinematic experience: she has worked, credited or uncredited, as an actor, a composer, a cinematographer, an editor, and a director.) The cues frequently evolve from sound effects. In fact, it is sometimes challenging, watching the movie, to know where the sound of a clanking tank or a distant piece of ordnance ends and the musical cue begins. This is truly ambient music, sourced from non-musical sounds but still presented musically, the opposite of the engineered bird sounds in *The Birds*, which were musically (or at least artificially) sourced but intended to be heard as "natural" sound.

All of Meade's cues are dark, and serve to underline the innate evil of the death machine that is war. The popular songs serve a different purpose. Though they function as background music, they are quasi-diegetic in the sense that they are songs of the era that all the Marines would certainly have heard. Kubrick arranges their appearance to correspond with the devolution of the film's sensibility from relatively light to exceedingly dark. The first song heard is the naïve country song, "Hello Vietnam," containing such clichés as "America has heard the bugle call." The last song, heard over the closing credits after the like-able lead character executes a female enemy, is the Rolling Stones' sinister "Paint It Black."

Kubrick's final completed film, *Eyes Wide Shut* (1999), blends pre-viously composed pieces with original cues by composer Jocelyn Pook. Pook's contributions are restricted for the most part to placements of a short piano motive taken from a Ligeti chamber music work. The effect is minimal and atmospheric—precisely the opposite of the functional use to which music was put in *2001* and *Barry Lyndon*. At his peak, Kubrick put music front and center in his films. By the time of his last film, however, he had repositioned music as a secondary feature.

The only other modern filmmaker to use previously composed music as much as Kubrick did is Woody Allen. A Woody Allen film is immedi-ately recognizable from two things in the opening seconds: the visual style of the credits, and the use of classic jazz or standard popular music over the credits. There are exceptions, especially among his earlier films, but for the most part Allen uses the visual and musical elements of his opening credits like a stamp that says "Film by Woody Allen."

The most effective use of previously composed music in an Allen film is, in this writer's view, the Gershwin score for *Manhattan* (1978). Beginning with the opening of Gershwin's *Rhapsody in Blue* as the film's writer-hero attempts various starts at a new novel, Gershwin's music dominates the emotional tone of this tale of confused love. Most of the cues are orchestral versions of the popular songs George com-posed with lyricist-brother Ira Gershwin, performed by no less than the New York Philharmonic under the baton of Zubin Mehta. Many are well-known, such as "Someone to Watch Over Me" and "Embraceable You." But the most effective include relative unknowns, such as "Land of the Gay Caballero" and "Bronco Busters."

The last scene tugs at the heartstrings musically as well as narrative-ly. The Woody Allen character has rejected the love of a seventeen-year-old girl (Mariel Hemingway) as being somehow immature and inappropriate—though he never uses those words—for him, a middle-aged man. But he has neglected to note the flip side of immaturity in the purity of the girl's love, and when he is rejected by a more "mature" woman (Diane Keaton), he rushes to the seventeen-year-old in the sudden realization that this innocence, and not the sophistication of the worldly Keaton character, is what he truly wants. Of course, it's too late. As he runs to her along the crowded Manhattan streets, the music is "Strike Up the Band," a spirited march full of hope and promise. When he finally reaches her, she is readying to leave for London and drama school. The music shifts to the melting "But Not for Me," a ballad of impossible love. Literalists have dismissed *Manhattan* as a pedophilic fantasy, because they fail to make note of the film's single, overpowering character: the city. (It's in the title!) Manhattan itself is the woman who fools the subject into thinking himself in love with her sophistication, when what he actually values is her endearing innocence, a simple amalgam of hope and trust at the core of a seemingly hard city. This dichotomy is known to all New Yorkers, and it is the very essence of Gershwin's jazzy/sweet music. Allen's story and his black-and-white visuals (another clue to his theme) are perfectly complemented by his use of the Gershwin tunes, something that may someday be recognized by a generation of movie critics less literalist and more open to symbolism than the crop that dismisses this minor masterpiece.

When director George Roy Hill conceived of *The Sting*, a buddy/revenge flick about two con men played by Paul Newman and Robert Redford, he heard ragtime in his head. It didn't fit the period of the film's action—*The Sting* (1973) takes place in the 1930s, and ragtime's era was roughly 1899–1914—but it suited the character of the film and especially the lead characters. Instead of giving in either to the standard-issue idea of an original score or the use of period songs from the 1930s, Hill stuck to his intuition and employed young Marvin Hamlisch, still a newcomer to Hollywood, to adapt and orchestrate ragtime pieces by the king of that genre, Scott Joplin. The result was not only a musical backdrop that brought out the stride and spirit of the characters, but a resurgence in ragtime's popularity. "The Entertainer," the rag that Hamlisch chose to serve as the main theme, enjoyed sudden hit status some sixty years after it had been forgotten.

The Sting was a perfect example of ready-made music finding its ideal cinematic counterpart. Another is Wes Anderson's *Moonrise Kingdom* (2012). Called a "pubescent love story," the film relates the bloom of love in two twelve-year-olds: Sam, a "Khaki Scout" (fictionalized boy scout) and Suzy, who lives on a New England island called New Penzance. During summer camp with the scouts, Sam discovers Suzy in a production of *Noye's Fludde*, an oratorio in Old English by the great twentieth-century English composer Benjamin Britten. It's the mid-1960s, when classical music played a larger role in young people's lives than it now does, so Anderson and music director Alexandre Desplat seized on that as an opportunity to infuse the entire film with bits of Britten as well as some Schubert and Saint-Saëns. Especially apt is the inclusion of Britten's *Young Person's Guide to the Orchestra*, which is heard at the start and the close of the film. That work is an introduction to the instruments of the orchestra and how they work together to make symphonic music. This is course parallels the love lessons learned by the pre-teen couple. Anderson has even gone so far as to say, regarding the use of Britten's music in *Moonrise Kingdom*, that "the film is sort of set to it." Some original tracks by Desplat are also included, but it would remain for Desplat to show his full powers in the extraordinary score to Anderson's *Grand Budapest Hotel* (2014).

Terrence Malick counts as one of filmdom's more musically knowledgeable directors, and by this I don't mean he's listened to a lot of the "right" music. He has a hands-on history in the film-scoring world, including a credit for composing the music to his graduation piece from the AFI Academy, *Lanton Mills* (1969). Ennio Morricone, who scored Malick's *Days of Heaven* (1978), has recalled the director making informed suggestions about the music. His sensitivity to music's place in film is further demonstrated in *The Thin Red Line* (1998), which we've noted in chapter 4 on epics. Malick's 2011 release, *The Tree of Life*, contains a perfect example of how to interpolate a classical piece into a film with meaning. The piece is *Les Barricades Mysterieuses* (The Mysterious Barricades) by the French baroque composer, François Couperin. The father in the film plays this piece, which does two things at once—one filmic, one musical. The musical thing is perhaps the more remarkable. The barricades of the piece's title have been disputed for centuries, with the usual, typically French conclusion being that they represent the "barricades to a woman's heart." In the context of Malick's film, which addresses the whole of being in a set of finite lives, it's clear that these barricades are the barriers to our very existence. The mystery is the mystery of what we are doing here on this plane of existence, barred as we are from understanding much beyond the limits of our daily lives. Malick thus at once solves the mystery of Couperin's title, and allows this solution to flood the premise of his story.

Some directors have added ready-mades to otherwise original scores, with mixed success. The most prominent examples are both Vietnam War films: Francis Ford Coppola's *Apocalypse Now*, and Oliver Stone's *Platoon*. In the former, Wagner's "Ride of the Valkyries" takes on an absurd significance compared to Carmine Coppola's cues, while in the latter, Georges Delerue's soundtrack screeches to a halt to make room for Samuel Barber's Adagio for Strings. There is also Ridley Scott's first *Alien* movie, with its sudden shift of musical mood from Jerry Goldsmith's edgy and compelling cues to the serene calm of Howard Hanson's Symphony No. 2 (the slow theme from the first movement). None of these work in my opinion, and show less than respect for their respective composers. It is one thing for a Kubrick to toss everything out and strip in music he understands. It is quite another for a director to allow outside pieces to swamp the composed score simply because he thinks these are a fit. I'm sure Goldsmith could have written measures as serene and lovely as the Hanson had he been given the chance.

Comedies frequently use previously written music to make some ridiculous bit even more ridiculous, usually by association. These are often sexual, such as when the Bo Derek's sex-bomb character in *10* (1979) runs in slow motion toward the camera to Ravel's *Bolero*. The most vulgar is probably Bizet's quintet from *Carmen* as it is played in its orchestral form while Ben Stiller masturbates to a picture of Cameron Diaz in *There's Something About Mary* (1998). The latter is all the more obvious to those familiar with Oscar Hammerstein's English version of the original French words: "Beat out that rhythm."

While it doesn't quite fit under the umbrella of ambient music/no music/ready-mades on the soundtrack, a certain controlled collision of two pieces of diegetic music in *Casablanca* (1942) must be mentioned somewhere, and this chapter is as close to a place for it as anywhere. It happens about halfway through the movie, when the Germans have essentially taken over Rick's Café Americain and are lustily singing the German call-to-war, "Die Wacht am Rhein." It is too much for Viktor Laszlo, the resistance fighter in hiding, who calls on the house band: "*La Marseillaise*! Play it!" Play it they do, and a weeping chanteuse with a guitar joins in as well, while the Germans continue singing their song of conquest. For a few amazing moments, the two songs continue in counterpoint, not clashing but complementing each other. At length, of course, the Germans stop and the French national anthem is taken up by everyone else in the bar. But that blending of disparate musical forces into one is powerful, and was almost certainly no accident. With no less than Max Steiner as the film's music director, it was surely a planned musico-cinematic event.

10

TRENDS, FORECASTS, AND INNOVATIONS

We have viewed the history of Hollywood film music as the story of the adaptation, by generations of composers, of the musical materials of late nineteenth- and early twentieth-century Western art music—"classical" music—with exceptions along the way that only go to prove the rule. The materials included a generally chromatic harmonic language, the instruments of the symphony orchestra, and a vocabulary of gestures that had come to "mean" such things as love (long-lined, slow melodies), hate or evil (diminished chords and dark orchestration), war (martial music, marches), and even nostalgia (simple melodies resembling folk songs). As genres took shape in the first two decades after talkies arrived, certain new gestures were developed unique to film scoring, such as the jazzy seductions of the saxophone accompanying Stanley Kowalski in *A Streetcar Named Desire* and Norma Desmond in *Sunset Boulevard*; the jagged rhythms and angular melodies of the Western, reaching their peak in Elmer Bernstein's *Magnificent Seven* and Jerome Moross's *The Big Country*; and the search for strange new sounds to accompany strange new worlds in Bernard Herrmann's *The Day the Earth Stood Still* and Jerry Goldsmith's *Planet of the Apes*.

We've then seen these significations challenged by innovators. Bernard Herrmann turned the sexy saxophone cue into a symbol of sleaze and decadence in *Taxi Driver*, Ennio Morricone wholly reinvented the musical soundscape of the Western in Sergio Leone's spaghetti Westerns, and John Williams tossed strange timbres out the window in favor of bringing epic grandeur to science fiction and fantasy. This leaves us without a clear path to cinematic musical identity. Anyone writing a Western score along the lines of Jerome Moross today would be laughed out of the studio. But Morricone's innovation was a onetime change-up: what to do now? Comedies seem to have become the biggest cinematic repository of pre-made pop songs, or if they do feature original music, the cues are brief and function basically as pleasant fill-ins for a temporary lack of dialogue, like Theodore Shapiro's music for *The Intern* (2015). Then there is the rise of the superhero movie, with its featureless Wall of Sound corresponding to the CGI and unceasing (and often meaningless) on-screen action.

This doesn't mean that composers and directors aren't pushing back against convention and ennui, but that such moves are to be found largely in smaller films—even if some of them are Oscar winners. Michael Keaton and Ed Norton are walking along a hot, crowded sidewalk in New York and as they talk (their chat turning to argument over artistic status vs. commercial appeal), we hear drums in the background. A drummer is playing a standard, medium rock beat as Keaton and Norton walk, and it fits the rhythm of their walk, making us assume we are hearing a background score. But then the pair pass a drummer—*the* drummer who is set up on the street, playing for tips, and whose beat we have been hearing the whole time. The background music has become diegetic—or revealed itself to have been diegetic all along—only to return to background again when the two proceed on their way after Keaton tips the drummer.

This scene from Alejandro G. Iñárritu's *Birdman (or The Unexpected Virtue of Ignorance)* not only blurs diegetic/background music, but puts percussion into the foreground where it has always been in the background. Drummer Antonio Sanchez provided all the original cues as drum-set solos. That they are improvised lends a natural feel to the score, but the spotting is exact, not random. For example, in another scene, as Keaton and Norton talk shop, we suddenly hear the "ding" of sticks on the crown of a ride cymbal and naturally wonder, "Why?" The question is answered immediately when Emma Stone enters the frame and meets the Norton character for the first time. As the dialogue proceeds, Sanchez's solo increases in complexity to match the instantly deepening complexity of the Norton-Stone relationship.

Birdman's scores balance Sanchez's originals with quotes from orchestral scores by Tchaikovsky and Mahler, as if to throw a strongly contrasting light on the old world of the theater and the contemporary realities of celebrity. Unfortunately for Sanchez, that meant the Academy could not nominate him for an Oscar, as the soundtrack depended too heavily on ready-mades.

The emergence of dramatic series such as *Breaking Bad, Madmen,* and *House of Cards* has come to employ many composers and led to a number of notable scorings. Jeff Beal's theme for *House of Cards* (2013) colors the feeling of every episode, and for excellent reason. It combines at least five distinct elements into a single statement: a syncopated rhythmic scheme in the treble, a demonic bass (the use of the *Jaws*-ish minor second interval again!) that Beal has said symbolizes the stubbornness of Frank (the politician "hero" of the piece), a solo flugelhorn theme that signals the national element at hand, and a very dark love theme in the lower strings emblematic of Frank's marriage. With all this at play, the theme somehow emerges as a single unit, and what is more, it ends with a magnificent ambivalence when the key of A minor changes to A major in the treble—but remains minor in the stubborn bass. The richness of Beal's theme—with every element pertinent to the show's characters and subject—could serve as a model for certain current "big screen" composers who, it seems, sometimes settle for any notes that feel right.

As we saw in Nino Rota's music for *The Godfather,* the confluence of background score with diegetic cues can be effective in evoking time and place as well as emotions. In Steve McQueen's *12 Years a Slave* (2013), Hans Zimmer's original score works hand-in-glove with Nicholas Britell's arrangements of spirituals and dance music. Britell, whose love of jazz led him also to produce *Whiplash* (2014), wrote original music for *The Big Short* (2015), a score that contains a kind of cue apparently coming into its own. This might be called the "music-over" cue. It consists of characters talking while music is played, except that the characters' words aren't heard. We are all used to music underlining dialogue and (when it's successful) throwing a light on the unspoken subtext. In the music-over cue, however, the music does all the talking.

In the scene using the music-over cue in *The Big Short,* we see the Steve Carell character talking with his wife about his brother's suicide. Director Adam McKay made a wise choice here in not allowing us to hear what almost certainly would have to have been the usual clichéd comforts of the wife: "You couldn't have done anything to stop him," "He died knowing you loved him," "He wouldn't want you to grieve like this," and so on. In such a case, it is the emotion that counts, not the predictable words. So McKay silences the dialogue soundtrack and lets Britell's music tell the tale.

Another instance of the music-over cue was found in a first-season episode of TV's *Better Call Saul*, the prequel to *Breaking Bad*. Jimmy McGill (Bob Odenkirk's character has yet to become "Saul Goodman") has just watched as two young men got their legs broken due to the outcome of his own scheme. As he sits with a hot date in a bar, he tries to engage in charming conversation, but cannot get the screams of the young men out of his head. We know this because, while we see him in the bar with his date, we hear only Dave Porter's music, a churning mix that grips the ear with terror, and as the music progresses, we see McGill's face slowly morph from forced glee to undisguised horror at what has happened.

New music sources including Sanchez's drums, new balances of diegetic and background music, and the potential for using music in new ways such as the music-over cue, point to some possibilities for the future. Music seems in many cases to be taking a back seat after a couple decades of riding shotgun. Howard Shore remains one of our best living film composers, though much of his energy recently has gone into writing classical scores, including an opera on *The Fly* and a piano concerto for Lang Lang. Still, his music for 2015's Oscar-winning best film, *Spotlight*, was barely present in only a handful of cues. John Williams experienced a temporary illness when Spielberg's *Bridge of Spies* was ready for scoring, so Thomas Newman took over. Newman's cues are perfectly serviceable, but one wonders what the film would have been with a Williams score. One imagines a quietly heroic theme for the Tom Hanks character, and possibly a sinister cue for the arrest of the young man. Williams's health improved in time for him to score the first installment in the latest Star Wars series of films, *The Force Awakens* (2015). But, for reasons that are unclear, he handed the job over to Michael Giacchino for *Rogue One* (2016). Giacchino had previously emulated Williams's style in *Jurassic World*, so it was a relatively seamless transition. Williams's themes and motives permeate Giacchino's musical homage to the master.

We take a moment to address a question concerning the future that earlier begged to be asked: Will women at last play a role in film composition in the coming years? After a decade or so of scoring BBC television shows and documentaries, English composer Rachel Portman emerged in the 1990s as a major composer for cinema, the first female to be commissioned the scores to major releases in succession. The history of most female film composers prior to Portman had been of doing a film or two, then being retired from the field; for example, Wendy Carlos's work on Kubrick's *Clockwork Orange* and *The Shining* did not lead to more films. Helping out in the background has also been a women's specialty in film music. Without Shirley Walker's help on orchestration, it is doubtful that Danny Elfman would have been able to tackle Batman, but Walker was uncredited. Lisa Gerrard co-composed the score to *Gladiator* (2000) with Hans Zimmer and *was* credited, yet when the Oscar nominations rolled around, only Zimmer's name was mentioned. Anne Dudley won an Oscar for her music for *The Full Monty* (1997) but has not enjoyed a high-profile career since then. The considerable talents of Angela Morley, a transgendered person, were kept primarily to the role of arranging orchestral scores of film musicals, such as Lerner and Loewe's *Little Prince* (1974). Morley did manage to become the first transgendered person to be nominated for an Oscar, first for her arrangements for *Little Prince*, and four years later for her arrangements of songs by the Sherman brothers for the animated feature, *The Slipper and the Rose*. Morley also penned a number of episodes of the TV series *Falcon Crest* and *Dallas*, and was an assistant to John Williams on the original *Star Wars* in 1977.

Whether the coming years will bring more women composers into the movie-music fold remains to be seen, though it is interesting to note that the world of the symphony orchestra has outrun filmdom in that arena. The ranks of classical composers and conductors include many women. Portman, at any rate, stands as a major female film composer, and perhaps as a model for others who aspire to that role. Her credits include *The Joy Luck Club* (1993); *To Wong Foo, Thanks for Everything, Julie Newmar* (1995); *Emma* (1996), for which she won an Oscar; *Chocolat* (2000), *The Manchurian Candidate* (2004); *The Lake House* (2006); *The Sisterhood of the Traveling Pants* (2008); and the Canadian feature, *The Right Kind of Wrong* (2013). To judge from her online biography, Portman's film activity may have slowed recently to accommodate her increasing work in composing for the stage.

In general it seems that as of 2016, film music is going in two directions: toward simpler and easier answers on the one hand, and toward greater sophistication on the other. Simplicity can be heard in the Wall of Sound typical of superhero scores, as well as in the increasing use of previously composed pop songs to fill in the gaps and serve as a score. Background cues seem to be fewer and farther between than in the past, if recent features such as *The Intern*, *The Martian*, and *Bridge of Spies* are any indication. This is neither good nor bad, and can actually be quite effective. Carter Burwell's cues in a typical Coen Brothers movie generally number only a handful. But in many cases (not in Burwell/Coens) the music feels like filler, as if any notes of a general nature would do just fine. This is taking the "unnoticed" half of the "film music must be unnoticed but indispensable" formula too far.

But increasing sophistication of means and methods is also evident. The jazz-drums-versus-classical-cuts score to *Birdman* is one example, and the emergence of what I have called the "music-over" cue is another. The blurring of diegetic and background music, the use of instruments or instrumental combinations other than symphony orchestra, and deploying cues where they previously were not typically used are all ways of pushing the film-scoring envelope. We will close with an example of a film score that does a little of all of these, and which manages to forge a union with the visual and dramatic components in a fresh yet masterly way: Alexandre Desplat's score for Wes Anderson's *The Grand Budapest Hotel* (2014).

The Academy of Motion Picture Arts and Sciences was right to award Desplat the Oscar that year for one of the most original and affective scores to come along in several years. Desplat's previous credits had included a range of both commercial and art films, such as *Syriana* (2005), *The Curious Case of Benjamin Button* (2008), *Harry Potter and the Deathly Hallows, Parts I and II* (2010 and 2011), Terrence Malick's *The Tree of Life* (2011), and *Argo* (2013). He had scored some cues for Anderson's *Moonrise Kingdom* (2012), but the music for that film consisted primarily of ready-mades by Benjamin Britten and other classical composers.

The Grand Budapest Hotel, with its strange mix of black comedy and romance, nostalgia and postmodern distance, exotic locales and familiar situations, must have seemed to the composer like a vein of golden opportunities, and he proceeded to mine every one of them. In a mythical eastern European country stands the Grand Budapest Hotel, a symbol for Europe itself in all its historicity, elegance, and class oppressions. The first thing we see is a young woman solemnly approaching the bust of one of that country's great authors. But before we see or know any of that, we hear something: three men singing in strange counterpoint, employing a vocal style that is almost a yodel (it will become a yodel at the end of the film). We hear the men before we see them, sitting on a bench as the woman passes. Thus, Desplat's music immediately puts us inside the film, and instantly suggests an alliance between the diegetic and the non-diegetic that will wax and wane throughout.

We know within a measure of his score that we are in some part of Europe remote from the charms of Italy or France. We suspect that we are in for an unusual tale—as indeed we are—from the probing, intertwining lines of the singers. The revered author, in a flashback, tells us of the great hotel, and the moment of its mention brings the signature sound of Desplat's score: a band of a dozen balalaikas, abetted by a zither to produce a sound that confirms that we are geographically in East Europe but also introduces the unique color of the plucked instrument. The group is the Osipov State Russian Balalaika Orchestra, and their tight ensemble forms the foundation of Desplat's score. Desplat uses the balalaikas in three ways: traditionally, to produce a folk song–like backdrop; classically, to suggest a Haydn-esque ambiance for the well-to-do who populate the Grand Budapest's lobby; and as a stand-in for the orchestra's usual role (though, as the score unfolds, he will also introduce instruments of the traditional orchestra). An early example of the latter use occurs when a train wreck of tremolo-ing balalaikas accompanies the news of the dowager's death—the event that will kick off the plot of the movie.

Throughout the score, glockenspiel or other bells indicate winter. This is first heard in connection with the dowager, who is in the winter of her life, but it will more often be heard during a snowscaped scene. The first full sound of the orchestra is heard when the train leaves, taking Gustave, the Grand Budapest's fabled manager, and his lobby boy Zero to the dowager's funeral. Full orchestra shows up rarely, mostly in the connective tissue of the plot; Desplat wisely leaves the majority of the sound lean. Desplat is not above some Mickey Mousing for fun, as when, during an investigation, the camera pans from eye to eye of the participants and, as it does, the sudden changes are signaled by perfectly spotted timpani strokes.

Slowly, as the story grows more and more arcane and new characters are introduced, different instruments arrive to enrich the music. The organ plays the roles of church signifier and bad-guy cue. Percussion instruments and effects increasingly crowd the score as the action intensifies. Timpani, snare drum, wood block, and hand-clapping have their roles to play. Desplat toys with rhythm to underline scenes of tension, as when the Jeff Goldblum character is followed into a darkened museum by bad guy Willem Dafoe. Two notes on the organ seesaw back and forth in hemiola (off-beat accents) against the balalaikas, which seem almost to be frantically trying to assert the beat.

One cue might be called a miracle of the diegetic interlacing with the non-diegetic, save that the source sound with which the music is coordinated is not music, but a sound effect. When Gustave and Zero are taking a cable car up an Alp to meet the witness to the dowager's murder, their car stops temporarily alongside another car, and as it does, the two cars swing back and forth, squeaking as they do. The snare drum, played with brushes, had previously set up a medium-tempo rhythmic pattern of long-short, long-short (6/8 or some other compound meter) and now, incredibly, the rhythm and the sound effect perfectly align. Of course, this could be a trick, for it's possible that the sound effect was no sound effect at all but rather yet another percussion instrument of some sort posing as a sound effect, and in the studio easily coordinated with the snare drum. But whether a trick or not, it remains an astonishingly perfect little moment of music-into-diegetic/sound effect. Immediately after this, we find ourselves in a monastery where the singing of the monks is also both course music and background score. It reminds us of the opening when three men sang the strange counterpoint, and implies a cultural relationship between the church and the people. Intriguingly, the balalaikas point in the other direction, toward secular folk music. To sing is to praise the divine, we might infer from this division, while to dance—and the end credits will feature a joyous dance played by the Osipov group—is to celebrate the here and now.

Desplat's music stands out as an example of a highly skilled job well done, but it's more than that because the composer did what every film composer, ideally, should do: grasp the core of the film, and express it in the cues. Every director who is more than just a mover of bodies and CGI supervisor has something to say, and as it is said of great philosophers—that the best have only one thing to say, but say it in myriad ways—so great directors say one thing over and over, as if by repetition they can make us "get it." Terrence Malick says, again and again, that we shine our light upon the world to bring it into authentic Being, as his onetime teacher, philosopher Martin Heidegger, famously taught. Every film by Joel and Ethan Coen remind us that courage is the only true virtue, whether it's the physical courage of *No Country for Old Men* and *True Grit*, or the personal courage confirmed in *Hail, Caesar*, and expressed via its very denial in *A Serious Man*.

Wes Anderson's One Thing is spoken clearly by Gustave when he assesses Agatha, the spunky girl who will become Zero's wife. This theme was already explored beautifully in *Moonrise Kingdom*. It is purity. Gustave's and Zero's and Agatha's purity is what makes them glow as human beings in the face of greedy aristocrats and fascist interlopers. Desplat's music is correspondingly pure. It makes no false moves, makes no moves at all in fact, that aren't simple and direct and, well, pure. No contrivance allowed. This is the true role of film music: to mirror in musical narrative not just the events on the screen, but the aesthetic of the director.

Film music has a short but amazing past, a promising present, and a wide-open future. Who knows what talents will arrive? What innovations will be made? What still-closer collaborations of director with composer will produce in the way of an integrated artistic product? The association of music with particular states of mind, actions, visuals, and emotions is ages old, and cinema arrived only yesterday. Long before film's arrival, nineteenth-century philosopher Arthur Schopenhauer wrote specifically about music's ability to underline the meaning of the visual, and the need to marry music to its appropriate visual mate. His statement could stand as a credo for film composers as well: "Music makes every picture, indeed every scene from real life and from the world, at once appear in enhanced significance, and this is, of course, all the greater, the more analogous its melody is to the inner spirit of the given phenomenon."

SELECTED READING

Adams, Doug. *The Music of* The Lord of the Rings *Films: A Comprehensive Account of Howard Shore's Scores*. Los Angeles and Van Nuys, CA: Alfred Music, 2010.

Audissino, Emilio. *John Williams's Film Music:* Jaws, Star Wars, Raiders of the Lost Ark, *and the Return of the Classical Hollywood Style*. Madison: University of Wisconsin Press, 2014.

Bushard, Anthony. *Leonard Bernstein's* On the Waterfront: *A Film Score Guide*. Lanham, MD: Scarecrow Press, 2013.

Chaplin, Charlie. *My Autobiography*. New York: Simon & Schuster, 1964.

Cooke, Mervyn. *A History of Film Music*. Cambridge: Cambridge University Press, 2008.

Cooper, David. *Bernard Herrmann's* Vertigo: *A Film Score Handbook*. Westport, CT: Greenwood, 2001.

Davison, Annette. *Alex North's* A Streetcar Named Desire: *A Film Score Guide*. Lanham, MD: Scarecrow Press, 2009.

Kalinak, Kathryn. *Film Music: A Very Short Introduction*. New York: Oxford University Press, 2010.

Kobel, Peter. *Silent Movies: The Birth of Film and the Triumph of Movie Culture*. New York: Little, Brown and Co., 2007.

LaFave, Kenneth. *Experiencing Leonard Bernstein: A Listener's Companion*. Lanham, MD: Rowman & Littlefield, 2014.

Leinberger, Charles. *Ennio Morricone's* The Good, the Bad and the Ugly: *A Film Score Guide*. Lanham, MD: Scarecrow Press, 2005.

Levant, Oscar. *A Smattering of Ignorance*. Garden City, NY: Garden City Publishing, 1942.

Palmer, Christopher. *The Composer in Hollywood*. London: Marion Boyars, 1990.

———. *Dimitri Tiomkin: A Portrait*. London: T. E. Books, 1984.

Previn, Andre. *No Minor Chords*. New York: Doubleday, 1991.

Raksin, David. *The Bad and the Beautiful: My Life in a Golden Age of Film Music*. Kindle Edition, 2012.

Rozsa, Miklos. *A Double Life*. New York: Wynwood Press, 1989.

Sartre, Jean-Paul. *The Words: The Autobiography of Jean-Paul Sartre*. New York: Vintage, 1981 (1964).

Sciannameo, Franco. *Nino Rota's* The Godfather Trilogy: *A Film Score Guide*. Lanham, MD: Scarecrow Press, 2010.

Selznick, David. *Memo from David O. Selznick; The Making of* Gone with the Wind *and other Motion Picture Classics*. New York: Viking Press, 1972.

Smith, Steven C. *A Heart at Fire's Center: The Life and Music of Bernard Herrmann*. Berkeley: University of California Press, 1991.

Sullivan, Jack. *Hitchcock's Music*. New Haven, CT: Yale University Press, 2008.

Timm, Larry M. *The Soul of Cinema: An Appreciation of Film Music*. Needham Heights, MA: Pearson Custom Publishing, 1998.

Whitner, Mariana. *Jerome Moross's* The Big Country: *A Film Score Guide*. Lanham, MD: Scarecrow Press, 2012.

Wierzbicki, James. *Film Music: A History*. New York: Routledge, 2009.

———. *Louis and Bebe Barron's* Forbidden Planet: *A Film Score Guide*. Lanham, MD: Scarecrow Press, 2005.

———, ed. *Music, Sound, and Filmmakers' Sonic Style in Cinema*. New York: Routledge, 2012.

Winters, Ben. *Erich Wolfgang Korngold's* The Adventures of Robin Hood: *A Film Score Guide*. Lanham, MD: Scarecrow Press, 2007.

SELECTED LISTENING

This book has dealt with background music for films, and the experience of that music as part of the overall cinematic experience. But sometimes music is listened to on its own, apart from the film it was written for. This makes music unique among filmic elements. It is not possible to abstract the cinematography from a film and somehow enjoy it by itself, nor is it possible to isolate the actors' skills from the story or the direction and appreciate it. It is possible to read a film script apart from its realization on the screen, and this is occasionally done via published scripts, but only musical soundtracks, among all the other elements of film, exist as artistic and commercial entities in a market all their own.

An official list of the top twenty best-selling movie soundtracks consists primarily of film musicals and concert films, and not the background scores that are our subject. It's hardly surprising that the soundtrack from *Grease* and the soundtrack from Prince's *Purple Rain* concert film are, respectively, the ninth and third best-selling soundtracks ever. It would be surprising indeed if those slots were filled by Elmer Bernstein's score for *To Kill a Mockingbird* and Jerry Goldsmith's music for *Chinatown*, or even Henry Mancini's *Breakfast at Tiffany's* and Ennio Morricone's *The Good, The Bad and The Ugly*. Since its inception, film music has had an affinity with "classical" music, in that it largely employs symphonic instruments and the harmonic language that descends from late romantic symphonic music via film music's earliest practitioners. In the current pop world, that is hardly a recipe for commercial success.

Yet, the best-selling soundtrack of all time is neither a musical nor a concert film. It is the contemporary drama, *The Bodyguard* (1992), but that film does not use a standard background score. Starring Whitney Houston, *The Bodyguard*, like an increasing number of movies since the 1980s, capitalized on previously written pop songs. The soundtrack, comprising hits by Houston and others, sold 17 million units, far more than could ever be imagined for symphonic music by Max Steiner or Maurice Jarre. Other top-selling soundtracks made primarily or wholly of pop song catalogs include *Top Gun, Saturday Night Fever*, and *Forrest Gump*. One has to dig pretty deep to find an original symphonic score that is also a best-seller—with one exception.

James Horner's score for *Titanic* (1997) sneaked into that list, selling 11 million units and ranking fifth, just below *Dirty Dancing* (a catalog soundtrack) and *The Lion King* (a musical). It did so on the strength of only one track, the song "My Heart Will Go On," as sung by Celine Dion. If the millions who bought the soundtrack expected an album stuffed with other pop songs, they were surely disappointed. Instead, they got Horner's dramatic cues, the only such album to make the top twenty soundtracks. Even John Williams's original *Star Wars* (1977), while it sold a very respectable one million units and thus earning platinum status, did not approach the multiplatinum stature of the pop catalog scores, concert films, and musicals.

We'll list our own twenty original soundtracks in no particular order, beginning with *Titanic* in homage to Horner's surprise commercial success. I've chosen the other nineteen from a combination of personal taste and historic importance, with a preference for soundtracks that stand on their own, at least to some extent. This means that some great film scores will not appear in the top twenty soundtracks because their cues are so tightly tied to the film that listening to them apart from the visuals and dialogue is without particular interest, except, perhaps, as a reminder of what one has seen on the screen. Remember our formula: a good film score serves the film, and is both indispensable and unnoticed. Remember, too, that there are exceptions, and that sometimes we notice a musical cue or three in the same way that we notice a moment of brilliant camera work or an actor's delivery of a certain line. The scores on our top twenty movie-music listening list belong largely to those exceptions. Therefore, you will find extroverted scores like *Lawrence of Arabia*, *Breakfast at Tiffany's*, and *The Godfather* in their entirety, but subtler sets of cues such as *Chinatown* and *Vertigo* in excerpts.

Included are some original soundtracks, some scores re-created long after a movie's release, and compilations. All are available on compact disc, and most are available via streaming.

James Horner: *Titanic* (1997), original soundtrack or Collector's Anniversary edition. The single-disc soundtrack gives you Horner's well-crafted orchestral cues and evocations of rough-hewn Irish folk music. The four-disc (!) commemorative contains everything from the movie to songs from the era. Both, of course, feature Celine Dion singing "My Heart Will Go On."

Maurice Jarre: *Lawrence of Arabia* (1962), original soundtrack. Though it has been re-recorded and widely performed by symphony orchestras worldwide, the original soundtrack to this acknowledged masterpiece of film music remains a must-have for all film-music fans. Jarre's sweeping main theme and the many colorful cues are a perfect match for David Lean's visuals, and evoke them splendidly when heard by themselves.

Max Steiner: *Gone with the Wind* (1939), original soundtrack. The flagship of all epic cinema music. Steiner teaches listeners how to hear big and important (the famous "Tara" theme), relentlessly tragic ("Twelve Oaks in Ruin"), the supercilious ("Scarlett Prepares for the Barbecue"), and more. Late romantic symphonic music became the sound of movies, thanks largely to Steiner.

Elmer Bernstein: *The Magnificent Seven* (1960), original soundtrack or Phoenix Symphony reconstruction. This fabled score was lost and unavailable in 1994 when conductor James Sedares and the Phoenix Symphony had it painstakingly reconstructed and recorded by the KOCH label. Years later, the soundtrack was rediscovered and reissued, but the vibrantly played Sedares/Phoenix Symphony recording has the advantage of a warmer sound and superior engineering.

Leonard Bernstein: *On the Waterfront* (1954) Symphonic Suite. The original soundtrack is available and has the attraction of containing all of Bernstein's cues. But the twenty-minute Symphonic Suite from *On the Waterfront* carries all the punch of the original, with the bonus of symphonic tautness. Bernstein masterfully shaped the two central themes—the love theme and the main theme—so as to magically coalesce at the end; the result resembles a one-movement symphony more than a suite. Bernstein conducts the suite on a Sony CD that also features his Symphonic Dances from *West Side Story.*

John Williams: Star Wars Trilogy, original soundtrack anthology. The four-CD set, first brought out in 1993, contains the original soundtracks of all three films, plus a bonus disc made of previously unreleased material and alternate cues. A thick booklet discusses the origins and impact of Williams's music. As you listen, note the growth and development of certain motives throughout the scores.

Terence Blanchard: *Jazz in Film.* Trumpeter-composer Blanchard, with guest saxophonist Joe Henderson and others, essays nine jazz-flavored themes from films released between 1951 and 1995, including Elmer Bernstein's *The Man with the Golden Arm,* Jerry Goldsmith's *Chinatown,* Andre Previn's *The Subterraneans,* Bernard Herrmann's *Taxi Driver,* and Henderson's own *Clockers.*

Alfred Newman: *How the West Was Won* (1962), original soundtrack. A quintessential Western-movie score, with deeply beautiful arrangements of folk songs (see the treatment of "He's Gone Away" in the cue, "He's Linus's Son") and rugged "cowboy" music with strong percussive accents. The overture and the entr'acte (an overture for the movie's second half) contain some authentic American folk songs without the orchestral dressing.

Ennio Morricone: *The Mission* (1986), original soundtrack. A masterpiece by any stretch. Every cue commands attention. Among them, "Gabriel's Oboe" has become a pops concert standard, covered by oboists and many other melody instruments. "On Earth as It Is in Heaven" provides choral music of mastery rarely found in motion pictures. "The River" evokes native American music with purity and grace.

Henry Mancini: *Breakfast at Tiffany's* (1961). Pass on *The Pink Panther* and go instead for Mancini's most fully realized score, and probably the most musically gratifying score to any romantic comedy, ever. There's "Moon River," of course, but no less than Oscar Peterson has covered the title track, which has subtler but no less enriching charms. The party music is a time capsule of the early 1960s.

Jerry Goldsmith: *40 Years of Film Music.* Goldsmith's output was so varied that a single soundtrack doesn't get it. I suggest instead this tribute set, four CDs containing soundtrack excerpts that hail both from popular hit films, plus a few rather obscure releases for which Goldsmith ended up writing some of his most inspired music—*The Blue Max* and *The Wind and the Lion*, for example, and the vastly underrated *The Great Train Robbery* (sometimes called *The First Great Train Robbery*). Weirdly, however, there is nothing here from either *Planet of the Apes* or *Patton*.

Nino Rota: *The Godfather* (1972), original soundtrack. Avoid all compilations from the trilogy and stick to Rota's original, which contains the main theme and love theme in their first incarnations, plus the extraordinary "Baptism" cue for organ, which breaks down the barrier between diegetic and background music.

John Barry: *The Lion in Winter* (1968), original soundtrack. Almost forgotten in the wake of Barry's James Bond scores and *Out of Africa*, this gem provides more choral cues than any other major release, including Christmas songs (the story takes place during that holiday) in English, French, and Latin, the three languages native to the court of the title character, Henry II. The score evokes the medieval era without resorting to cliché.

Howard Shore: *Lord of the Rings* Trilogy (2002–2004), original soundtrack. The question becomes: To listen as a spark to recalling the film? Or as music for its own sake? Do neither. Instead, listen to the three-disc set as background to your own re-imagining of Tolkien's fable. Shore's orchestral cues retain their power over the years, and the CDs also contain the vocal contributions of such performers as Enya and Annie Lennox.

Bernard Herrmann: *Essential Film Music Collection*. Here it is in a two-CD set of soundtrack excerpts: music from *Citizen Kane*, *The Day the Earth Stood Still*, *The Trouble with Harry*, *Vertigo*, *North by Northwest*, *Psycho*, *Taxi Driver*, and more. The true Herrmann fan will want to start here, but not stop before seeking out the composer's concert works, widely available on CD.

John Corigliano: *The Red Violin* (1998). This Oscar winner is a study in how to shape a theme that supplies within its measures all the material needed for love scenes, scenes of high drama and tension, epic passages, and more. The solo violin is, of course, the main musical voice here, and it doesn't hurt that the soloist is Joshua Bell.

2001: A Space Odyssey (1968) and *Alex North's 2001: World Premiere Recording* (1993). Comparing the "temp" score put in place by director Stanley Kubrick, which eventually (and famously) became the actual soundtrack, with the music Alex North created to match it is an education in the film composer's craft. Though the score was dumped by Kubrick, North's cues found the light of day after his death, when his old friend Jerry Goldsmith recorded it as an album.

Miklos Rozsa: Various. Looking for representative Rozsa recordings is perhaps the most frustrating of all film-music searches. The composer conducted what was then a groundbreaking recording in 1977 called "Rozsa Conducts Rozsa," containing cues from a number of his scores including *Spellbound*, *Ben-Hur*, and *The Private Life of Sherlock Holmes*. Though excerpts can be found on YouTube, the recording is out of print and doesn't even show up as used copies available on Amazon. The soundtrack for the original *Ben-Hur*, sturdy as it is, does the composer only partial justice, and one might finally be better off buying violinist Jascha Heifetz's recording of Rozsa's incredibly beautiful Violin Concerto, which served as the theme for *The Private Life of Sherlock Holmes*.

The Sea Hawk: The Classic Film Scores of Erich Wolfgang Korngold. Buckles learned to swash under the musical pen of one of Europe's most gifted classical composers. Here, re-created by conductor Charles Gerhardt and the National Philharmonic Orchestra, are cues from *The Sea Hawk*, *Captain Blood*, *The Adventures of Robin Hood*, *Anthony Adverse*, and other classics from the 1930s.

Sunset Boulevard: The Classic Film Scores of Franz Waxman. Here are conductor Gerhardt and the National Philharmonic again, this time tracing the career of one of Hollywood's first-generation composers, from the horror of *The Bride of Frankenstein* to the very different horror of the title film, to his playful, almost Gershwin-esque cues for the romantic comedy, *The Philadelphia Story*.

INDEX

ABOUT THE AUTHOR

Kenneth LaFave has published thousands of articles about music in newspapers and magazines; composed works on commission for such organizations as the Phoenix Symphony, the Tucson Symphony Orchestra, the Kansas City Chorale, and the Chicago String Quartet; and studied philosophy, culminating in a PhD in the subject. His previous book in this series was *Experiencing Leonard Bernstein*. LaFave lives in Scottsdale and is currently at work on a series of books on philosophical subjects.